ETHNIC NATIONALISM AND STATE POWER

Ethnic Nationalism and State Power

The Rise of Irish Nationalism, Afrikaner Nationalism and Zionism

Mark Suzman
Washington Correspondent
Financial Times

First published in Great Britain 1999 by
MACMILLAN PRESS LTD
Houndmills, Basingstoke, Hampshire RG21 6XS and London
Companies and representatives throughout the world

A catalogue record for this book is available from the British Library.

ISBN 0–333–73373–8

First published in the United States of America 1999 by
ST. MARTIN'S PRESS, INC.,
Scholarly and Reference Division,
175 Fifth Avenue, New York, N.Y. 10010

ISBN 0–312–22028–6

Library of Congress Cataloging-in-Publication Data
Suzman, Mark, 1968–
Ethnic nationalism and state power : the rise of Irish
nationalism, Afrikaner nationalism and zionism / Mark Suzman.
   p.   cm.
Includes bibliographical references and index.
ISBN 0–312–22028–6 (cloth)
1. Nationalism.   2. Nationalism—Case studies.   3. Afrikaners–
–South Africa—History.   4. Zionism—History.   5. Nationalism–
–Ireland—History.   I. Title
JC311.S9   1999
320.54—dc21   98–47533
                                                                                CIP

This book is printed on paper suitable for recycling and made from fully managed and
sustained forest sources.

10   9   8   7   6   5   4   3   2   1
08   07   06   05   04   03   02   01   00   99

Printed and bound in Great Britain by
Antony Rowe Ltd, Chippenham, Wiltshire

Contents

Preface

The origins of this book lie in an attempt to understand the apparent durability of the apartheid state in South Africa during the late-1980s. At the time, it was widely accepted that part of the reason for the regime's strength was the fact that it was underpinned by the monolithic and unbending force of Afrikaner nationalism. That prompted me to investigate the forces which had allowed those nationalists to take power in 1948 in the hope that understanding the origins of the movement would help me better understand its future. The more I explored the issue, however, the clearer it became that Afrikaner nationalism had never been the undifferentiated movement its leaders portrayed but was the product of a complex coalition of forces that was then in the process of fracturing.

That conclusion was soon borne out by the release of Nelson Mandela from prison in 1990 and the start of negotiations that would lead to the end of apartheid. Nevertheless, I remained fascinated by the question of how nationalist movements mobilised, and turned my attention to the manner in which the Zionists and the Irish, two other movements widely seen to be driven by a powerful, uncompromising nationalist sentiment, had come to power. This book, which had its origins in a doctoral thesis at the University of Oxford, is the final result of those investigations.

In the midst of writing the dissertation, I took a job with the *Financial Times* as a Johannesburg correspondent to cover the period leading up to and after the historic 1994 elections that brought Nelson Mandela to power. The chance to observe first-hand the final demise of a movement whose rise had so fascinated me was a unique and unmissable opportunity. Although South Africa remains deeply divided and the wounds caused by apartheid will take decades to heal, the country has now opened a new chapter in its history that holds out promise for the future. At a time when peace negotiations are continuing on a stop–start basis in both Israel and Ireland, this book is written in the hope that both those countries will soon be able to turn the page on their own troubled pasts.

Acknowledgements

There are many people who have helped in the writing of this book. I would particularly like to thank John Hall, who first stimulated my interest in nationalism, Anthony Smith, who helped me to sharpen my understanding of the topic, and Michael Hart whose able assistance allowed me to navigate the many pitfalls of what often seemed a hopelessly over-ambitious project. Erica Benner and Jack Spence also made a number of very helpful comments on how to improve the structure and argument of the book. I would also like to express gratitude to the Rhodes Trust, which financed research trips to Israel and Ireland. And last, but by no means least, I would like to thank my family for unstinting encouragement throughout.

Introduction

AIM AND DEFINITIONS

As the past decade has proved, nationalism is far from a moribund force in international politics. Precipitated in large part by the collapse of the Soviet Empire, old nationalist movements[1] have been revitalized and new ones have proliferated across much of Europe, Asia and Africa. These events have also reignited scholarly interest in nationalism, generating numerous new studies seeking answers to the old questions of what nationalism is, why it remains so pervasive and what its future impact is likely to be. While critically important, however, such overarching topics beg a far more practical and less well understood problem: how do nationalist movements transform themselves from small social groups to rulers of sovereign, independent nation-states? The primary aim of this book is to shed light on this question by studying how three such movements, the Irish, the Afrikaners and the Zionists, came to power in the first part of the century.

For the purposes of this investigation, *nationalism* can be broadly defined as a political ideology insisting that the 'state' be controlled by the 'nation'.[2] The *state* is a legal and political organisation with sovereignty over a designated territory and population. It exists simultaneously as an internationally recognised member of the community of states, and as a compulsory organisation run along bureaucratic lines with control over the legislative, administrative, judicial and coercive functions of society.[3] An *ethnic group* can be defined as one with a common myth of descent, shared culture, an association with a specific territory and a sense of solidarity.[4] The *nation*, in this conception, is a politically mobilised ethnic group seeking to secure state power.[5] Members of such a movement are expected to give their highest political loyalties to the nation in an attempt to establish a unified *nation-state*: one where the apparatus of the state is firmly under the control of the nation.

WHY THE IRISH, AFRIKANERS AND ZIONISTS?

Existing studies of Afrikaner nationalism, Zionism and Irish nationalism are diverse and contentious. Many have implicit (and sometimes

1

explicit) political agendas and are often characterised by varying degrees of polemic. But while the histories of each movement are well-researched, the historiographies are in the main parochial and limited. Irish historians give prominence to nationalism, but make little attempt to flesh out the concept in any rigorous social scientific manner. By contrast, analysts of Afrikaners and Zionists make substantial use of broader ideas and concepts in the social sciences, but pay only limited attention to theories of nationalism.[6] In addition, most students – and inhabitants – of Ireland, South Africa and Israel commonly see their situation as unique because of their distinctive geographic, cultural and religious contexts.[7]

In practice, however, while there are no direct parallels between them in the same way as, for example, nationalist movements in nineteenth-century eastern Europe, the three share many characteristics. Over the past decade, attempts at conflict resolution in all three countries have highlighted some of these similarities, although most commonly the comparison is made with Northern Ireland's Protestant community alone.[8] In such comparisons, however, the central dynamic at work is rarely seen as nationalism, but more often race or religion. Indeed, Donald Harman Akenson's study of 'God's Peoples', explicitly focuses on the religious aspect, asserting that all three groups are primarily shaped by the injunctions of the Old Testament. He asserts that

> [u]nless one uses the lens of the ancient Hebrew covenant as the primary mode (not sole but primary) of viewing the Ulster-Scots, the Afrikaner and the Israeli, then…neither their history nor their future will make much sense.[9]

That perception remains a dominant one in all three cases. The strength and power of each movement is seen as being derived from the ineluctable forces of language, culture and especially religion. This study, which focuses on Irish Catholics rather than Protestants, acknowledges that such factors were critically important in the *formation* of each movement. However, it argues that such a focus obscures more than it reveals about the manner in which each movement developed. Its central argument is that the evolution – and ultimate success – of Irish nationalism, Afrikaner nationalism and Zionism depended much more heavily on political, economic and organisational factors that were shaped by the similar nature of their struggles for state power.

METHODOLOGY

The study of both nationalism and the state has always been poised uneasily between political scientists and sociologists focusing on their domestic elements and international relations theorists interested in their global ramifications. Such divisions are unjustified in most cases and clearly untenable for the study of nationalism. Understanding how nationalist movements come to create or control new states requires looking at both 'domestic' and 'international' factors. In particular, it requires answers to two separate but related questions: first, how nationalist movements develop, and second how their strategies work towards building or controlling a state in the international system.

Comparative history is well suited to seek an answer to such questions. As seminal studies such as Barrington Moore's analysis of dictatorship and democracy show, it allows for the application of social theory to history and takes advantage of the strengths of each field.[10] The cases share a wide range of rarely noticed similarities that make it appropriate to study parallels between them. First, the movements under investigation are roughly contemporary. Second, each struggled both against a competing ethnic group and an imperial power. Third, in each case the latter conflict was directed against the same great power, the British Empire. At the same time, however, important differences help clarify the relationship between nationalist movements, the state and the international community. Most striking is the divergent end-result of each campaign: Ireland ultimately achieved independence through partition, Israel through the effective expulsion of most of its Palestinian population, and the Afrikaners assumed exclusive ethnic control of a multiethnic state. A comparative study of the three, therefore, requires us to exploit the parallels to understand better how nationalist movements develop and grow and then explain the different outcomes in each case.

Although this book first develops and then applies a broad analytical framework to carry out the study, it is not seeking to posit a new general theory on the nature and origins of nationalism. Indeed, as will become apparent, one conclusion of this study is that such a general theory is probably impossible. Also, while it is to be hoped that the work will prove of interest to specialist historians – and it does make significant use of primary materials – it is not intended to comprise a radical revision of the history of any of the case studies. Instead it aims to shed new light on relevant historical events by approaching them from a different theoretical perspective. As Theda Skocpol comments in her comparative study of social revolution:

> The comparative historian's task – and potential distinctive scholarly contribution – lies not in revealing new data about particular aspects of the large time periods and diverse places surveyed in the comparative study, but rather in establishing the interest and *prima facie* validity of an overall argument about causal regularities across the various historical cases. The comparativist has neither the time nor (all of) the appropriate skills to do the primary research that necessarily constitutes, in large amounts, the foundation upon which comparative studies are built. Instead, the comparativist must concentrate upon searching out and systematically surveying specialists' publications that deal with the issues defined as important by theoretical considerations and by the logic of comparative analysis. If, as is often the case, the points debated by specialists about a particular historical epoch or event are not exactly the ones that seem most important from a comparative perspective then the comparative analyst must be prepared to adapt the evidence presented in the work of the specialists to analytic purposes somewhat more tangential to those originally envisaged.[11]

OUTLINE

Chapter 1 seeks to set out a suitable analytical framework for this study. Adapting new insights in social movement theory to nationalism it argues that the investigation must be grounded in an analysis of the conditioning effect of structural opportunities and changes on nationalist movements, in particular the nature of the state in which mobilisation takes place. Within this overarching framework, it suggests that the study must analyse four broad factors. First, it needs to examine the social and cultural background to national mobilisation, relating the emerging nationalist ideology to the ethnic context in which it was derived. Second, it must look at the resulting organisational networks set up by nationalists, encompassing the role of material factors in persuading people to give their allegiance to the movement. Third, it must analyse the impact of ethnic conflict and how it helped shape nationalist strategies. Finally, it must examine the impact of the international state system on each movement.

Chapter 2 begins the historical analysis by looking at the origins and early development of a full-blown ethnic nationalist movement in the three cases. It argues that the foundation of each movement was predicated on the prior existence of a common ethnic consciousness among a substantial proportion of a largely literate population in a modernising state. It shows first how this consciousness arose in each case and then how the emerging intelligentsia within each group developed a nationalist ideology. The chapter examines the early history of these groups and argues that, while enjoying some success, they were unable to make substantial headway against the dominant political organisations in each respective society relying on cultural, linguistic and religious arguments alone.

Chapter 3 argues that a critical element in changing this proved to be greater involvement in the economic arena. It shows how in each case the role of the state in supplying or denying material welfare to members of the ethnic group became a key part of the nationalist debate. It demonstrates that each movement was able to broaden its appeal significantly by setting up new organisations, such as trade unions and banks, that were able to combine ethnic and class interests. At the same time, the chapter shows how the new groups set up to push forward this process combined with the cultural and political organisations to comprise a powerful new bureaucratic infrastructure centred on nationalist ideals. Driven by an overlapping, highly sophisticated, elite leadership, it argues that these organisations became the chief engine driving the process of national mobilisation.

Chapter 4 focuses on the issue of ethnic conflict. It shows how both the ideological and organisational factors examined in Chapters 2 and 3 were strongly reinforced, and to some extent directly shaped, by such clashes. For the Irish, Afrikaners and Zionists alike, the nationalist struggle was waged simultaneously against two different 'others' – the British on one side and, respectively, the Protestants, blacks and Palestinians on the other. The chapter shows how a wide range of cultural and material issues, ranging from competition over scarce economic resources to demands for mother-tongue education, resulted in vehement, frequently violent, demonstrations against ethnic opponents. It demonstrates how this fuelled national solidarity and prompted the formation of military wings dedicated to attacks and reprisals while attempts at reconciliation became progressively less popular with the general public. This resulted ultimately in plans for the Catholicisation of the Irish state, the development of apartheid in

South Africa, and the subordination and expulsion of Palestinians from the prospective state of Israel.

Chapter 5 examines the international aspects of the nationalist struggle. It suggests that this had two dimensions: on the one hand international events and broader geopolitical shifts had direct repercussions on both the shape of nationalist strategies and the strength of their development. On the other, because the ultimate objective was control of the state, each movement had to develop political strategies designed to secure international approval and recognition for their endeavours. With regard to the first issue, the chapter argues that extraneous geopolitical events from the Boer War to the Great Depression strongly influenced the nature and outcome of the nationalist struggle in each of the case studies. In particular, it shows that global conflicts with no direct impact on each territory – the First World War for the Irish, the Second for the Zionists and Afrikaners – were critical catalysts in the process of national mobilisation. On the second issue, the chapter argues that nationalist leaders were always painfully aware of the need to achieve *de jure* recognition for their claims from the international community as well as *de facto* control over their respective states and embarked on a series of diplomatic initiatives to achieve this. It suggests that these strategies, while dependent on the exigencies of international power politics, ultimately combined with domestic mobilisation activities to help secure both internal and international legitimacy, thereby propelling each movement to power.

The conclusion returns to the analytical framework set out in the first chapter and reassesses each of its major elements in the light of the subsequent historical discussion. It establishes that each movement followed a roughly similar progression in the long transformation from fringe political group to ruler of a sovereign state. The development of political, cultural, economic and military organisations based on nationalist ideology and stimulated by intense ethnic conflict acted as a set of self-reinforcing building blocks, leading to the creation of a powerful bureaucratic edifice dedicated to national advancement. It also argues that differences in the timing, manner and outcome of mobilisation across the three cases were largely the result of differing domestic and international structural constraints. Finally, it briefly comments on the study's implications for the broader understanding of nationalism.

1 An Analytical Framework

INTRODUCTION

Nationalism is a protean concept. There are at least two types – civic and ethnic – and several theorists see many more.[1] It can also be analysed in at least four different ways: as an ideology, a group sentiment, a process of 'nation-building,' or a collective movement. This study is primarily preoccupied with the last of these. It is comparing three cases of nationalism as an *ethnic* movement with a *political* goal: achieving state power. This chapter seeks to develop an appropriate theoretical framework to help analyse how ethnic nationalist movements transform themselves from small social groups into the rulers of sovereign, independent nation-states.

The key issue to be addressed in this investigation is not how nationalist movements form, but what makes them successful. Most theorists of nationalism – and committed nationalists – conflate these issues, implicitly arguing that the causes are also the main reason for the doctrine's success. As a result, the spread of nationalism is all too often seen teleologically: once the spark has been struck it is believed to spread rapidly and inexorably over populations, transforming the political debate and in the process reshaping the international system. But in practice only a relatively small proportion of nationalist movements ever meet their goal of taking state power. What distinguishes the successes from the failures? Is there an identifiable set of characteristics that such nationalist movements share? The aim in this chapter is to identify the key areas of analysis to be applied to the case studies to help answer those questions.

NATIONALISM AS A SOCIAL MOVEMENT

The vast majority of studies of nationalism neglect to examine the role of the movement itself.[2] In an excellent synthesis of recent advances in the understanding of social movements, Doug McAdam, John McCarthy and Mayer Zald argue that there are three broad sets of factors that condition their formation and development: the structure of the political opportunities and constraints they face, the forms of organisation (both formal and informal) available to them and the collective processes of interpretation and social construction that shape their actions.[3] Although these parameters were developed from the study of relatively small or localised movements, their utility in analysing broader topics has been increasingly recognised and they serve as a useful starting point for the study of nationalist movements. Nevertheless nationalism is clearly a very distinct type of collective mobilisation. Accordingly, rather than applying these three sets of factors to the case studies directly, this chapter seeks to adapt them to the study of nationalism. First it briefly examines the relationship between structural change, the state and nationalism. Then it sets out a framework focusing on the relationship between nationalist ideology and ethnicity, the role of organisation and material issues, the effects of ethnic conflict, and the impact of the international system.

STRUCTURAL CHANGE AND THE STATE

Most social movements and revolutions are sparked by structural changes that 'render the established social order more vulnerable or receptive to challenge'.[4] Alterations to the prevailing political and economic environment create disequilibria within society which create structural opportunities for particular groups to mobilise. They also help define the manner in which political and social movements shape their organisational responses and general strategies.[5] Derived from the work of Ernest Gellner, many theorists accept the connection between nationalism and structural change, regarding the doctrine as a functional response to the process of uneven development that inevitably occurs during industrialisation.[6] Their basic argument is that the structural changes wrought by capitalism and the development of the modern state accentuate pre-existing, societal fault lines of a cultural or religious nature. Successful nationalist movements are those best able to reinforce those fault lines by politicising them through a combination of ethnic and material arguments. The spread of the doctrine is achieved by elites within a modernising and literate society exploiting popular dissatisfaction with economic dislocation amongst the masses. Movements succeed in their goals when they are able to put their arguments across to a receptive, literate audience via mass education and other institutions of the modern state.

But while such approaches convincingly point to the need to examine the effect of underlying changes in the structure of economy and society on nationalism, they provide a limited understanding of its development. The process of modernisation is ongoing in most societies, but national mobilisation is not. In part this is due to variations in the specific ideologies, organisations and the leaders who develop them. But it is also a reflection of the changing nature of the state itself. It is now well established that the strategies of social movements are often related to and conditioned by state structures.[7] It makes sense that this should be especially true for nationalist movements, where the struggle is focused directly on the state itself. As John Breuilly has argued, nationalism

> clearly builds on some sense of cultural identity. It is clearly connected with new forms of mass participation in politics made possible by changes in the structure of communications. The growth of capitalism has created these social groups and objectives.... but nationalism cannot be linked to any particular type of cultural attribute or social arrangement; or to any particular structure of communications; or to any particular class interest; or to any particular psychological state or need; or to any particular social function or objective... the key to an understanding of nationalism lies in the character of the modern state which nationalism both opposes and claims for its own.[8]

For Breuilly, the development of an effective nationalist movement is directly related to the structure of the state in which it operates. This broadly accords with the ideas put forward by 'political process' theorists in social movement theory. They argue that collective mobilisation is conditioned by factors such as the relative openness of the prevailing political system, the presence of allies or enemies in the existing power structure, and the state's capacity and propensity for repression.[9] All these factors necessarily condition nationalist strategies and need to be a central focus of this study.

IDEOLOGY AND ETHNICITY

In recent years, social movement theorists have focused increasingly on the importance of 'framing processes' in collective mobilisation. These can be defined as 'conscious strategic efforts by groups of people to fashion shared understandings of the world and of themselves that legitimate and motivate collective action'.[10] Essentially they encompass the subjective motivations of participants: the shared sentiments, beliefs and conception of goals that help bind members of a movement closer together and shape their tactics and strategies. In the case of nationalism, it points particularly to the need to assess the importance of the ideology itself and the cultural context in which it is articulated.

Broadly speaking, the idea of the nation as a specific community striving for political autonomy was derived from the eighteenth-century writings of Johan Gottfried Herder[11] on the distinctiveness of linguistic and cultural groups. This notion was expanded by Johann Gottlieb Fichte at the beginning of the nineteenth century, who argued that each distinctive language group constituted a separate nation and as such should have and control its own state.[12] By making an explicit connection between language and polity, Fichte shifted the demands of the nation from the cultural sphere to the political one. From these origins, a broad doctrine of nationalism was developed. In ideal-typical form it can be reduced to five basic propositions:

1. The world is naturally divided into nations, each with its own unique culture, normally based on language but sometimes on religion or other factors
2. All people must belong to a nation.
3. All nations must seek full political autonomy, or statehood.
4. Only within an independent nation can an individual find true spiritual and political fulfilment.
5. Only a world of free and sovereign nations can provide international order and stability.

At root most nationalists believe that it is the innate power of these ideas – which are seen to reflect a fundamental insight into the nature of human social identity – that accounts for the popular appeal of nationalism in the modern world. It is also an interpretation broadly shared by many theorists, the most prominent of whom has been Elie Kedourie. Although he rejects the validity of most of its claims, Kedourie regards nationalism as essentially invented by the intelligentsia – a 'comprehensive doctrine which leads to a distinctive style of politics'.[13] The process of mobilisation and achievement of statehood is seen as a direct consequence of the intrinsic resonance of nationalism *vis-à-vis* other competing ideologies.[14]

In practice, however, while the ideology itself is clearly sufficient motivation for some nationalist supporters to support such a movement, it does not adequately explain the doctrine's appeal to the masses. Part of the answer to this problem lies in the nature of the relationship between nationalism and ethnicity. Some theorists, most notably Anthony Smith, have argued that there is an 'ethnic core' at the centre of successful attempts to construct a nation. Sidestepping the primor-dialist/ instrumentalist debate that preoccupies many theorists of eth-nicity he suggests that this core adapts over time to changing political contexts, and in the modern era is manifest as nationalism.[15] The notion that this means the roots of nationalism necessarily lie in antiquity should not be automatically endorsed (the Afrikaners, and the language that defined them, did not even exist until the late nine-teenth century). However, Smith's contention that the success of nationalist movements depends in large part on whether the newly articulated ideological appeal resonates with broader, pre-existing ethnic sentiments merits close analysis.

ECONOMY AND ORGANISATION

While psychological propensities to mobilisation may be a necessary factor in collective mobilisation, they are rarely sufficient.[16] This has led several theorists to suggest that another key factor in the success or failure of social movements is the *resources* available to them, most importantly the strength and durability of the formal organisational structures they are able to establish. These in turn are conditioned by a number of other structural variables ranging from the state's propen-sity for coercion against the group and the strength and nature of political alignments with, or opposition from, other organisations.[17] Further studies have also demonstrated the importance of related factors such as the political capabilities of the mass base and the existence of indigenous social frameworks (for example religious or recreation groups) that can be taken over and utilised by a move-ment.[18]

Once those organisations are formed, moreover, they become inde-pendent actors. The responses of the people they seek to recruit or influence and the prevailing political powers they oppose become partly shaped by the groups themselves and the particular strategies they undertake. For example, there is some evidence that when social movements use force, their longer-term goals are more likely to be met than if they stick to peaceful protest.[19] Also, many social movements appear to benefit from so-called 'radical flank' effects – where the existence of a radical wing helps legitimise the activities of the more moderate centre.[20] The extent to which either of these is true for nationalist movements needs to be studied. Is there a distinctive manner in which they articulate their goals and shape their mobilisation strategies?

Finally, it is also necessary to examine the economic dimensions of such mobilisation. On one level, to fund and sustain their struggle, nationalist movements clearly need to accumulate economic resources themselves. On another, strengthening the power of the nation-state, and by extension the material wealth of the nation's constituents is a key goal of nationalist economic policies. Most commonly this leads to the promotion of autarkic domestic policies and mercantilist stance on international trade issues, all of which carry implicit material rewards for the members of the nation.[21] But there are also often direct, micro-level economic benefits promised to or provided for members of nationalist movements. As Daniel Bell has pointed out, one reason ethnic appeals tend to be more successful than class ones is specifically because they can combine economic interests with emotional arguments.[22] The manner and extent to which this is a feature of nationalist mobilisation needs to be explicitly addressed.

ETHNIC CONFLICT AND STATE-MAKING

The process of mobilisation can also be spurred on by various external pressures, most notably conflict with other groups. This is well established in the study of nationalism, where there is widespread evidence that ethnic divisions can often precipitate or intensify nationalist feelings.[23] What has rarely been recognised, however, is the fact that such conflict can also be a spur to forming new organisational structures. Charles Tilly has shown how conflict between the emerging states of early modern Western Europe helped stimulate the formation of new bureaucracies, innovative forms of revenue enhancement, and the creation of broader, more efficient institutional structures. Central to all these processes, he suggests, was coercive power, encompassing not only the monopoly of domestic force but, as important, the ability to make war with other states.[24]

Although Tilly's focus is on existing states (and he regards nation-building as merely a functional response to state development designed to impose cultural homogeneity on society) we do not have to accept such an instrumentalist perspective to recognise the importance of these ideas to the study of ethnic nationalism. In the case of nationalist movements not yet in control of the state, it reinforces the need to examine their organisational activities. Bureaucracies are necessary to the exercise of power, and nationalist movements engaged in sustained conflict with the existing government and/or other groups frequently seek to establish their own power bases separate from the state. The extent to which ethnic conflict shaped the bureaucratic structure of each nationalist movement and their willingness and capacity to use force in pursuit of their goals needs to be examined.

THE INTERNATIONAL SYSTEM AND LEGITIMACY

While analysts of nationalism often marginalise the importance of extra-statal events, international relations theorists have for the most part neglected nationalist movements. In practice, however the international system can have a profound impact on the internal dynamics of states.[25] It is only logical, therefore, that global crises and other extraneous events can have a significant effect on nationalist movements operating within states. At the same time, nationalist movements should themselves be seen as international actors with political goals.[26] Indeed, one of the most distinctive aspects of nationalist mobilisation compared to most other social movements is that it has always had an explicit international dimension. All such movements are at least partly guided by the doctrine of national self-determination: the idea that every nation has the right to an independent state.[27] This means that aspiring states also need to achieve international legitimacy – the acceptance, or at least acquiescence of other states of their right to exist.[28] Whether such recognition is forthcoming depends in large part on the attitude of countries, especially great powers, with interests in the particular region or territory in which the nationalist movement operates.[29] Accordingly, the extent to which nationalist movements have to develop strategies for international diplomacy to further their goals needs to be a key part of the analysis.

In addition to international legitimacy, however, nationalist movements also need to attack the domestic legitimacy of the existing order: the popular acceptance of, or acquiescence in, its right to exist and govern. Nationalist movements, by definition, insist that the only legitimate form of government for a state is a national one. This is a normative claim that aims to undermine non-nationalist conceptions of the state order. Any increase in the power and influence of nationalist movements must, therefore, at least partly reflect a shift in popular perceptions about the legitimacy of the existing political order. In domestic politics, transfers of power often take place when the existing state suffers some form of 'legitimacy crisis' as a consequence of which the population loses its faith in the existing state order and seeks to replace it.[30] In such cases, moreover, the key for groups seeking to usurp state power is not necessarily to win over a majority of the overall population (in South Africa, for example, until the 1980s most domestic politics was focused exclusively on the white population). Rather, as David Held puts it, 'what matters most is not the moral approval of a society's members...but the approval of dominant groups...[amongst whom] the politically powerful and mobilised, including the state's personnel, are particularly important'.[31] The extent to which nationalist movements are able to do this by engineering or taking advantage of such legitimacy crises also needs to be investigated.

CONCLUSIONS

Understanding how nationalist movements develop is clearly a complex, interdisciplinary task. This chapter has sought to set out an analytical framework to study their growth and development. It argues that understanding the nature of the struggle for power by nationalist movements requires studying two complex but related phenomena: nation-building and state-making. The former involves the process of ethnic mobilisation around nationalist organisations that develop, promote and disseminate an ethnically exclusive ideology premised on state control. The latter involves the carving out of a new state in the international system or the usurpation of control of an existing state.

To understand how this process takes place, it is necessary to be aware of the conditioning effects of structural changes – particularly the political and economic opportunities permitted by the prevailing state – on the strategies and development of nationalist movements. But to explain properly how nationalist movements took advantage of structural opportunities to mobilise and take power, several other issues need to be addressed. First, the study needs to analyse the nationalist ideology and the manner and extent to which its articulation and dissemination were conditioned and shaped by ethno-cultural issues such as language and religion. Second, it needs to encompass the organisations which grew up to articulate this ideology and lead the struggle for power, examining the manner in which they were shaped by factors such as ethnic conflict and material issues. Finally, it must also include the international context of national mobilisation, examining the impact of external powers and events on the nationalist struggle.

The next four chapters will examine these issues – and the interaction between them – in the three case studies. Chapters 2 and 3 look at the organisational development of the nationalist movements in relation to the state with a focus on ethno-cultural and economic factors respectively. Chapter 4 examines how each movement was affected by, and sought to influence, ethnic conflict. Finally, Chapter 5 examines the impact of external geopolitical factors on each struggle as well as the diplomatic attempts to secure international sovereignty. Although I have tried to keep the narrative broadly chronological, the thematic nature of each chapter means that there is occasionally some overlap, and where appropriate, I have made references in the text.

2 Ethnicity and Ideology

INTRODUCTION

The prior existence of some kind of ethnic consciousness among a substantial proportion of the target population is critical for the emergence of ethnic nationalism. The exploitation of ethnic links via nationalist ideology necessarily draws on various historical, cultural and religious elements related to ethnic identity. Accordingly, the most important initial requirement of a nationalist movement is the construction and dissemination of a suitable ideological foundation for nurturing national sentiment and executing the political struggle of national independence. This chapter shows how ethnic nationalism first arose in each country and examines each movement's early attempts at political mobilisation. It argues that while these efforts manage to win over a committed core of support, ultimately each movement was fundamentally handicapped by the structural limitations of its nascent national organisation. It shows that while the development of a nationalist ideology grounded in language, culture and religion was essential to the establishment and early development of each movement, it was not nearly sufficient to meet the goal of taking control of the state.

IRELAND

This section argues that ethnic nationalism, in the sense of a nationalist political ideology linked to explicit ethno-cultural and linguistic demands, did not become a significant force in Ireland until the end of the nineteenth century. It suggests that prior nationalist movements and uprisings all contributed, in the context of a modernising Irish state, to a growing ethnic consciousness amongst the intelligentsia and the middle classes. Only once this was in place, and a constitutional approach to addressing national aspirations partially discredited, was a new, ethnic-based mass movement focusing on Catholic political and cultural autonomy able to establish itself.

The section begins by analysing the various nationalist and quasi-nationalist movements of the early and mid-nineteenth century. It then looks at the Land War of the 1870s and the Home Rule strategies of

Charles Stewart Parnell. Following this it examines the early movements of the new nationalism such as the Gaelic League and Gaelic Athletic Association and suggests that these marked the foundation of an ethnic nationalism. Finally it turns to the political origins of Sinn Fein and analyses the party's early activities while seeking to explain its limited political success.

The Origins of Irish Nationalism

When Ireland was granted restricted political autonomy from Great Britain in 1782 Sir Henry Grattan, leader of the new Dublin parliament, declared that 'Ireland is now a nation'. The term 'nation' was also widely used in Wolfe Tone's United Irishmen movement in the period up to the failed revolt against British rule that he had led in 1798. According to the standard nationalist interpretation of Irish history, this was the period when modern Irish nationalism was born. It was under Tone that the first elements of nationalist iconography became widely used and recognised, notably the display of the green flag with the Harp of Erin. But while both Tone's republicanism and Grattan's parliamentarianism undoubtedly contained nationalist elements, neither grouping remotely constituted a mass-based, ethnic nationalist movement. Nor, in the first part of the nineteenth century, did Daniel O'Connell's Catholic Association and Repeal Movement even though the organisations pursued limited ethnic mobilisation along religious lines to secure, respectively, Catholic social and political rights and the repeal of the Act of Union.[1] Indeed, O'Connell came under withering criticism from later nationalist leaders for his neglect of issues of Irish language and history.

A far more influential precursor to Irish ethnic nationalism was the Young Ireland movement. Started by a Protestant, Thomas Davis, in the 1840s it was self-consciously styled on emerging European nationalist movements in Germany and Italy. Young Ireland introduced the romantic element critical for the emotional commitment demanded by ethnic nationalism. As one of Davis's chief lieutenants, Charles Gavan Duffy, put it, the nationalism they promoted sought to be non-sectarian, 'inspiring genuine emotion and comprising noble ends'.[2] Centred on the *Nation* newspaper, the movement began to develop and propound a new, nationalist history of Ireland. It extolled the activities of Tone and the United Irishmen, and started to write about and popularise a glorious Irish past – a field which had hitherto been the preserve of only a small coterie of Protestant history enthusiasts.[3] In tandem with the histories came a new nationalist iconography of Irish symbols, extolling Gaelic heroes of yore such as Cuchulain and Brian Boru as proof of a distinctive Irish identity.

The newspaper was a great success, eventually garnering the astonishing readership of 250 000.[4] Inspired by this, one of Davis's more radical supporters John Mitchel, founded another publication, *United Irishman*, which took an increasingly militant and confrontational attitude to Britain, particularly at the time of the potato famine. A typical issue decried British connivance in the 'famine and plague [that] have been slaughtering our countrymen' and strove to promote the 'holy hatred of foreign dominion'.[5] Mitchel was ultimately arrested and deported although some of his followers under Smith O'Brien launched an abortive and easily quashed rebellion in 1848. Despite its ineffectiveness, that revolt marked the successful launch of a powerful new symbol of Irish nationalism – the tricolour flag of orange, green and white that, ironically, was designed to symbolise unity between Protestants and Catholics, but ultimately came to represent Catholic exclusivism.[6]

By the end of the Famine, Young Ireland and its offshoots were already fading from the political scene. Their effect, however, had been significant. While the organisation's ostensibly non-sectarian ideology, combined with a largely Protestant leadership, precluded it from promoting an exclusively ethnic nationalist movement, Young Ireland had inadvertently laid the ideological foundations for such a movement to arise. It had introduced the growing Catholic elite – already politicised along ethnic lines by O'Connell – to a new nationalist history and iconography that was defiantly anti-British. This helped establish an ethnic consciousness among the broader Catholic community and plant the seeds of ethnic nationalism in its small but growing intelligentsia.

Nevertheless, after the disappointments of 1848, the cultural and political initiative among Irish nationalists shifted to the growing population of American expatriates.[7] In 1858, with American influence, the Irish Republican Brotherhood, a semi-secret organisation aiming at the violent overthrow of British rule, was formed. Popularly known as Fenians (after the Fianna warriors of ancient Ireland) they built up a wide-ranging but inchoate movement with members spread through small towns and villages. But although later nationalists liked to paint a picture of committed revolutionaries in constant struggle against the British, in practice, many members only joined so as to take advantage of the many recreational activities, circumventing the harsh social strictures imposed by the Church. As such, the group provided a 'forum for fraternal association and communal self-expression' for the great majority of poorer Irishmen still frozen out of the parliamentary political process by the restricted franchise.[8] The Fenians did manage to expand in rural Ireland, eventually building up a membership of 200 000.[9] But while they may have been relatively effective mobilisers, as revolutionaries the Fenians were conspicuous failures. An IRB-sponsored uprising in 1867 failed to garner significant support and proved a pitiful affair, quickly crushed by the British.

Following the disastrous rebellion, the group reorganised itself into a smaller and more clandestine organisation while setting up a formal leadership in the form of a Supreme Council. Its new constitution stated, unambiguously if somewhat optimistically, that

> [t]he object of the Irish Republican Brotherhood is to establish and maintain a free and independent Republican government in Ireland .... The Supreme Council of the IRB is hereby declared to be in fact as well as by name, the sole government of the Irish Republic.[10]

In practice, however, the IRB represented even less of a cohesive nationalist movement than had Young Ireland. Its importance was to sustain the anti-British republican tradition rather than introduce or spread a coherent nationalist doctrine and political programme. Nonetheless, by dint of its predominantly Catholic membership it helped nurture the growth of a religious-based, ethnic political awareness in Ireland.

The Land War and Parnellism

In the late 1870s, following a series of particularly poor harvests, a new grouping, the Land League, was formed to address land grievances. Led by Michael Davitt, an IRB member, the League aimed at becoming a country-wide organisation that would single out, and target for protest, landlords responsible for unfair evictions while at the same time demanding the passage of major reforms at Westminster. With its dynamic, centralised leadership and a powerful message that had immediate resonance for most Irishmen, the League spread quickly through the country, even in towns. In doing so, it generated a degree of active, mass support for its goal that was unprecedented in modern Irish history. More importantly, it established a cohesive, organisational network that allowed for the countrywide coordination of popular action.

This in turn laid the groundwork for what came to be called the 'New Departure' in parliamentary politics under the leadership of the Protestant landlord, Charles Stewart Parnell. Parnell was a member of the Home Rule movement, a loose coalition of Irish parliamentarians at Westminster under the leadership of Isaac Butt. Following the extension of the franchise in the United Kingdom after the passage of Reform Acts in 1867 and 1884, for the first time a significant proportion of Irish voters were Catholics. The Home Rule faction was a new political grouping that, relying on a mixture of Protestant and Catholic electoral support, sought to secure for the Irish 'the right and privilege of managing our own affairs'.[11] Following the Land League's suppression by the British authorities, Parnell allied himself with Davitt in a new organisation called the National Land League. At the same time he became leader of the Home Rule movement at parliament, with the faction becoming known as the Irish Parliamentary Party, or simply the Parliamentary Party. In doing so, Parnell innovatively wedded the two traditions of parliamentary and extra-parliamentary politics in Ireland. Also, by briefly joining the IRB and professing sympathy with their goals (and serving a short jail sentence), Parnell was largely able to neutralise hardline opposition to his policies from more radical, revolutionary nationalists. The result was that he became the undisputed leader of a powerful, new movement aimed at the establishment of an independent Ireland.[12] As T.W. Moody puts it, 'the struggle for land and the struggle for independence became merged in a mass movement without a precedent in Irish history'.[13]

Combining demands for national self-government with those for land reform proved a powerful rallying call. In the 1885 elections Parnell was able to gain overwhelming support from voters outside the North-East and Dublin. Entering an alliance with Gladstone's Liberals following the latter's public conversion to the cause of Home Rule, the Irish Party's haul of 85 seats gave it the balance of power. Despite this, the resultant bill was defeated in parliament by the newly formed Unionists and the Liberals forced from office. Parnell continued to agitate at Westminster, but in the face of a determined British government he was unable to achieve anything substantive. In 1890, he was brought down in an adultery scandal. Condemned by the Catholic Church, most of his political allies, including Gladstone, refused to stand by him. The issue split the party, leaving it a directionless and largely powerless shell. Parnell died the next year, a broken man.

Despite the Parliamentary Party's ultimate failure, the 1880s are commonly regarded by historians as the high point of 'constitutional nationalism'.[14] Nonetheless, there is a real question as to just how strong Parnell's nationalist credentials were. He was certainly willing to use stirring rhetoric (such as his most famous rallying cry that 'No man can set bounds to the march of a nation'), but he himself showed little attachment to nationalist ideology. The Parliamentary Party's general neglect of national symbols, history, or support for Irish national culture further supports this claim. Even Parnell's political goals were highly circumscribed: the Home Rule bill he had been prepared to accept approved only a very limited form of self-government. Nonetheless, the underlying fact was that the Land War and Parnellism had together mobilised and politicised Ireland in an unprecedented manner. The political movements directed by O'Connell in the 1820s and 1830s, the nationalist history and icono-graphy used by Young Ireland in the 1840s and the republicanism and militancy of the IRB in the 1860s and 70s had all combined to generate a high degree of ethnic consciousness and political awareness. Under Parnell, for the first time, these sentiments were used to galvanise Irish support under a broad, if ill-defined, nationalist banner.

The political and economic structure of Ireland helped dictate the shape and dimensions of this emerging national challenge. During the course of the century, the literacy rate rose dramatically in response to both the continued spread of priest-driven Catholic schools and some educational reforms undertaken by the government following the famine. Also, while there may have been no industrial bourgeoisie of significance in Ireland, through the agency of the state, a modern infrastructure was gradually being set up while a broader middle and lower middle class became established in the towns and villages. Better transport and communications systems combined with a committed leadership, allowed for the formation of country-wide organisations. At the same time, the process of gradual enfranchisement had redir-ected political debate, at least among the wealthier and better edu-cated Catholic elite who now became voters, away from revolutionary means towards constitutional, parliamentary agitation. If the Fenian movement had been, at least in part, an attempt by the disenfranchised Catholics to pursue their goal of political independence, Parnellism was an attempt to harness those shock troops in support of parliament-ary politics. Following the Land War, the focus of both the IRB and Home Rulers shifted to Westminster and away from demands for full political independence or republicanism achieved via revolution.

The Gaelic Revival

But if ethnic consciousness now existed in Ireland, no fully articulated ethnic nationalism yet did. Young Ireland had begun the process, and the gradual growth in popularity of symbols, such as songs, flags and new monuments testified to a spreading awareness of a cultural basis to Irish national identity, but no cohesive ethno-national ideological or organisational network was in place to direct these feelings. Nevertheless, indications of the gradual emergence of such a movement were increasingly evident from the 1870s onwards. In 1876, the Society for the Preservation of the Irish Language was established by a small group of Gaelic supporters. This marked the first serious attempt to extol Gaelic as part of Irish ethnic identity after well over a century of neglect. Three years later it was buttressed by the establishment of a Gaelic Union and in 1892 a National Literary Society was formed to promote traditional Irish literature and poetry. Although small and largely confined to the intelligentsia – schoolteachers, clergy and the like – these groups provided a new outlet for the further elaboration and dissemination of national histories and verse. Ultimately, several regional literary societies were formed too, the most important and influential being the Cork Literary Society.

From 1892, the selling of such a romantic approach to Irish history and literature was diligently undertaken by a new organisation, the Gaelic League. The League was dedicated to the development and spread of the Gaelic language and sought to repackage and broaden the ideology introduced by Young Ireland with a new, Gaelic gloss. It was led by another Protestant, Douglas Hyde and Eoin Macneill, a poet and writer. Officially a non-political, cultural organisation, the League claimed to seek national regeneration through the resurrection of the Gaelic language and a literary revival which together would serve to 'tend the flame of national pride'.[15] This focus on language allowed for the articulation of a new ethnic political discourse. As Hyde put it (using the eugenicist terminology that was becoming increasingly fashionable throughout contemporary Europe), 'the Celtic race' that comprised the core of modern Irish identity was being swamped by pernicious 'Anglicisation'.[16] To counteract this devilish force he urged that Gaelic be formally introduced in schools, and called for all people, places, sports, history and literature to be re-'Gaelicised'. The League itself was formed

lest we the nation should forget that the sacred pain of nationality –
which is the driving force and vital breath of all our struggles, the
spell which makes hope enchanting, the consecration which lifts us
above the paltry contention of the hour and makes even suffering
and failure sweet – has its origins deep in the recesses of the past,
among the old associations of which the Gaelic language is the very
living voice and soul.[17]

Not only did this mark the politicisation of ethnicity, but the new
emphasis on racial and linguistic characteristics implicitly excluded
Protestants. With the notable exception of Hyde, the Gaelic League's
membership was almost exclusively Catholic. Prominent in the leadership throughout, moreover, was a solid IRB element including Mac-
Neill himself. The Brotherhood was attracted to the ideals of the
League and saw it as a useful vehicle for spreading its own gospel of
violent resistance. Using such ethnic-based ideological arguments, the
new movement grew rapidly. Employing educational classes, drama,
and social events (increasingly described in traditional Gaelic terms
such as *feisanna*), it established a broad social network to promote its
cultural core. By 1897, the League had 43 branches, and its books and
music were reaching an ever-widening audience.[18] By explicitly linking
its cultural claims to traditional anti-British grievances in making the
core policy one of 'De-Anglicisation', they found a new means of
reasserting their secular authority. It also issued an ongoing series of
books along the lines of 'Love Songs of Ireland' and 'Irish Fairy Tales'.
    In 1899, a more ambitious, and self-consciously literary movement
was established in the guise of the Irish National Theatre. Formed by
the Protestant poet W.B. Yeats, this new body hoped to minister to the
intellectual and spiritual needs of the Irish nation through poetry and
plays.[19] Yeats and his allies sought not just national independence but
the establishment and institutionalisation of an all-encompassing Irish
national cultural heritage.[20] They felt that Ireland had a unique opportunity to develop a mass national literature of genuine literary merit and
complained bitterly of the 'melodrama' of Young Ireland tradition and
its shallow, romanticised historics. Their aim was to establish a model of
the Irish nation through the Arts that would strike a popular chord and
help the pursuit of national independence. But, the Irish public proved
resistant to such highbrow attempts at nation-building. At the Abbey
Theatre, Yeats's own play *Cathleen ni Houlihan* proved relatively successful, but others, most notoriously J. M. Synge's *Playboy of the Western
World* were publicly condemned for their perceived denigration of 'true'

Irish culture. In practice, the Irish masses remained far more receptive to the cheap popularism of the Davisite tradition than the convoluted intellectual approach of the poet and his cohorts. The public wanted heroes first and literature second. By supplying national myths in easily accessible forms, the Gaelic League established the foundations for a genuine mass, ethnic nationalist movement.

Initially, however, the League's appeal was largely limited to the intelligentsia and upper middle class. Schoolteachers were very prominent, as were some junior clergy and a wide number of civil servants.[21] As the self-appointed guardians of the Irish literary historical heritage, such figures' livelihood and authority within their town and village communities depended in large part on public interest in literature and history. Two events, however, combined to widen interest and support from the wider population. The first of these was the centenary celebration for the 1798 uprising. With national histories disseminated in pamphlet, newspaper and song, the League (largely under the influence of its IRB members) organised a highly successful set of countrywide festivities culminating in a mass celebration at Tone's grave at Bodenstown. Forgotten was the essential ambiguity of Tone's personality and the unrepresentative nature of his movement and revolt – he was now the first great martyr of modern Irish nationalism, the man who started a chain of resistance to the British occupation that led in turn to the uprisings of 1805, 1848 and 1867. His story became inspiration to the masses and his burial place was effectively transformed into a sacred national site to which committed nationalists would now make pilgrimage.

The second event was the Anglo-Boer War of 1899–1901. The sight of a small 'nation' struggling for freedom against the might of the oppressive British Empire struck a resonant chord with the Irish. A brigade of volunteers went out to fight for the Boers, and nearly all Irish political leaders from the parliamentarians to the IRB made public statements of solidarity with the embattled Afrikaners. Collections were held, songs written and even some streets renamed in their honour. This spilled over into a new articulation of Irish ethnic pride, a sentiment that the League was ideally placed to tap and direct. By 1904, it had expanded to 600 branches with over 50 000 members and many more consumers of its literature.[22] Three years later, it had increased to 75 000.[23] The message of a distinctive national cultural and linguistic tradition that separated the Irish from the English at all levels of society proved increasingly persuasive. Nearly all the history and most of the traditional occasions were 'imagined' but their success testified to the new existence of a shared ethnic consciousness amongst the Irish people.

The Athletic Association, the Church and Irish Ireland

Popular though it became, however, a different kind of organisation was needed to bring the message of the Gaelic revival to the attention of the mass populace. The Gaelic Athletic Association, a group which had been founded in 1884 to revive the ancient Irish sports of hurling and Gaelic football, came to fill this role. Within a year of its formation it was drawing an average of 15 000 spectators a match. Like the League, it was officially non-political while in practice being strongly nationalist. An early resolution adopted by the Association stated that '[t]he GAA shall not be used in any way to oppose any nationalist movement which has the confidence and support of the leaders of the Irish people'.[24] In reality, however, the Association was always strongly associated with the IRB and the Catholic Church. A messy and divisive power struggle between those two bodies over which would directly control the GAA continued throughout much of the 1890s and was ultimately decided in the IRB's favour.

Like the League, the GAA benefited greatly from the national sentiment stirred by the Boer War, and even named some of their teams after Afrikaners. One official was heard to observe that 'sooner or later Irishmen would adopt Boer tactics – the sooner the better'.[25] By the end of the war, membership had expanded hugely and Gaelic games were regularly attracting crowds of 32 000 and more. This was comparable to the crowds drawn by soccer in England and was a stunning testament to the GAA's success given the smaller size and wider distribution of the Irish population. As W. F. Mandle has put it

> The growth of the Gaelic games enabled the myth and self-consciousness of a Celtic past to be brought to people untouched by the earnestly middle-class Gaelic League, by Yeats's *Oisin* or by Hyde's *Love Songs of Connacht*.[26]

This in turn allowed the GAA to establish a wide-ranging network of associated clubs in most Irish schools and colleges. Its activities also became widely publicised and reported in the popular press, including accounts of hurling and Irish football together with the standard history lessons, poems, songs and literature.[27]

The combination of all these factors served to raise Irish ethno-national consciousness dramatically amongst GAA members and supporters. It was, moreover, an exclusively Catholic ethnic conscious-ness. The GAA's internal newspaper, *The Champion*, explicitly identi-fied Irish games with Catholics, and, even though it lost official control of the Association, the Catholic Church remained highly influential among GAA leadership throughout its existence, with prelates often acting as official sponsors of the Association's activities. As important, the GAA proved a prime recruiting ground for various other nation-alist movements, especially the IRB. This drew the attention of the police, who were openly worried about its role as a forum for 'rebel-lious and seditious ideas'.[28] At the same time, the GAA constitution forbade any members of the army or constabulary to play in its teams and such social ostracism acted as a disincentive for young Irishmen seeking careers in either of those fields.

Although Catholicism was a key ingredient in the Gaelic Revival – and despite its direct involvement in the GAA – the Catholic Church itself had an ambiguous relationship with the growing ethnic national-ist movement. Building on religious revivalist movements that arose in the latter part of the century, its traditional sectarian authority over the Irish people was consolidated and expanded – a growth that was aided by the disestablishment of the Church of Ireland in 1869.[29] Outside the religious realm, however, the Church was primarily concerned with maintaining clerical control over education, not questions of sover-eignty.[30] Although it supported nationalist principles, the Church preached submission to civil power and condemned violence. By and large, this meant giving qualified support to the Parliamentary Party, although it did encourage the Gaelic League, which it saw as an antidote to the 'immoral' publications arriving from England. The leaders of the Gaelic Revival also preached respect for St Patrick as a symbol of Irish nationalism and this enabled the Church to use nationalist ideology to promote its own agenda. But while the hierar-chy vacillated, many junior clergymen were actively supportive of, and often directly involved in, the national movement. As teachers, priests drummed these ideas into schoolchildren, immersing a new generation in clerical-nationalist principles.

The growing ethnic exclusivity of the nationalist movement was becoming increasingly evident. Most notably, D.P. Moran, a prominent journalist, began propounding the notion of 'Irish Ireland' – a veiled phrase essentially meaning non-Protestant – via the pages of his newspaper, *The Leader*. Moran extolled the Gaelic language and Catholicism in similar but more emphatic vein than O'Brien:

We must retrace our steps and take as much of our inspiration as possible from our own country and its history. We must be original Irish and not imitation English. Above all we must relearn our language and become a bilingual people. For the great connecting link between us and the real Ireland which few of us know anything about, is the Gaelic tongue.[31]

Moran was visceral on the subject of O'Connell, whom he saw as having contributed to the destruction of Gaelic, and lukewarm about all other nationalist leaders from Tone to Parnell. He also criticised Yeats for continuing to write Anglicised versions of national history. More strikingly, in his public statements, Moran made the Catholic element of the Gaelic movement explicit, charging that 'in the main non-Catholic Ireland looks upon itself as British or Anglo-Irish' and that 'the Irish nation is *de facto* a Catholic nation'.[32]

In such a conception, therefore, an independent Ireland that was not both Catholic and grounded in Gaelic language and history would be worthless. Political sovereignty was seen not as an end in itself (as it was for Grattan or even Parnell) but a means to fulfilling the special nature of the nation through its own ethnic characteristics such as language and religion. Issues of language and culture rather than calls for Home Rule or republic, had become the core element of the nascent ethnic nationalist movement. Cultural issues became political ones. Although relatively few people agreed with the extreme line taken by Moran, the Gaelic movement was clearly proving to be a particularly effective and emotionally resonant mobilising tool. The League began to expand its influence by giving classes in Gaelic to nearly 250 000 people. Despite the fervour of its leadership, however, the League made little progress in reclaiming the linguistic ground lost to English. At a purely practical level, this was unsurprising. By the beginning of the 1890s fewer than one in seven Irish people spoke Gaelic.[33] Nonetheless, while it lost the battle for Gaelic as a spoken language, the League was slowly winning the war for Irish support as awareness of and respect for the Gaelic heritage steadily grew.

Political Dimensions

In 1899, Arthur Griffith, a journalist recently returned from several years in South Africa, founded a new nationalist paper called *Sinn Fein* – 'Ourselves'. Its first issue declared:

Lest there be any doubt in any mind, we will say that we accept the nationalism of '98, '48, and '67 as the true nationalism and Grattan's cry 'Live Ireland, Perish the Empire!' as the watchword of patriotism.[34]

A year later, he formed a loose political grouping, *Cumann na nGaedhael*, to focus on Irish regeneration in language, music, history and industry. In 1905 it combined with a number of other small nationalist groups to form a new umbrella organisation that also went by the name Sinn Fein and promoted self-sufficiency in all spheres of life. Declaring that 'between the individual and humanity stands and must continue to stand a great fact – the nation', Griffith staked a new middle ground between the traditional political poles of parliamentary agitation and violent revolution. [35]

He favoured a conscious imitation of the successful *Ausgleich* of 1867 that had led to the establishment of Hungarian political autonomy within the Austro-Hungarian empire, and urged all Irish MPs to boycott Westminster until Britain granted independence. But although it was nominally open to Protestants, Sinn Fein was in practice a more exclusively Catholic organisation than its political predecessors. As a later member put it, the organisation's key aim was to turn Ireland into the 'working model of a modern Catholic state'.[36] Meanwhile, a new generation of leaders had taken over the IRB and the organisation was beginning to expand once more. IRB members secretly joined and came to dominate first the GAA and then the Gaelic League and both organisations became important sources of recruitment.[37] While it never came to control Sinn Fein, significant overlapping membership meant that the links between the two groups soon became extensive and Griffith himself was briefly an IRB member. Both had an activist membership that was predominantly young, Catholic, male, drawn from the intelligentsia and petty bourgeoisie – shopkeepers, teachers, and the like.[38] Reflecting these new links, the IRB itself began to take on a more ethnic nationalist persona. The vague revolutionary republicanism of the 1860s and 70s was evolving into a sophisticated ethno-national agenda. Together with Sinn Fein, the IRB stood at the centre of a countrywide organisational network with a powerful core of committed members.

But despite the rising profile of these groups, by far the most prominent political actors in Ireland remained Parnell's successors in the Irish Parliamentary party. After a decade divided between pro and anti-Parnellites, a new grassroots group, the United Irish League forced the factions to reunite in 1901 under the leadership of John Redmond. This allowed the party once again to pursue Parnell's strategy of making common cause with the Liberals in exchange for a promise of Home Rule, while hoping for the balance of members in a hung parliament. Redmond and his fellow party members would openly use nationalist language in and outside Parliament, but retained their focus on political rather than cultural goals.[39] Nevertheless, the Parliamentary party did not take up the cause or language of ethnic nationalism. Organisationally too it had serious deficiencies and garnered little support among poorer urban dwellers or in the countryside.[40] Its success was largely a result of the prevailing political structure. Given the fact that most Irishmen now had the vote, a constitutional approach to addressing Irish grievances still seemed the most logical approach. Playing balance of power politics in Westminster was a strategy that had come close to success under Parnell and appeared to have a realistic chance of working in the future.

Conclusions

While the struggle for political independence had a long pedigree in Irish history, it was not until Parnell's death that an overtly ethnic nationalist movement based on the Catholic population and its Gaelic heritage came into being. Before a viable ethnic nationalist movement could be established a literate Catholic intelligentsia had to form, and the weak form of political nationalism derived from Grattan that sought constitutional redress of Irish grievances had to be discredited. O'Connell's Repeal Movement, Young Ireland and the Land League all helped raise ethnic consciousness and increase the propensity for political organisation, but none explicitly undertook ethnic mobilisation under a nationalist banner. Following Parnell's death, however, the new, educated, and increasingly urbanised Catholic community that had grown up over the course of the century became more receptive to the ethnic ideology promoted by the different organisations underpinning the Gaelic revival. By 1906, Sinn Fein, the IRB and, if not the hierarchy of the Catholic Church, many of its clergy, stood at the head of a wide-ranging organisational network comprising movements involved in culture, language, literature and athletics.

The common factor across all the constituent groups was their concern with more than simply political sovereignty. Political independence was the primary goal, but the means mattered as well – the route to power would be through ethnic mobilisation. In the 20 years following Parnell's death, Irish nationalism changed both its character and strategies. A significant, exclusivist, Gaelic-Catholic strain had come to political prominence. But while these new nationalist groups had a strong impact on the local political and cultural scene, they were still very far from taking power. Despite its faults, the Parliamentary Party retained its dominance.

This continued constitutionalism was primarily a result of the political structure of Ireland. As the franchise had been extended to an increasing number of Catholics in the latter part of the nineteenth century, the possibility of using Parliament to redress Irish grievances helped restrict the popularity of alternative tactics of revolution and secession. Had the Irish been completely denied the vote, then a broader and more violent ethnic nationalism would almost certainly have grown up far earlier in the century. With the parliamentary outlet, however, such alternative strategies could achieve only limited popularity. Nevertheless, Sinn Fein's continued political weakness and the Gaelic movement's failure to effect the resurrection of Gaelic as a spoken language despite its successes in raising it to the status of national icon, clearly showed the political limitations of a strategy built around ethno-cultural arguments alone. Historical, cultural and religious appeals to a common ethnicity made for a powerful mix that could command the loyalty of a significant sector of the population. But as election results (and the lack of rural mobilisation among the disenfranchised) clearly demonstrated, the mass of the population remained either firmly wedded to the constitutional approach of the Parliamentary Party or oblivious to the political struggle. The ideological message propounded by the new ethno-nationalists was not strong enough to deliver power to Sinn Fein and statehood to Ireland.

THE AFRIKANERS

This section looks at the early development of the cultural and linguistic elements of an exclusive Afrikaner nationalism in South Africa. It argues that neither the nineteenth-century Boer Republics nor the Cape Afrikaners were genuine nationalists but suggests that they were nonetheless critical in helping politicise Afrikaners along ethnic lines. An authentic ethnic nationalism only arose with the formation of the Broederbond and its cultural offshoots in the 1920s and the Purified National Party (GNP) in the early 1930s. These organisations were able to capitalise on the foundations laid by the earlier movements and establish a fully articulated ethnic nationalist ideology together with a solid organisational base around which to build a nationalist movement.

The section opens by examining the republics and the Cape Afrikaners during the nineteenth century. It then looks at the Christian National Movement that arose in the wake of the Boer War. It analyses the activities of Hertzog's National Party in the new South African state and then examines the formation of the Afrikaner Broederbond. It looks at the Broederbond's early activities in the cultural sphere and assesses its importance to the development of ethnic nationalism. Finally it turns to the establishment of the GNP in 1933 and the nation-building activities undertaken by these groups through the course of the 1930s.

Afrikaner Ethnic Consciousness

Although it is now well established that the Great Trek of the 1830s and 40s was not in practice the first manifestation of self-conscious Afrikaner nationalists seeking independence on the frontier, it did nonetheless indicate that a separate Afrikaner ethnic consciousness had developed. The weak Boer republics of the Transvaal and the Orange Free State, established in the 1850s, were places where a few tens of thousands of Afrikaners lived on sprawling, poorly run farms in semi-literate communities united by bonds of religion and common lifestyle. But they were far from constituting a nation, and there is no evidence that they thought of themselves in such terms. It was only after the British annexation of the Transvaal in 1879, and the subsequent winning back of independence as a result of the Battle of Majuba Hill in 1881, that the first inklings of a self-described 'national mission' emerged. Both republics had loose parliamentary *volksraads* – parliaments – and national flags, and were recognised by Treaty with the British, but remained politically and geographically divided.[41]

For those Afrikaners who stayed in the Cape, gradual exposure to British culture and education did eventually lead to the establishment of a small intelligentsia. In the late 1860s, a wealthy farmer, Jan Hendrik Hofmeyr started an Afrikaner Farmers Union and a Dutch newspaper, *De Zuid Afrikaan*. At the same time, under the guidance of Reverend S.J. Du Toit, what came to be known as the First Language Movement was launched. Du Toit founded the first Afrikaans language newspaper, *Die Patriot*, in 1876 along with the first Afrikaner cultural society, the *Genootskap van Regte Afrikaners* and then drew up the first

Afrikaans grammar and school readers.[42] In addition, he wrote an Afrikaans history of the region entitled *The History of our Country in the Language of our People*, which was the first work to assert that a new nation, the Afrikaners, had been forged by dint of their unique history in South Africa. As his paper unequivocally put it:

> If any Africander asks us what our purpose is, our answer is TO STAND FOR OUR LANGUAGE, OUR NATION AND OUR COUNTRY.[43]

Not unlike Young Ireland, Du Toit and his followers were able to create a sense of national identity and lay the foundation of a national myth, but could not translate it into a political movement. When an Afrikaner-based political party, the Afrikaner Bond, was formed in 1880, it did not adopt nationalist platforms. Rather, under Hofmeyr's guidance, it pursued a generally moderate programme aimed at addressing local economic grievances, with only limited demands for language and religious rights. The party platform, moreover, did not demand national independence or the expulsion of the British.[44] Hofmeyr's nationalism was highly inclusive. When he called for 'Africa for the Africanders' he included English-speaking inhabitants who gave their first loyalty to South Africa. As he put it in his autobiography:

> My definition [of an Afrikaner] embraces everyone who, having settled in this country, wants to stay here to help promote the common interest.[45]

This message proved relatively successful among Cape Afrikaners. By 1887 the Bond claimed over 2000 members, growing to 10 000 over the next twelve years and enjoying significant electoral success in the Cape Parliament.[46] As in Ireland, therefore, the use of parliamentary politics was directly shaped by prevailing political structure. With a gradually expanding property franchise from the 1850s onwards, the Cape Afrikaners, like wealthier Irish Catholics, had access to the ballot box and sought first to address their grievances through constitutional means.

Although Du Toit made vague intimations about an Afrikaner republic stretching from the Cape to the Zambesi, Hofmeyr's message achieved far greater resonance. Neither the Cape Language Movement nor the governments of the two Boer Republics to the north displayed much inclination towards the creation of a pan-South African Afrikaner identity. As late as the 1890s, the Transvaal's President Paul Kruger explicitly asserted that no-one whose descendants had not been part of the Great Trek could regard themselves as Afrikaners. At the same time, rather than pursuing an inflexibly anti-British line, the Afrikaner Bond allied for a time with the arch-imperialist Cecil Rhodes.

But while there was no nationalism in the sense of an explicit ideology calling for an Afrikaner state, there was increasing awareness amongst Afrikaners of the ethnic bonds of language and religion and history. This became particularly acute after the discovery of gold in 1886 in the Transvaal. Britain exploited the grievances of the newly arrived, foreign *uitlander* population of gold-rush followers gradually to increase its influence in the region, leading to the Jameson Raid in 1895 and finally culminating in the outbreak of the Boer War in 1899.[47] It was this conflict that first established a nascent national solidarity between Cape and Republican Afrikaners. The sentiment was encapsulated by a famous pamphlet drafted by the Stellenbosch- and Oxford-educated Jan Smuts, Transvaal's young attorney general. Entitled *A Century of Wrong* it lamented that

> [o]nce more the day has dawned in our blood-written history when we are compelled to take up arms and renew the struggle for liberty and existence and to entrust our national cause to that Providence which has led our people by miracles to South Africa.[48]

Like the opening statement in *Sinn Fein* newspaper in Ireland, it showed how retroactive historical myth-making was taking root among Afrikaners. The groundwork was being laid for a separate political identity built around an ethnic core of language and history.

After three years of bitter war, the British finally vanquished the Boers. Many thousands of Boer men had been killed in the conflict, and those who survived returned to farms and towns destroyed by Lord Kitchener's scorched-earth policy. The death from disease and starvation of 26 000 women and children in British concentration camps was a further devastating loss. Under the authority of Lord Milner and a group of associates, later dubbed his 'kindergarten', the British sought to remove the threat of renewed conflict with the Afrikaners by ruthlessly suppressing them. They pursued a strict Anglicisation policy, forbidding the teaching of Dutch or Afrikaans in schools or use of those languages in government. At the same time, they encouraged mass British immigration to dilute the Afrikaner population. As a later Afrikaner historian described it, emotionally but not altogether inaccurately:

[t]he Boers now found themselves under the hard, heartless government of Milner, who ruled as a dictator and was determined to break
the back of Afrikanerdom.[49]

A new organisation, the Christian National Education movement, was
founded in 1903 in opposition to the required teaching of English in
Afrikaans schools. This group became the driving force of the Second
Language Movement and began to revive and expand the notion of a
unique Afrikaner religious and linguistic background. Like the Gaelic
League's resurrection of Davisite ideas, the Christian Nationalists
sought to take Du Toit's message and use it to spearhead their own
opposition to Anglicisation. Also like the League, the progenitors of
this movement comprised an emerging intelligentsia.[50] Most were
professionals or teachers, including many churchmen, a disproportionately large number of whom harked from the small, highly conservative, Dopper sect.[51] But although a stubborn racism and a firm
commitment to Calvinist ethics were prevalent in the movement,
these values did not lead to the propagation of any explicitly nationalist
sentiments. Nevertheless, this clergy-driven education movement in
the North developed links with new language movements in the
Cape. This coincided with a new lyric poetry movement. Led by Totius
and C.J. Langenhoven, the advent of a genuine Afrikaans literature
provided a new source of ethno-linguistic pride and inspiration, not
unlike that promoted by Yeats and his followers.

In 1907, after the return to power of the Liberals in Britain, the new
Prime Minister, Sir Henry Campbell-Bannerman, granted the Transvaal and Orange Free State responsible government. The move caused
much trepidation among Tory backbenchers who feared that it set an
unhealthy precedent for other parts of the Empire, particularly Ireland. But in practice the new parliaments were dominated by conciliatory Afrikaner parties, largely in the spirit of Hofmeyr's old Afrikaner
Bond – *Het Volk* in the Transvaal under Boer War generals Louis
Botha and Jan Smuts and *Orangia Unie* in the Free State under
General De La Rey. Neither party was overtly nationalistic, but both
were strongly influenced by the Christian National Movement, and
pushed for the right to mother tongue education. In the Free State the
Education Minister, General J.B.M. Hertzog, passed a set of bills
calling for the equal teaching of Dutch and English in schools and a
certain number of hours of bible study. This marked the first battle-
ground of a nascent nationalism. Like the Gaelic revival movement the
active role of a growing intelligentsia in promoting issues of language

in education, marked the incursion of ethno-national sentiments in the political sphere.

Structural Effects of Union

In 1910, after lengthy negotiations between the four provinces, South Africa was established as a unitary state.[52] During the unification talks between 1907–10 by far the most contentious issue was the question of whether blacks should be granted the franchise. Hostility towards blacks, and more particularly the insistence that they should have no say in political matters, had long been a central tenet of Afrikaner belief. Nevertheless, the Cape colony had been successfully run on the basis of a colour-blind franchise that involved a small property qualification since 1853. Both these models provided possible precedents for a South African state. Arrayed firmly against the notion of a black vote were the Transvaal and the Orange Free State. On the other side, the Cape, under the leadership of Liberal Prime Minister John X. Merriman, pressed for the universal adoption of its own system.[53] After a bruising battle, the Afrikaner colonies won the issue, although the Cape was allowed to retain its own franchise system.[54] All Afrikaners were living in the same political unit for the first time since the 1830s, when little Afrikaner ethnic consciousness, let alone a national identity, had existed. Not only did politico-structural factors now create a context within which ethnic mobilisation was possible – they defined the shape which that mobilisation was most likely to take.

Most importantly, the franchise meant that if Afrikaners, who constituted 52 per cent of whites in 1911 and, due to a higher birth rate, a growing proportion thereafter, were ever able to orchestrate a successful mobilisation on an ethnic basis, they would be able to gain political power in a state in which they constituted a tiny minority. Without the all-white franchise it is extremely unlikely that an Afrikaner nationalist movement would ever have been able to take power by constitutional means. Even the relatively small number of blacks who would have been allowed to vote under the property franchise might have been sufficient to leave Afrikaners a minority among voters. Under such a situation, it is quite conceivable that Afrikaners would have shifted the focus of their political allegiance, either supporting an all-white alliance or splitting along class lines.

The racial franchise, therefore, was an essential prerequisite for the ability of an exclusive Afrikaner nationalism to take control of the state through normal political channels. The political structure of the South

African state implicitly encouraged the pursuit of ethnic political strategies by Afrikaners. As they had the vote, and thus direct influence over the established state structure, the Afrikaner nationalist movement, when it developed, had a great deal of political and economic space in which to pursue its goals. To follow successfully a nationalist strategy, Afrikaners would have to build up their own power base independent of English-speakers and ensure the continued political isolation of blacks. This meant that any Afrikaner nationalist political strategy would most likely focus on opposition to these two groups. Thus, the structure of the South African state encouraged the formation of an ethnic politics by Afrikaners founded on the principles of racism and opposition to English speakers. It entrenched hostilities that had built up over the nineteenth century and predisposed them to becoming integral parts of a nationalist ideology.

The National Party and the Boer Rebellion

The new language and cultural movements stimulated a growing ethnic awareness among urban Afrikaners throughout the country that was soon to have political repercussions. From 1910, the country was led by the new South African Party headed by Botha and Smuts. Their stated aim was conciliation between the two white races. Hertzog, however, now Minister of Justice, continued to push the issue of language rights from within the cabinet. After a series of combative speeches, he was forced out of government. In response, in 1914 he founded a new party, the National Party, to promote his goal of 'two streams' to white South African life, which he argued would allow for full cultural expression by the Afrikaner. His guiding principle, however was a relatively mild one that '…when the interests of South Africa came into conflict with the interests of the Empire, then the interests of South Africa came first'.[55]

The new party soon received a tremendous boost from the advent of the First World War. When South Africa entered the conflict on the side of the British, some disaffected Afrikaners who could not bear the thought of allying with their great enemy so soon after the Boer War rebelled. The horseback-led uprising was quickly crushed by the Union's newly mechanised armed forces. Nevertheless, the NP took advantage of increased Afrikaner hostility to Botha and Smuts to win 26 seats to the SAP's 54 in the 1915 election. Significantly, the party did best in the Orange Free State, which was where most of the rebels had come from. As Hertzog's original power base, it was also the only area in which the party had a strong organisational infrastructure. Nevertheless, the small party also generated support in the Western Cape, the base of D.F. Malan, one of Hertzog's chief lieutenants. Malan, a preacher, in 1915 became editor of a new paper, *Die Burger*, that came to serve as a mouthpiece for the NP. Its opening issue bemoaned the demise of the volk and called for national upliftment of the Afrikaner 'rooted in the love of God'.[56] Its printing marked the beginning of a broader Afrikaans publishing revolution, encompassing new papers, magazines and a publishing house, the *Nasionale Pers* devoted to Afrikaans language books and, importantly, school texts. While only 92 Afrikaans books had been published before the turn of the century, *Nasionale Pers* and other new publishers began steadily to increase both the output and distribution of such works.[57] This helped spread Afrikaner ethnic ideas in much the same way that the Gaelic League's Library of Ireland had for the Irish.

Smuts became Prime Minister following Botha's death in 1919. Soon after, he merged the SAP with the old English-speaking Unionist party to offset the increasing leakage of Afrikaner votes to the NP. Hertzog made great political capital out of this, accusing Smuts, fresh from a stint in the Imperial war cabinet, of selling out his people for the British Empire – a highly emotive charge in the wake of the war and the rebellion. Building on this and other examples of Smuts's heavy-handedness, most notably his harsh suppression of the Rand Rebellion in 1923, NP support grew steadily. In 1924, on a platform of securing full political independence from the British Empire and protecting the white worker against black competition, Hertzog came to power at the head of a Pact government. Incongruously allied with the socialist-oriented, English-speaking Labour Party, but having gained a clear majority of Afrikaner votes, Hertzog and the National Party had taken political power. This did not however demonstrate the existence or strength of full-blown Afrikaner nationalism, but merely continued hostility to Britain and increased support for the idea of Afrikaner cultural independence.

The Pact Government

Once in power, Hertzog sought permanently to secure the place of Afrikaans language and culture in South African society. The new government made Afrikaans, rather than Dutch an official language in 1925 and introduced a bilingualism requirement for civil service jobs. In the emerging nationalist discourse, there was also a need for new national symbols, particularly a flag and anthem to supersede the Union Jack and 'God Save the Queen'. As Malan, the new minister overseeing the process, argued:

> A flag is not merely a bit of cloth; a flag symbolises the national existence. A flag is a living thing, it is the repository of national sentiment....For a flag a nation will live; for its flag a nation will fight and can die.[58]

As in Ireland, therefore, the creation of a national iconography was seen as critical to the overall formation of separate national identity that would formally demonstrate South Africa's separation from the British. Significantly, however, the anthem, taken from an Afrikaans poem called *Die Stem van Suid Afrika* – 'The Voice of South Africa' – was given an English version, while the final flag retained a small Union Jack in the centre, together with the old flags of the Boer Republics. Hertzog did not insist on the removal of all the symbols of British power and influence – just their equal status with Afrikaner ones.

Despite the rhetoric from Malan, whose policies certainly had begun to verge on full-blown ethnic nationalism, no comprehensive nationalist political ideology was being propagated by Hertzog. The political demands articulated by the NP did not assert the absolute primacy of the Afrikaner nation in the South African state – as its alliance with the Labour Party illustrated. Although the party theoretically favoured the creation of a republic, Hertzog's pursuit of this goal represented more an attempt to be free of British political influence than an articulation of Afrikaner nationalism. Even Hertzog's definition of 'Afrikaners', was, as Hofmeyr's had been, inclusive. He believed that English speakers who subscribed to the idea of 'South Africa First' should also be regarded as Afrikaners, and was never committed to the political dominance of Afrikaans speakers. Although there was a movement towards cultural and linguistic exclusivism among Afrikaners it had not yet translated into ethno-nationalist political demands. Nonetheless, it was increasingly apparent that there was now a real possibility that such mobilisation could take place. As one prominent (and prescient) observer put it in 1929:

> [i]t has been shown that on a purely racial appeal with a considerable measure of anti-British propaganda in the rural districts, the Dutch can obtain a clear majority in the South African parliament. Under such conditions it is only a question of time before ... an exclusively Dutch government rules the Union.[59]

Before that could take place, however, a broad organisational move-ment dedicated to such an aim needed to be established.

The Broederbond and the FAK

In 1918, a small group of educated Afrikaners made the decision to 'develop an organisation in which Afrikaners could find each other'.[60] The society, initially called Young South Africa, soon changed its name to the *Afrikaner Broederbond*, and in 1921 became secret. Its manifesto charged members

> [t]o carry the Afrikaner volk towards its sense of identity to inspire self-respect and to nurture and cultivate love for language, history, land, volk and law.[61]

The Broederbond thus recognised that political unity among Afri-kaners on the basis of ethnic identity was a prerequisite for political power. All the key motifs of ethnic nationalism were emphasised: culture, language, religion and loyalty to a specific territory with which the ethnic group had an historical attachment. Structurally the group was built around local cells of between 5 and 50 members. Each cell was responsible only to the 12–man executive council and had no formal contact with each other. The Council was elected on a bi-annual basis by representatives from each division and was responsible for all important Broederbond policy and activity.[62] Membership expanded slowly and by 1925 the organisation contained only 8 cells and 162 members. Of these, nearly half were teachers or clergymen, reflecting the controlling influence of the Afrikaner intelligentsia (although it was officially open to all Afrikaners, heavy dues effectively prevented working-class membership). This meant that the Broederbond from the start became a self-consciously elite group devoted to developing and promoting an exclusive Afrikaner ideology.

In its early years, the organisation had no real direction and was wracked by factionalism. In 1927, however, prompted by Hertzog's rejection of a republic, the organisation declared its intention to 'take an active role in the life of the community, leaving no avenue neglected'.[63] Not wanting to become directly involved in politics, the Bond members sought a new means of tapping the Afrikaner national sentiment and expanding their ideological influence. The logical arena for expansion was the cultural one – to use the Afrikaans language in the same way that the Gaelic League had begun to orchestrate a shift in Irish national sentiments away from political nationalism towards a more exclusive Catholic-Irish identity.

Greater literacy and better education was already making the Afrikaner population more receptive to such mobilisation. In addition to *Die Burger* and other Afrikaans newspapers, a new Afrikaans magazine, *Die Huisgenoot*, was established. This devoted itself to serious articles on issues relevant to Afrikaners and had achieved a readership of 13 500 by the early 1920s, a significant number for a self-consciously upmarket publication. In 1925, it ran a long celebration of the centenary of Kruger's birth, and used the occasion to call for the formation of a new, national language and cultural organisation for Afrikaners.[64] Acting on this advice, in 1927 the Broederbond formed a new organization called the Federation of Afrikaans Culture (FAK) to act as its public front. Declaring that culture was the 'name given to the common spiritual possessions of a people', the FAK invited all recognised Afrikaner cultural groups in the country to a conference on the issue of cultural identity in 1929. From that time on it became a national coordinating body aimed at encouraging closer cooperation between Afrikaner institutions dedicated to asserting cultural and linguistic independence.

The FAK was the first major organisation to devote itself explicitly to the pursuit and dissemination of an ethno-cultural ideology, and it took up the task with vigour. Covering activities from school drama to literary societies, it spread through towns and cities all over the country, sponsoring ethnic activities among Afrikaners and working actively towards the creation of a self-conscious Afrikaner identity. Its influence was so pervasive that, after 1929, virtually every Afrikaner cultural organisation in South Africa came under its indirect control. By 1937, it encompassed over 300 groups countrywide, and had successfully spread the central tenets of the new nationalist history and ideals throughout the country. A central element of this message became the political affirmation of national identity through cultural and linguistic means. Events included recreational activities – dances, songs, sporting events and the like – supplying a similar, all-enveloping cultural atmosphere promoted by the Gaelic Revival in Ireland.

Encompassing this, a wide range of alternative Afrikaner organisations in other spheres of life was established. Small, but particularly prominent was the *Afrikaner Nasionale Studentebond*, an Afrikaans student group under the leadership of Piet Meyer which broke away from the predominantly Anglophone National Union of Students of South Africa and managed to attract, and politicise, a new generation of Afrikaner intellectuals. Most of its leaders became Broederbond members and several, after studying in Nazi Germany, made major contributions to the nationalist *oeuvre*. In this way, the vague Christian National ideas first put forward after the Boer War began to coalesce into a comprehensive national political ideology. Nico Diedrichs, a leading member, declared forthrightly that the development of the Afrikaner nation was occurring according to divine law.[65] Meyer himself, in a book called simply *Die Afrikaner*, insisted that a true 'sense of nationhood' was the special task of Afrikaners that could only be achieved through the 'national language' – arguments that were classically Fichtean in origin.[66]

Throughout this process, the Dutch Reformed Church (DRC), to which nearly all Afrikaners belonged, provided a forum for the discussion and dissemination of nationalist ideas and policies. Many individual churchmembers were heavily involved in the articulation and defence of Afrikaner nationalist ideals. Both D.F. Malan and the first President of the Broederbond, for example, were DRC preachers. At the same time, several Afrikaans newspapers moved away from supporting Hertzog and started to promote more exclusive nationalist ideals among the broader reading public. H.F. Verwoerd, later to become the primary architect of apartheid, was also a newspaper editor, of the Transvaal-based *Vaderland*. Thus, while the seeds of the Christian National ideal were for the first time being actively disseminated among the masses through the FAK, the foundation of an ethnic nationalist movement was laid. By placing existing organisations under the guidance of the FAK and using the Church and press to spread nationalist ideology, the Broederbond was able to make use of indigenous Afrikaner groups and turn them into part of the broader nationalist movement. Through its indirect control of all these different bodies, the Bond spread the notion of an independent Afrikaner cultural and linguistic identity within South Africa beyond the ranks of the intelligentsia.

The Purified National Party

The Broederbond did not, however, restrict its activities to the social and cultural spheres. Although the organisation officially declared that it had no interest in politics, its activities were always carried out with an eye to political events and actors and became widely known as *kultuurpolitiek*, to distinguish it from the *partypolitiek* being carried out in parliament. It actively promoted republican ideals among

Afrikaners by extolling their exclusive cultural identity and emphasising the need for a political homeland in which that identity could flourish away from alien British influences. Such a framework is the essence of ethnic nationalism, preaching political liberty and spiritual fulfilment through the nation. In response to this new activism, Bond membership grew to 1023 by 1933 and began to include more civil servants and urban professionals.[67] The Bond also started to recruit politicians as members and provide assistance to individual candidates who campaigned on behalf of Afrikaner nationalism.

In the wake of the economic and political chaos caused by the Great Depression, however, Hertzog was forced to accept fusion of the NP and SAP into the new United Party in 1934 to stay in power. He believed that most of his goals had been achieved, and in the context of a national crisis, was prepared to compromise with Smuts. Unwilling to serve with a man now regarded as a betrayer of Afrikanerdom, Malan and a group of MPs broke away to form the Purified National Party (GNP). This marked the creation, for the first time, of a political organisation explicitly committed to exclusive ethnic nationalism. More importantly, it represented the first major effort by exponents of Christian Nationalism to seek exclusive political power. As the nationalist intellectuals worked at building up the ideological backbone of Afrikaner nationalism through the course of the 1930s, the GNP consistently adopted these new ideas for its own. The GNP's ideological parallels to the Broederbond soon allowed for the forging of strong links between the two groups, not unlike those between the IRB and Sinn Fein in Ireland.

These connections were essential to the growth of the nationalist movement because the newly formed GNP was essentially a regional party based in the Cape. The Broederbond, with its strength based in the Transvaal and the Free State was able to provide a core support group in these areas, where the GNP became 'little more than the Broederbond writ large'.[68] In addition, Malan himself and other senior members of the party soon became members of the Broederbond – though not its leadership. In this way, a close relationship was established between the two primary organisations of Afrikaner nationalism. While the Broederbond never came to control the GNP, it exerted a strong influence on the party, its leaders and its platform. For these two groups, Afrikaners were no longer any whites who gave allegiance to South Africa as Hertzog had suggested but were defined first and foremost by their language, religion and culture. Nonetheless, they remained very far from political power. The GNP won only 14 seats to the UP's 133 in the 1934 election, making clear that most Afrikaners, remained content with Hertzog's achievements on language, culture and the constitution.

Conclusions

A developing Afrikaner ethnic consciousness, in the guise of Christian Nationalism, had been slowly built up in the period following the Boer War on the nineteenth-century foundations laid by the First Language Movement in the Cape and the Boer Republics. After the union of South Africa in 1910, first Hertzog's National Party, and later the Broederbond and its satellites were able to generate popular support for nationalist ideals by appealing to the common socialization experiences and ethnic heritage of Afrikaners. This appeal was made through the construction of a national ideology centred on language and religion. As the very name Afrikaner took root in the society, so did its connotations – these were people of Africa, not Europe. The development of a formal grammar and literature for Afrikaans, the articulation and spread of a national history, and the all-pervasive sense of opposition to the alien British, particularly after the severe trauma of the Boer War, comprised a powerful ideological message that these new organisations could propagate.

In order to do this successfully, however, the movement could not simply rely on psychological appeals to an alienated populace. Rather, it exploited the political structure of the state and the racial franchise, to establish a solid organisational foundation. Given the fact that the Afrikaners – unlike their Irish counterparts – were rarely under threat of any coercive reprisals by the state, it was possible to create such groups in virtually every sphere of society. The resulting institutionalisation of Afrikaans culture, history and language provided the foundation for a unified Afrikaner front capable of mounting a political challenge. As with the myriad organisations built around Sinn Fein, the IRB and the Gaelic League before 1914, the overlapping leadership of the Broederbond, the FAK and the GNP in the 1930s, was able to use this new organisational infrastructure to propagate the demand that the Afrikaner nation should control South Africa. The establishment of these organisations helped spread ethnic nationalist ideology and ethnic messages of solidarity. Nevertheless, while firmly established it was largely powerless. The United Party continued to enjoy overwhelming support from the white population, including most Afrikaners.

THE ZIONISTS

The political mobilisation of Jews under the Zionist banner only became significant after the outbreak of secular anti-semitism in Europe and Russia in the late nineteenth century. This prompted the search for a political solution, led by assimilated Western European Jews, that would secure Great Power support for Zionist goals. This section argues that it was only by integrating the demand for a state with Jewish cultural and religious precepts that the movement was able to establish a mass base and attract the first immigrants to Palestine. It suggests that these precepts were institutionalised by these early immigrants through a wide set of organisations in political and cultural spheres that effectively transformed Zionism into an ethnic nationalist movement. In particular, by taking advantage of the political structure of the Ottoman empire, the Zionists were able to establish a wide range of organisations in Palestine dedicated to both the resurrection of Hebrew and the establishment of a viable national community.

The section opens by looking at the first Zionist ideologues in late nineteenth-century Russia and the activities of early Jewish communities in Palestine. It then turns to the formation of the World Zionist Organisation and its early strategies. It examines both the Zionist movement's diplomatic activity and the first practical initiatives in nation-building undertaken by immigrants to Palestine. In particular it focuses on the new political parties established by these newcomers and the manner in which they undertook the promotion of Zionist ideology.

The Origins of Zionist Ideology

In the decades following the growth of Western liberalism after the French Revolution, many European countries emancipated and gave full citizenship to their Jewish inhabitants for the first time. Even in the Russian empire, which, by the mid-nineteenth century, contained some five million of the continent's seven million Jews in a vast swathe of territory stretching from Lithuania to Galicia called the Pale, a partial programme of Jewish emancipation was implemented. Although these Jews were overwhelmingly literate, and long conscious of their identity as an ethnic group, they had made little attempt to mobilise politically. The vast majority were content to live according to traditional religious precepts in ethnic enclaves or ghettos, while those who didn't sought to assimilate into the mainstream of the countries they lived in. By the latter part of the century, however, liberal ideals, which had once been seen as synonymous with nationalism, now began to be threatened by the doctrine's exclusivist claims. This in turn led to growing intolerance of ethnic minorities in central and eastern Europe, among whom Jews were the most conspicuous. This had two important repercussions. First, it generated a new, more virulent form of anti-semitism that saw Jews as ineradicably foreign people rather than merely misguided non-believers who could be saved by conversion to Christianity. Second, it forced some Jews to start thinking of themselves as a separate nation.

In 1862, inspired by the Italian Risorgimento, Moses Hess, a German Jew, wrote a book called *Rome and Jerusalem* calling on the scattered Jewish people to band together and create a new country which would become a socialist paradise.[69] Hess's arguments received little attention and his work languished in obscurity for two decades. In 1881, however, following the assassination of Tsar Alexander II, a new pogrom in Russia marked the end of reformism there. It resulted in the deaths of thousands of Jews and caused many to despair of the goal of equal citizenship. Into this receptive atmosphere, a Russian Jew, Leo Pinsker, published a new pamphlet called *Autoemanzipation*. This brief document told Jews that assimilation was an unattainable dream and the only solution to the persistent problem of anti-semitism was the creation of a separate Jewish state. Apart from his own people, Pinsker suggested, the Jew was doomed to be an object of scorn and hatred throughout his life.

> [f]or the living the Jew is a dead man; for the natives, an alien; for property holders, a beggar; for the poor, an exploiter and a million-aire; for patriots a man without a country; for all classes a hated rival.[70]

The solution was to create a state where Jews could live with one another and hence lose this stigma.

In response to this call, a group of Jews set up an organisation called *Hovevei Zion*, which had the express aim of setting up a Jewish state in Palestine, the site of the ancient Jewish kingdom of Israel. Following a conference in Katowice, Poland, in 1884, a Jewish youth group sent several thousand emigrants to Palestine in what became known as the 1st *Aliyah*. Over the next twenty years some 25 000 settlers joined the existing Jewish community numbering some 24 000.[71] One of these new arrivals, Ben Yehudah, undertook the mammoth task of transforming Hebrew into a modern, living language, compiling a dictionary and grammar to be used by Zionists. However, the original residents were predominantly religious Jews, congregating around various holy towns, particularly Jerusalem, with little interest in the Zionist precepts of the newcomers. Once in Palestine, moreover, then a province of the Ottoman empire, many of the immigrants rapidly assimilated into the Arab community, often speaking and dressing as Arabs, with some becoming local landlords.

Those who did not attempted to set up separate Jewish communities outside the existing settlements. These enterprises proved unproductive. Many new arrivals were forced to return home and by 1902 some 65 per cent of the original immigrants had departed.[72] The remainder survived only through the generosity of the French Baron Edmond de Rothschild who subsidised several of the settlements, paying above market prices for their produce and eventually investing some 10 million pounds into the project. But by 1902, there were only 21 such colonies in place with 5000 inhabitants. While significant, this did not represent any sort of recognizable progress towards statehood. Back in Europe too, Zionist ideas gained little headway. Despite vigorous intellectual debates on the nature of the future Jewish state among members of the Jewish community in Poland, Lithuania and Russia, little practical action was taken to turn Zionism into anything more than a fringe ideology of appeal only to a few secularised Jewish intellectuals. As in the Afrikaner and Irish cases, however, it was notable that issues of religion and culture were primarily taken up by the intelligentsia.

The Formation of the Zionist Movement

In 1896, a secular Austrian Jew working in Paris, Theodor Herzl, was prompted by the Dreyfus affair to write *The Jewish State*, a new book which argued that the only place in which Jews would be forever safe from persecution would be their own state. That, he suggested would simultaneously rid the world of the Jewish problem and Jews of anti-semitic discrimination. It would be a state complete with laws, army and flag, 'for which people live and die'.[73] Unlike his forerunners, however, Herzl was able to bring organisation and leadership to an otherwise inchoate movement. In 1897, he single-handedly brought together a group of like-minded Jews to serve as delegates to the inaugural Zionist Congress in Basle, Switzerland. There he founded the World Zionist Organisation (WZO) and became its first chairman.

The new group was designed as an elected body that would meet at regular intervals to pursue its aims. Its constituents would be all Jews worldwide who paid a 'shekel' membership fee.

In its founding declaration the WZO announced that its ultimate aim was 'to create for the Jewish people a home in Palestine secured by public law'.[74] Its opening manifesto charged Zionists to

> secure for the Jewish people a publicly recognised, legally secured home in Palestine. For the achievement of its purpose, the Congress envisages the following methods:
> 1. The programmatic encouragement of the settlement of Palestine with Jewish agricultural workers, labourers and those pursuing other trades.
> 2. The unification and organisation of all Jewry into local and wider groups in accordance with the laws of their respective countries.
> 3. The strengthening of Jewish self-awareness and national consciousness.
> 4. Preparatory steps to obtain the consent of the various governments necessary for the fulfilment of the aims of Zionism.[75]

These aims were far more detailed and wide-ranging than the manifestos put forward by any Irish or Afrikaner groups and reflected the much greater obstacles faced by the Zionists than the other two groups. Spread across many countries and without any significant base in its target territory, national mobilisation had to take place in conjunction with promoting emigration to Palestine and political diplomacy with existing powers.

From the beginning, therefore, the Zionists explicitly linked organisation, ideology and nation-building. The establishment of a permanent organisation would provide a suitable means of continuing the ethnic mobilisation of world Jewry behind the Zionist cause in a rational and deliberate manner. The promotion of Jewish colonisation marked an awareness of the need to build a Jewish presence within Palestine itself that would ultimately constitute a viable national community. The campaign for internationally recognised legal rights demonstrated the Zionists' realisation that the other two aims were irrelevant unless they could secure the support of existing states. The leadership of the WZO was aware from the beginning that statehood required both domestic sovereignty and international legitimacy. It therefore sought to achieve both these aims together. Nation and state building would have to interlock.

Culture and Politics

The WZO's formation had a powerful impact on the global Jewish community. Within three years the organisation had a membership of over 100 000. In the face of increasingly rampant anti-semitism that was partly generated by other nationalist movements' opposition to Jewish minorities, a call for Jewish solidarity had a significant impact. As the organisation grew, moreover, it developed factions: the dominant bourgeois General Zionists, the religious *Mizrahi* and a smaller socialist wing. All, however, were united by a sense of ethnic solidarity and common purpose. As with the Afrikaners and Irish, symbols too were important. For a flag, Herzl suggested a banner with seven gold stars on a white background, but the movement eventually settled on the Star of David in blue on a white background. An anthem, the *Hatikvah*, was also established. Its lyrics clearly reflected the sense of Jewish national history behind Zionism:

> Our hope is not lost
> The two thousand year hope
> To be a free nation in our land
> The land of Zion, Jerusalem.[76]

Reinforcing this emerging sense of national community, a loose coalition of 'cultural Zionists', was formed which cut across all three factions in the WZO and was deeply concerned with creating an environment that would nurture the Hebrew language and Jewish arts and culture. Inspired by the Russian Asher Ginsburg, who took the Hebrew name Ahad Ha'am, most cultural Zionists took seriously the injunction in Isaiah that Jews should be a 'light unto the nations'. This meant creating not just a political refuge but a spiritual home in which Jewish culture could be carefully nurtured.[77] The key for Ha'am and his followers was 'not the saving of the Jews by ameliorating their physical existence but the preservation and development of the Jewish spirit'.[78]

But these cultural nationalists, most of whom came from the Pale, were also unashamedly nationalist. As Chaim Weizmann, a young Russian Zionist, put it in a letter in 1903:

> we regard the concepts of Zionism and nationalism as identical.... Zionism is a national movement... [its]whole mission is to the furtherance of all activities that contribute to the creation of Jewish national values.[79]

For Weizmann, and more especially Ha'am, it was only through their cultural identity as Jews that a Jewish state could or should be fought for. The only possible territory for such a state was the Biblical territory of Israel – an area which many felt had 'an organic connection' to the Jewish People.[80] As in the Irish and Afrikaner cases, political demands came to mesh with cultural ones and such ethnic sentiments were used to mobilise support for the final political goal of statehood.

While the Zionists were united on the need to build a strong national base to secure this goal, they were divided over how best to do so. Herzl placed great emphasis on 'political Zionism', seeking to achieve a Zionist state through negotiation and diplomacy. Opposed to this were the 'practical Zionists', who advocated the incremental development of a state apparatus through gradual immigration. Initially, Herzl hoped to persuade the wealthier Jews of western Europe to provide funds that he could offer the Ottomans in exchange for Jewish sovereignty in Palestine, and proposed this to the Ottoman Sultan, Abdul Hamid. Herzl was, however, unable to raise much money or support from assimilated Western Jewry and the Ottomans remained resolutely opposed. Undaunted, he sought, and briefly gained, the support of Kaiser Wilhelm II of Germany for his goals while also campaigning for support in England and attempting to purchase the Sinai peninsula.[81] Herzl even briefly flirted with the anti-semitic Russians following a new pogrom in 1903, trying to persuade them that the best solution to their domestic 'Jewish problem' was to support the establishment of a Jewish homeland to which these unwanted subjects could be sent.

The same year brought Herzl's first and only concrete offer: the British suggested the Zionists should take control of the African territory of Uganda as a homeland. The proposal precipitated a divisive debate within the Zionist movement and forced the clarification of the WZO's self-appointed mission. Was Zionism an ethno-cultural nationalist movement centred on Jewish culture and thus irrevocably committed to Palestine as a homeland, or was it a purely political attempt to find a practical solution to the Jewish problem? Herzl favoured the Ugandan option, as did a slight majority of the WZO's delegates. But for the vocal cultural Zionist faction, which included most of the Russian Jews for whom the Zionist project was intended, the issue of Palestine was non-negotiable. Their prevailing belief, as one of Ha'am's followers later put it was that:

[o]nly in Palestine can the Jew become once more a Hebrew. There and only there can he take up the thread of his national history and begin over again the eternal pursuit of his ideal. There and only there can the Hebrew spirit find a body and become effectively a force making for absolute righteousness.[82]

For cultural Zionists it was this ethno-cultural core built around the Jewish religion, the Hebrew language, and the Bible that linked the two, that was at the heart of Zionism. Palestine, as the Biblical Land of Israel, was irrevocably connected with these factors. The offer was accordingly refused. But while none of Herzl's diplomacy produced tangible results it did have the significant effect of the profile of the Zionist movement within the international community. Not unlike the confused state of Irish nationalism after Parnell's demise, by the time of Herzl's own premature death in 1904, the Zionist question was freely discussed among the capitals of Europe.

After a few years of stagnation, in 1907, Weizmann became the leading figure in the WZO. He resurrected Herzl's political ideas in the context of a policy of 'synthetic Zionism', which sought to combine practical and political strategies. He had already called for a practical programme that would provide political training, education, and the knowledge of Hebrew language and culture for new recruits.[83] Now he sought to combine the ethno-cultural process of promoting national sentiment to that of political mobilisation. This position was endorsed by the WZO executive, and Weizmann, now based in Britain, began a long and sustained process of winning over British policy-makers, newspapermen and other influential figures to the Zionist cause, hoping that an opportunity might present itself to secure British sponsorship. Ultimately, however, in the prevailing geopolitical context this was unfeasible. There was no real reason for Britain or any other power to offer support when such backing would only alienate the Ottomans.

Nevertheless, the international weakness of the Ottoman empire and its peculiar domestic political structure gave the Jews a critical opportunity to gain a foothold in Palestine. First, under a system known as the 'Capitulations' the Ottomans had given all Europeans immunity from local jurisdiction. Also, the empire was traditionally governed through *millets* which granted each religious group within the empire a degree of autonomy. In such a political structure, Jewish immigrants, as both foreign citizens and non-Muslims, had a relatively large degree of freedom for internal political and economic organisation. Second, much of Palestine was owned by absentee Arab landlords who were generally willing to sell to foreigners. The combination of these factors meant that, even without any military support, the Jews were able to immigrate, organise, and purchase land in Palestine despite official Ottoman opposition. From 1904 until 1914 a new wave of around 40 000 immigrants, known collectively as the 2nd *Aliyah*, did just that.

Nation-Building in Palestine

The new arrivals saw their role as agents of the Zionist goal of building a Jewish state in the land of their forefathers – 'to work the soil and defend it'.[84] Their activities in Palestine were accordingly very different from those of their predecessors. Predominantly young, Russian and male, they brought with them a tradition of socialist and communist thought and a corresponding belief in the possibility of social transformation. Nevertheless, their fundamental political aim was the creation of a Jewish state. Having deliberately chosen Palestine over the more attractive destination of the United States, they were already ideologically committed to the broad principles of Zionism. Often the children of intellectuals, nearly all were literate and some 45 per cent were able to speak Hebrew before arrival.[85] As such they were the perfect group to begin the process of establishing a Jewish homeland. By 1906 they had already formed two political parties. Both were left-leaning, with *Poale Zion* dedicated to helping the Jews become part of the coming world socialist revolution and the more pragmatic *Ha'poel Ha'tzair* promoting a domestic programme calling for the 'conquest of labour'.[86]

The newcomers had a distinct social and cultural agenda. In addition to ordinary schools, one of their first acts, in 1905, was to establish a school of art, which flourished.[87] Most important of all, however, was promoting the use of Hebrew as a spoken language as many of the immigrants only spoke Yiddish or other European or Arab languages. In 1903 a Union of Hebrew teachers was founded and two years later the first Hebrew-language secondary school was founded.[88] The first of many Hebrew newspapers was established soon after and informal literary groups and recreational organisations centred on the language spread quickly, reinforced by a growing amount of books and poetry. A national history was developed and taught which extolled the heroic days of the ancient kingdom of Israel under the rule of David and Solomon and largely ignored the stateless wanderings of the Diaspora.

After early dissension over the issue, the new political parties too spent much of their time promoting the language and conducted most official business in Hebrew.

Nevertheless, the language struggle with European Jews persisted through the first decade of the century. The schools only managed to keep Hebrew as the primary language of instruction after teachers had gone on strike to achieve it – initially classes were taught in French, German or English, depending on which Zionist chapter was funding them. When a Technical College was established at Haifa in 1913, its German financiers wanted German to be the language of instruction and only after a bitter fight, and Weizmann's personal intervention, was the issue decided in favour of Hebrew.[89] When a university was first mooted, the debate over the role of Hebrew as an academic language was another acrimonious one. There too, as with the Gaelic campaign in the Irish universities, Hebrew triumphed. Weizmann later referred to the Hebrew University of Jerusalem, eventually founded in 1918 (though not formally opened until 1925), as the Zionists' 'greatest national project' in Palestine.[90]

Deeply involved in this entire process were *Mizrahi*, the faction of religious Zionists in the WZO. Although generally prepared to keep a low profile in political matters, as among the Irish and Afrikaner priesthood, the portion of the rabbinate who did lend their support to the Zionist cause insisted upon the central role of religion in education. As a condition for its support for the dominant General Zionist faction, *Mizrahi* came to directly control nearly a third of all Jewish schools in Palestine and ran compulsory Bible study programmes in most of the others. In this way, religious precepts became firmly embedded in the emerging Zionist ideology being imbibed by a new generation of Jews growing up in Palestine.

These initiatives were the primary means by which the Zionist movement developed and reinforced its nationalist ideology in all spheres of Jewish life in Palestine. The speaking and teaching of Hebrew was a self-consciously Zionist act. The fact that the immigrants often came from different linguistic backgrounds meant that Hebrew was particularly important both as a means of communication and as an everyday assertion of common purpose. Yiddish, spoken by most of the Germans and Russians had been a more likely candidate for a common language on purely practical grounds, but it was regarded as the language of 'sadness, of exile, of loss and of persecution' – not sentiments to be encouraged in the new Israel.[91] Hebrew emphasized the Jews' ethnic kinship and their historical claims to their ancestral homeland, and was thus a central pillar of the entire nation-building process. As David Ben Gurion, one of the new arrivals put it

the rebirth of Hebrew as the Jewish national language was a great victory and a great affirmation of our links to our ancient past.[92]

Another very important dimension of Jewish development in Palestine was in the military sphere. Initially, most guard duty was performed by local Bedouin tribesmen who hired themselves out for the tasks. Ben Gurion and his colleague Yitzhak Ben Zvi, however, felt that this left the Jews vulnerable to both blackmail and violence. In 1907, to counter the perception of Jewish passivity, they formed a group called *Bar Giora* to train and arm Jewish farmers so that they could act as guards for their own settlements. This soon became part of a slightly larger group called *Hashomer*. Although poorly equipped, by 1914 a force of 100 trained fighters was in operation, the kernel of a formal Zionist military wing. It was also a hugely important symbol of national pride and a key aspect of seeking national self-reliance.

All these activities combined to begin the process of founding a separate Jewish state. The separateness of the Zionist community in Palestine far exceeded the religious divisions that had traditionally marked the Ottoman empire. The foundations of a self-contained, armed, politicised ethnic group with a strong sense of national pride and attachment to language and territory had been laid. As a disillusioned Arab observed in 1910:

They do not mix with the Ottomans, and do not buy anything from them ... They have a blue flag in the middle of which is a 'Star of David' and below that is a Hebrew word meaning Zion ... They raise this flag instead of the Ottoman flag at their celebrations and gatherings; and they sing the Zionist anthem ... they settle their claims and differences among themselves without the knowledge of the [Ottoman] administrator ... They have a special postal service, special stamps, etc., which proves that they have begun setting up their political aims and establishing their imaginary government.[93]

As with the Irish and the Afrikaners, the symbols of language, flag and anthem were combined with cultural and religious messages promoted by a wider range of organisation to strengthen the bonds of ethnic nationalism among the population. Unlike in Ireland and South Africa, however, where the ethnic group merely had to be persuaded of the merits of national mobilisation, most of the Zionists' constituents still overwhelmingly lived outside Palestine, and the WZO had limited success in persuading most of them to move there. Many Orthodox Jews thought that returning to Israel before the advent of the messiah was blasphemous, while liberal assimilationists feared it would reinforce anti-semitic stereotypes.

Even the great majority of Jews who despaired of assimilation sought solutions other than Zionism for their salvation. In Russia, far more joined the Jewish Bund, a large-scale social democratic group campaigning for Jewish political autonomy within the Pale. Indeed the Bund was highly successful and for a long while commanded the allegiance of a majority of politically active Russian Jews. Others joined socialist and communist parties in the belief that anti-semitism would be subsumed beneath class solidarity. A very large number eschewed all these options and emigrated. Over 2.25 million Jews left eastern Europe for the United States alone between 1872–1914, and many hundreds of thousands more departed for England, South Africa, Australia and Latin America.[94] In fact, over this period, only some 3–4 per cent of all Jewish emigrants from Europe chose to go to Palestine. Despite 17 years of campaigning, by 1914 only 130 000 Jews were members of the WZO out of a global population of some 15 million – barely more than in 1901.[95] The call of nationalism and the establishment of a political and material base for Jewish settlement in Palestine were inadequate to the task of beginning a process of state-building.

Conclusions

After forming in response to anti-semitism and the growth of nationalism in Europe in the late nineteenth century, the Zionist movement focused all its energies on the establishment of a Jewish state. Within the framework of a nationalist organisation, the Zionists developed a three-pronged strategy to achieve their goals: extending nationalist sentiment throughout the world's Jewish population, pursuing international support for these goals, and promoting Jewish development in Palestine. When the first two of these factors proved difficult to pursue in the prevailing international context, emphasis was given to the third. Funding was provided for immigration and the activities of the 2nd *Aliyah*. Through education, cultural initiatives, the promotion of a resurrected language, the establishment of political parties and a military and economic base, a viable Zionist settlement in Palestine was developed and nurtured. Although it comprised only a very small number of people, this was an important first step in the long-term strategy of expanding the Jewish presence there.

If nationalist solidarity underlay the formation and maintenance of the WZO and the early settlement in Palestine, it was the strategies articulated in the Basle doctrine that marked how the movement sought independence. Although political Zionists had hoped for immediate results, when these failed to materialise they were nevertheless able to continue pursuing their overall goals by other means. By exploiting the limited openings available to them through land purchase and immigration they continually reinforced the ideological ethno-nationalist core of Zionism. This was done through schools, newspapers, political parties and other organisations, all of which contributed to the promotion of Hebrew as a modern, spoken and written language. The flexibility of this strategy linking the practical task of building a national community and the political one of international recognition was critical. In the absence of international success, continued domestic development managed to maintain momentum for the overall campaign. Some years later Weizmann asserted that the years up to 1914 'laid the foundations of institutions' for the national home.[96] But they were no more than foundations. An enormous gulf remained between the reality of Jewish Palestine and Herzl's dream of a Jewish state.

GENERAL CONCLUSIONS

The initial process of national mobilisation followed strikingly similar routes for Irish Catholics, Zionists and Afrikaners, albeit within vastly different structural frameworks. As the societies within which each group lived gradually modernised, a small group of professionals, including an intelligentsia, slowly developed. These men (there were few women) acted as cultural entrepreneurs, creating ideologies that sought to involve and politicise members of each ethnic group. The three cornerstones of this nascent ethnic identity were a common religious faith, a shared language and historic ties to a particular territory. Of these, language was the most important, providing the means of linking the cultural and historical identity of each people. Gaelic, Afrikaans and Hebrew were not widely spoken or written at the time that ethnic mobilisation began and the process was premised on the work of such people as Douglas Hyde, S. J. Du Toit and Ben Yehuda in establishing each as a modern language. New literary figures featured prominently in all three movements employing both history and religion in new forms of nationalist poetry and literature which were spread amongst members of each ethnic group through a growing number of books and newspapers.

More importantly, each language was popularised by organisations like the Gaelic League, the FAK and the various WZO branches both in and out of Palestine, as well as being continually reinforced through a wide range of recreation activities. The battles over, and ultimate victories for, Afrikaans and Hebrew allowed for the reinforcement of a separate, and authentic, national identity. While Gaelic never re-established itself as a spoken language this reflected a pragmatic acceptance of the *status quo* rather than real failure on the part of the nationalists. English was the language of the oppressor, but it had less of a stigma for the Irish than had Yiddish (as the language of the oppressed) for the Zionists. Also, while a majority of Jews already had a working knowledge of Hebrew from religious ritual, the same was not true of the Irish, where only very few understood any Gaelic by the time the revival started. At the same time, the Irish proved able to create a distinctive national voice within English literature anyway. Even so, Gaelic became a powerful symbol of cultural differentiation from the Protestants and the English – a fact that was demonstrated by the successful campaign to have the language made compulsory at schools and the new Catholic universities.

In each case, this linguistic identity was always linked directly to religion. The Jews' use of Hebrew marked the explicit secularisation of a unique religious identity in order to facilitate political mobilisation. Similarly, the Irish emphasised their position as the heirs of St Patrick and the medieval monasteries that were islands of light in an era of darkness (despite the fact that such events had little or no connection to more ancient, pagan, Gaelic traditions). Meanwhile the Afrikaners invented their role as a Calvinist outpost amongst the heathens of Africa. Given the pre-existence of a set of belief systems that could easily be encompassed by an ethnic nationalist ideology, in all three cases this proved a powerful adjunct to the process of building a national identity. Meanwhile the religious organisations came to provide political platforms for the process of national mobilisation, in effect supplying a wide-ranging institutional support system.

Despite this, it is worth emphasising that although religion was integral to the broader process of building a national identity, it was clearly not the driving force. While individual churchmen or rabbis were prominent in the leadership and membership of each nationalist movement, religious authorities were never at the forefront of national mobilisation. Rather, the Catholic and Dutch Reformed churches, like the Zionist religious faction *Mizrahi*, concentrated on issues that directly impinged on their sectarian authority. In particular, they demanded, and by and large achieved, a powerful say in the growing educational systems that helped spread the ethnic nationalist gospel. There they supported the nationalist struggle over the means of instruction as evidenced in Church-run schools in Ireland, and, more dramatically, in the struggle for Hebrew in Palestine and the Second Language Movement's resistance to Milner's Anglicisation, in exchange for insisting on compulsory religious instruction at all schools.

The initial focus of the early ethnic nationalist leadership in each case was on cultural pursuits that would reinforce a sense of national identity rather than full political autonomy. Powerful political vehicles such as the Irish Parliamentary Party, the NP and Afrikaner Bond and the Jewish Bund in Russia all sought constitutional redress for their grievances within the prevailing political order. As the process of nation-building developed, however, an ethno-national ideology began to be promoted by newer political parties which sought to build an independent state: some Russian Jews rejected assimilation or the Bund for the WZO, Sinn Fein was established in Ireland, and the GNP was carved out of Hertzog's more moderate National Party in South Africa. These groupings soon came to act as the primary political agents of the process of national mobilisation.

In both South Africa and Ireland, meanwhile, a semi-secret group, dedicated to a hardline ethnic nationalist argument became involved in, and frequently assumed control over, cultural and political organisations involved in the broader nation-building process. Despite the fact that the IRB in the 1890s and 1900s was ostensibly dedicated to violent revolution while the Broederbond in the 1920s and 1930s was nominally a cultural organisation, they followed very similar strategies. Both retained a small, elite membership which worked at infiltrating and influencing the broader range of ethnic nationalist organisations in cultural, recreational and political spheres. The new labour-oriented parties in Palestine in effect pursued a similar role – driving the process of political and cultural mobilisation in Palestine while seeking to influence the WZO from within.

Despite these similarities, however, there were obvious differences between each movement, most of them a function of the different structural context within which each group operated. The growth of

Irish national consciousness, for example, began much earlier than in the other two cases. This was a direct reflection of the relative spread of modernisation across the different communities. A Catholic intelligentsia and professional class, operating within an increasingly literate and urbanised populace emerged as early as the 1820s and 30s. Thus, by the time of Young Ireland, there was already a thriving newspaper industry and room for a national literature. Politically, however (failed rebellions notwithstanding), the existence of the Westminster system led many nationalist leaders from O'Connell to Parnell, to maintain a focus on parliamentary politics. As Home Rule still had many Protestant proponents, an exclusive ethnic, Catholic-based movement was not only inappropriate but unlikely to succeed. It was only when parliamentary politics appeared to fail (after having politicised a new generation of voters during the course of the 1880s) that the opportunity arose for a more exclusive ethnic nationalism to arise.

In nineteenth-century South Africa the political divisions between the states in the region, combined with the lack of a viable language and literature or sizeable intellectual class amongst Afrikaners, effectively prevented the emergence of a full-blown ethnic nationalism until after the Boer War. Even after union in 1910, moreover, despite the formation of the Christian National movement, a parliamentary approach focusing only on cultural and linguistic rights rather than ethnic hegemony predominated. Only when it became clear that Hertzog's inclusive nationalism would not bring about exclusive Afrikaner government did the Broederbond, then a tiny elite organisation, begin its involvement in the broader national struggle by founding the FAK. By contrast, although Jews had a long-standing ethnic identity, the community only developed a modern, secular intelligentsia once Europe began to permit them access to education and jobs outside the traditional ghettos. The origins of Zionism lay in the confrontation between a new class of Jewish intellectuals and the reality of modern anti-semitism in the late nineteenth century. Similarly, the complexity of the Zionists' early political agenda compared to the slower evolution of strategies developed by Irish and Afrikaners was in large part a reflection of the more complicated structural obstacles facing the Jews. They had to mobilise across state boundaries to achieve statehood in a territory where they had no numerical presence.

The three movements followed broadly similar strategies of building up a nationalist ideology that both inspired, and was promoted by, an organisational network of ethnically focused political, cultural and social organisations. After initially focusing on cultural rights alone, these organisations refined and successfully disseminated a nationalist ideology with the core demand being control of the state by the newly identified, ethnically based nation. At the same time, the common themes of language, religion and culture – the key elements of ethnic solidarity – were continually reinforced within the organisations and throughout the broader community by means of religious institutions, schools, and newspapers. By accessing pre-existing ethnic sentiments and developing them into an historical and cultural package that helped promote and nurture national pride, nationalist ideology acted as the cement which held the organisational building blocks of the nationalist movement together. In all three cases this message reached only a relatively small proportion of the target ethnic group, but each movement had successfully created a base from which to orchestrate future expansion.

3 Economy and Organisation

INTRODUCTION

Nationalist movements aim for state power, and their strategies for achieving this are directly related to the structural context within which they operate. This encompasses not only the avenues for political and cultural mobilisation made available by the existing state structure, but demographic factors such as population distribution, relative wealth, and education levels. Also critically important is the role of the state in supplying or denying material welfare to its citizens and the impact this has on both mobilisation structures and strategies. This chapter examines these factors and argues that the organisational networks established by each of the nationalist movements were in large part shaped by such factors. It suggests that it was those organisations, rather than the ideology underlying them, that were the key to their resilience. In particular, it argues that each movement utilised patronage – ranging from the direct provision of jobs and pensions, to the promise of future material benefits – as an important element in the consolidation of national support.

IRELAND

This section aims to study the broader impact of state structure on the development of Irish nationalism in the years before the First World War. It argues that the modernisation of the state apparatus was necessary to the process of national development and conditioned many of the strategies undertaken by nationalist organisers. It also demonstrates that economic issues were, from the beginning, a major element of the national enterprise. The section details how Sinn Fein and the broader ethnic nationalist movement sought to incorporate the notion of indigenous economic development into the nationalist platform while nationalist and socialist ideas became closely linked through the development of the small Irish socialist movement. It suggests that, given the nature of the state and the traditional Irish focus on land rather than industrial issues, these initiatives met with limited success but nevertheless represented an important strand in the overall development of the nationalist movement.

The section opens by looking at the country's steady modernisation during the nineteenth century on Irish nationalism. It re-examines the effects of the Land War of the 1870s on the nationalist movement before turning to the economic agenda proposed by Arthur Griffith and early attempts by Sinn Fein to build up its own sources of economic wealth. It suggests that this marked a partially successful attempt to demonstrate the efficacy of ethnic industry while trying to attract the loyalty of new supporters with the promise of material gain helping to generate ethnic pride. It then analyses the Socialist and Trade Union movements and their relationship to Irish nationalism. Finally it examines the resurgence of the Parliamentary Party in the wake of the British constitutional crisis of 1909–10.

THE IRISH STATE

Ireland in the nineteenth and early twentieth centuries has traditionally been seen as backward and underdeveloped. Such an assessment, however, misrepresents the widespread social and structural changes that occurred in the country during that period. As Chapter 2 noted, literacy and education levels rose steadily through the latter part of the century. In conjunction with this, the British administration undertook the modernisation of Ireland's transport and communications infrastructure. A countrywide railway system was put into place, as was a centralised post office and a telegraph network. Urbanisation rose to 24 per cent in 1881 and then to 33.5 per cent in 1911.[1] Along with this infrastructural development, the Irish state itself was rapidly transformed. Between 1861–1911, the size of the bureaucracy increased tenfold, from 990 to 9821.[2] Indeed, by the beginning of the twentieth century Ireland had 'one of the most advanced, centralised and rationalised administrative machines in Europe'.[3] Just as important, a steadily growing proportion of state employees and professionals were Catholic. Partly as a result of pressure from various nationalist movements, by 1911 Catholics filled 44 per cent of all legal posts and comprised 48 per cent of medical officers and 39 per cent of official government posts.[4] While the southern part of the island failed to industrialise, therefore, on balance it modernised as rapidly as any other area in Europe between 1845–1918.[5]

These complex and interlinked processes had a powerful impact on domestic nationalist politics, particularly with regard to the economy and the still dominant agricultural sector. Following the massive dislocation of the Great Famine, agriculture too became rapidly modernised and more commercially oriented.[6] Already the balance of power had been shifting away from the old landlords who used tenant labour to run their estates and towards a new class of independent, small farmers. Now the change in rural class structure was dramatically accelerated. Between 1841 and 1881, the proportion of independent farmers and graziers rose from 25.4 per cent of the working population to 44.3 per cent.[7] This meant that land, for both the new graziers and the remaining tenants, remained the most important political priority for the great bulk of Irishmen.

The Land War

Reflecting this, movements from Young Ireland onwards continually sought to introduce an economic dimension to their political campaigns. Davis himself opposed the process of 'English' industrialisation in its entirety, saying that he would far prefer to see the establishment of small cottage industries.[8] His more pragmatic chief lieutenant, Charles Gavan Duffy was quick to reassure that 'the capitalist, merchant and trader has nothing to fear' and promised that it was only landowners who would be replaced should Ireland come under nationalist rule.[9] However contradictory the specific prescriptions, these assertions came to underpin a powerful and persistent theme in Irish nationalism: Britain was responsible for Irish poverty through its misappropriation and gross misuse of Irish land, and the suppression of indigenous Irish industries.

This linkage was upheld by the nationalist movement of the early twentieth century. John Redmond, the Parliamentary Party leader, regularly charged that Britain was responsible for Irish poverty and called for an end to 'excessive taxation and general underdevelopment'.[10] Similar but more emphatic sentiments also appeared in much of the writing and speeches that fuelled the Gaelic Revival, including its more radical exponents. The most inflexibly ideological of Revivalists, D.P. Moran, warned that Ireland was being 'run by British commercial interests' who were misappropriating the country's wealth.[11] Even political radicals in the IRB such as Patrick Pearse, the messianic, romantic nationalist who was to meet his fate in the Easter Rebellion, promised that:

[a] free Ireland would provide food and export it. It would drain the bogs...would nationalise the railways, would improve agriculture, would protect fisheries, would foster industries, would beautify the cities, would educate the workers.[12]

But despite such glamorous visions, the structure of the Irish economy meant that the issue of greatest popular concern was always land. This fact was clearly evidenced in the succession of rural disturbances through the course of the nineteenth century and, most dramatically, in the Land War. Although the Land League was later harnessed by Parnell in his Home Rule campaign, the phenomenon itself had been primarily a reaction to the new evictions of agricultural labourers under-taken by the landlords in response to the lingering recession of the 1870s. Groups of men would forcibly seize tracts of land from land-owners and demand them for their own use, only to be removed by the authorities. Unlike earlier forms of land unrest, which tended to fizzle out as quickly as they started, the League was able to sustain protest for several years. One reason for this was that, despite the struggle's rural focus, a major portion of its membership came not from the countryside but the towns and the recently urbanised petty bourgeois, who were better able to coordinate activities with other branches.[13]

But while its leaders used nationalist rhetoric, the mass response that the movement elicited owed much more to the League's apparent success in airing and addressing economic grievances than political ones. The Fenians' nationalist platform had proved capable of rallying fewer than a thousand people for their failed revolt in 1867, but when land was made the central issue, tens of thousands joined the protest. Just as important was its powerful organisational framework which by 1886 had over 1200 branches.[14] While land hunger may have been the underlying impetus of the movement 'mobilization rather than . . . dis-content' was the key to the success of the Land League's new social protest.[15] Economic arguments had to be linked to viable organisa-tional networks to succeed in mobilising large numbers of people around a purportedly nationalist agenda.

Ultimately, however, a succession of Land Bills in the 1880s and 90s undermined the movement. The British government addressed many of the most pressing grievances, including granting the 3 Fs – freehold, fair rent and fixity of tenure. This process culminated in the Wyndham Land Act of 1903 – legislation which effectively marked the final demise of old-style Irish landlordism by providing for the purchase of land from the landlords by the state and its redistribution to tenants.

Over the next two decades vast tracts were handed over, dramatically accelerating the process that had begun after the Famine. At the same time, a wide range of governmental agencies were established by the authorities to help improve the lot of Irish farmers and peasants, including the Land Commission (1881), the Congested Districts Board (1891), the County Councils (1898) and the Department of Agricultural and Technical Instruction (1899). Several of these were bodies created at the instigation of the Protestant reformer Arthur Plunkett aimed at helping solve the land problem. By developing Irish land management and agricultural techniques and by improving the material lot of farmers, he hoped to persuade them to drop their nationalist support while regenerating the spirit of the Irish people.[16]

This programme, a deliberate attempt by successive Unionist governments to defuse tension in Ireland through economic means so as to prevent a resurgence of political unrest, proved highly successful. Although by 1906 sporadic outbreaks of cattle rustling and land stealing had re-emerged, the late 1880s through to the early 1900s was a relatively peaceful time for Ireland in terms of land protests.[17] The various nationalist movements managed to establish themselves in the Irish political firmament but proved able to recruit relatively few people. While the Irish farmers may have been unsure about the spiritual dimension of the land programmes promoted by Plunkett, there was no question that the succession of land reforms had largely addressed Irish grievances, at least outside the very poorest rural areas in the south and west.

Sinn Fein

Although the belief that 'Ireland as a free nation would be one of the most prosperous of states',[18] was always widely held by nationalists, the only major group to try to spell out in detail how such prosperity might come about was Sinn Fein. Griffith regarded economic issues as having as much, if not more, salience than political ones. Basing his arguments on the economic ideas of Friedrich List, the Austrian economist who argued for the central role of the state in economic development (a theory greatly disliked by English economists who extolled the virtue of free markets), Griffith vigorously promoted mercantilist policies.[19] If Ireland were to take control of its own trade rather than being forced to act as a captive market for English manufacturers and a supplier of raw materials to English industry, he argued, then the country would soon be able to realise its inherent wealth. Charging that '[t]he

Anglicisation of the Irish mind is best exhibited in its attitude to economics' he asserted that 'It is the task of national economics to accomplish the economical (*sic*) development of the nation'.[20] This required using the state as a vehicle of economic policy. Accordingly, Sinn Fein made the development of Irish industry and economy its top priority, ahead even of language and cultural issues.[21]

At the same time, Griffith also paid attention to micro-level economic initiatives and proposed the immediate development of a purely Irish section of the economy. He argued that the nationalist movement should establish its own system of local manufacturers – funded, owned and operated by Irishmen. These firms explicitly sought to give direct preference to the hiring of Gaelic speakers (hence Catholics). Between 1906–10 Griffith successfully established a bank premised on borrowing from and lending to Sinn Fein members and set up some shops and industries. By 1907 the party newspaper was already able to advertise proudly a range of small goods such as bicycles that had been 'manufactured with Irish components'.[22] Although the individual companies were never very successful (Griffith blamed the failure on the lack of a favourable tariff structure to protect the nascent enterprises from British competition) Sinn Fein nonetheless established a connection between nationalism and economic benefits in the public mind. By forming limited, ethnically exclusive, financial and industrial enterprises, Griffith was able to demonstrate to his party members that supporting an exclusive ethnic nationalism could provide them with tangible material benefits to complement the feelings of ethnic solidarity that the cultural bodies attached to the Gaelic Revival promoted.

By arguing that an Irish nationalist government, with control of an independent Irish state, could pursue such a programme of indigenous economic development far more effectively than a small political party, Sinn Fein linked the idea of nationalist control of the state explicitly to economic upliftment. These issues appealed greatly to the new Catholic middle classes. Civil servants, schoolteachers and the clergy became the driving force of the new nationalist movements. They were overwhelmingly young, male and Catholic, and many were also members of the League, the GAA and even the IRB.[23]

These arguments were never made in isolation from the central nationalist message that political liberation was an end in itself and that it was only through the establishment of an Irish state with full sovereignty that the cultural and economic initiatives could come to fruition. By 1908, a typical issue of *Sinn Fein* newspaper would begin by giving detailed news of the activities of the Gaelic League and GAA, thereby focusing primarily on the reinforcement of its central ideological message. It might then extol the workings of the party's bank, run an article promoting the further development of national banking and a national insurance scheme and exhort its members to join the civil service so as to help bring the state under the control of more nationalists. Finally, it would contain a nationalist poem or historical story to complement its advertisements for authentic Irish goods and cultural regalia such as 'Celtic Art Jewellery' or 'Wolfe Tone songbooks'.[24]

The Socialists

Although land remained the primary economic preoccupation of the Irish, during the late nineteenth century, the country's infant industrial sector spawned a small working class. Its constituents were overwhelmingly concentrated around Belfast and Dublin, although there were some smaller groupings in towns like Cork. In Belfast, a majority of the workers were Protestants who manned the shipbuilding and other heavy industries that had been established there in the latter part of the nineteenth century.[25] Nevertheless, the number of Catholic workers was steadily growing. To mobilise them, in 1896, James Connolly formed the Irish Socialist Republican Party, later to be supported by the Irish Transport and General Workers Union under James Larkin. Largely ignored by the British Trades Unions Congress and the emerging Labour Party in England, Irish Catholic workers were compelled to map out their own political agenda. They chose to set out their demands within a socialist framework that embraced nationalism rather than following classical Marxist doctrine and rejecting it as false consciousness.

Drawing comparisons between modern socialism and ancient Gaelic social arrangements Connolly argued that 'the cause of Ireland is the cause of labour; the cause of labour is the cause of Ireland'.[26] Between his writings and speeches and the trade unions' growing activism workers were mobilised for industrial action under a version of the Gaelic/Catholic nationalist ideology being propagated through the Gaelic Revival. Despite some common ideological ground, the movement did not build up any formal relationship with Sinn Fein, due primarily to Griffith's strong support for capitalism. Nevertheless, by 1909 the IGTWU was able to state a sizeable dock strike and a few years later it virtually shut down a section of Dublin in a vicious, protracted lockout with major employers. The Socialists thus became a small but significant force which managed to mobilise a portion of the Irish populace that had remained largely immune to the League and GAA – the Socialist party newspaper, *Irish Worker*, had a higher circulation than that of *Sinn Fein*.[27] Like Griffith, Connolly promoted a nationalist ideology that explicitly focused on the economic dimension of the state as a promoter of industrial development (even if those included policies, like nationalisation, that Griffith abhorred).

The New Home Rule Debate

Sinn Fein and its allies began to wean support away from the Parliamentary Party and its offshoots. Although it failed to win a seat in parliament in 1906, a creditable performance in a 1908 by-election demonstrated that the party was steadily growing in support levels and political clout. Most notably it helped lead the Gaelic League's successful campaign to ensure that Gaelic was taught in schools and the newly established Irish university system would have a faculty devoted to Irish Studies.[28] Significantly (and further evidence of the party's belief in the importance of linking cultural and economic initiatives) it also campaigned successfully for the inclusion of faculties of Economics, Commerce and Agriculture, all of which had initially been omitted.

Despite this, from 1909 onwards, support from Sinn Fein began to fall. This was primarily due to dramatic changes in British domestic politics. Under the leadership of John Redmond, the Parliamentary Party had largely recovered from its post-Parnellian decline and re-established itself as by far the most important player in domestic Irish politics.[29] Following the crisis over the Liberal budget in 1909, Redmond resurrected the old Parnellian strategy of offering electoral support to the Liberals in exchange for a promise of Home Rule. With the balance of power at Westminster finally within its grasp, the Parliamentary Party was able to reclaim the support of most of its old power base. By 1910 Sinn Fein still had around 150 affiliated clubs and societies, but in the 1911 elections it again failed to win a single seat as the Parliamentary Party swept Ireland outside of Ulster and helped keep the Liberals in power. The new administration promptly passed legislation removing the veto power of the House of Lords, substituting it with a two-session delay on any new legislation. Shortly after, in exchange for Redmond's backing in government, it introduced the Third Home Rule Bill to Parliament in 1912. With the House of Lords no longer able to veto it, Irish self-government was due to come into effect in 1915.

Redmond predictably portrayed this as the culmination of centuries of struggle and the final victory of Irish nationalism. In reality, however, the bill barely provided for Irish self-government let alone full political sovereignty. It allocated fewer independent responsibilities to Ireland than Gladstone had proposed in 1886, falling well short of the wide range of powers that the other self-governing parts of the British empire such as Canada and Australia, had begun to exercise.[30] Nevertheless, in an environment where land issues were less pressing than before, it was a political victory of note, and most of Ireland, including Sinn Fein and the ethnic nationalists, were prepared to suspend criticism. It seemed as if ethnic nationalism championed by Sinn Fein, even with an economic dimension to bolster its cultural and political initiatives, was destined to remain little more than a fringe group in Irish politics while the Parliamentary Party waited to assume power in Home Rule Ireland.

Conclusions

Throughout modern Irish history, economic demands, particularly with reference to land, were directly linked to the nationalist struggle. Indeed most Irish nationalists from Young Ireland onwards explicitly sought to link political liberation and economic prosperity. The period in which the broader movement for Irish independence had its greatest success was during and after the Land War. To attract mass support, the League showed how using economic issues in a strategic manner could give powerful impetus to its political demands. The continued growth of the modern Irish state and its increasingly interventionist attitude to the economy (most graphically illustrated in the land reforms and the new state agricultural bodies) promoted the link between state and economy in the minds of nationalists. Sinn Fein made an explicit connection between the economic policies of the state and ethnic nationalism arguing that independent Ireland would be able to develop the national economy through autarkic development policies. Just as important, the party worked to create an independent economic base that could provide tangible evidence of the efficacy of ethnic patronage as well as provide much needed financial resources for its activities. This strategy was a response to the broad structural changes that had occurred in Ireland over the preceding half-century. The creation of a cohesive administrative apparatus allowed for the articulation of a nationalist economic strategy predicated on the use of an interventionist state.

But while such economic demands and initiatives may have boosted the level of Sinn Fein's support they did not make it a dominant force in Irish politics. The party's organisational network, linked to the various Gaelic organisations, was sufficiently cohesive to maintain its status as a significant political force, but Sinn Fein failed to develop the kind of countrywide branch system with grass-roots involvement necessary to mobilise significant sections of the populace. Between 1906–9 support grew rapidly but was never large enough for the party to win a parliamentary seat. The success of the Gaelic Revival, and increasing popular support for historical tales or football matches, did not necessarily translate into direct electoral backing for ethnic nationalist policies.

The economic movement was able to reinforce the emotional messages of ethnic solidarity spread by the social and cultural movements with concrete material benefits and the promise of further support through state protection and patronage in an independent Ireland. But while the party did manage to help establish a few Irish manufacturers and a bank, the importance of these initiatives proved more symbolic than tangible. This focus on utilising the powers of the modern state for nationalist economic intervention was reinforced by Connolly's Socialists. Nevertheless, although it managed to gain the loyalty of the small working class, the labour movement was able to exert little power outside its Dublin base. By contrast, from 1910 the star of the far less ideological Parliamentary Party had moved into the ascendant once more.

In a context in which the Irish public continued to broadly accept the legitimacy of British rule, constitutional reform was still seen as the desired route to increasing Irish autonomy. Sinn Fein, together with the IRB and the broader ethno-nationalist movement had become important players on the Irish political scene, but they were far from dominant. Griffith's ethnic nationalism and economic promises helped build a powerful base across cultural, political and economic spheres. But in a situation where Home Rule seemed imminent and the most pressing land problems were being resolved via the Wyndham Land Act there was little to persuade the public to give its allegiance to ethnic nationalism.

THE AFRIKANERS

This section argues that a key aspect of the development of Afrikaner nationalism in the 1930s was its attempt to develop a viable economic agenda. It suggests that the Broederbond, inspired by Hertzog's use of the state for purposes of patronage and economic development, made nationalist economic policies and the promise of direct material benefits for Afrikaners a major part of its political platform. Given the growing population of Afrikaner workers, and an even greater number of languishing 'poor whites' this message had a natural constituency which, for the first time, responded to nationalist arguments. By embarking on a series of economic initiatives to complement its existing political and cultural ones, the Broederbond was able to introduce a crucial addition to its overall strategies for achieving power. Just as important, was the organisational sophistication of these initiatives which greatly helped the overall process of mobilising Afrikaners behind an ethno-nationalist banner.

The section opens by examining the nature of the modern South African state and its involvement in economic issues. It then shows how Hertzog and the National Party incorporated the protection of white labour into their party platform in the 1920s and how these initiatives influenced the Broederbond and its long-standing focus on patronage. It examines the Broederbond's involvement in the trade union movement and its articulation of a policy of *volkskapitalisme* ('people's capitalism') to try to develop Afrikaner economic interests. Finally the chapter looks at the attitude of Malan's GNP to economic issues and assesses the overall development of the nationalist movement.

The Modernisation of the South African State

The administrative structure of the modern South African state owed its existence primarily to Lord Milner.[31] Prior to the Boer War, the two states and two British colonies that comprised South Africa lacked even proper communication and transport links let alone a coordinated state bureaucracy. As High Commissioner in the conflict's aftermath, Milner dismantled the inchoate and inefficient legal and administrative apparatuses of the old republics. In their place, he built up a modern infrastructure supported by extensive rail links, upgraded roads, telegraph and telephone networks that for the first time linked the four colonies into one unit. This development was reflected in the provincial bureaucracies as Milner imported large numbers of well-trained British civil servants to fill important posts. In this manner, he laid the foundations for a meritocratic and technocratic civil service with few local political loyalties. The new administrative structure was set up explicitly to provide an efficient partner for the gold mines and to help generate income to develop the entire region while filling the imperial coffers in London.[32] The key element in this process was the control and regulation of black labour for the mines. From the development of the gold and diamond mining industries after 1867 and 1886 respectively, the need for a regular source of reliable labour became crucial for capital even prior to the development of a unitary South African state. Thereafter, a systematic programme of repressive labour legislation became the norm. The state became responsible for the recruitment of black labour on behalf of the mines through the formation of a monopsony, effectively preventing wage labour competition among blacks and thus cutting labour costs for the mines.

Despite other differences between the white political parties after union in 1910, there was consensus on the need to control black labour. Over the next decade as the black presence in the mines grew, there were a series of increasingly violent white strikes. These culminated in the Rand Revolt of 1923 in which thousands of mine-workers rampaged through the streets of Johannesburg illogically demanding that 'Workers of the World Unite and Fight for a White South Africa'. The government, now led by Smuts following Botha's death, reacted swiftly and violently, using troops to snuff out the uprising and hanging the ringleaders. This prompted Hertzog to pay closer attention to white, working-class grievances. In the wake of the revolt, he formed an electoral alliance, known as 'The Pact', with the socialist Labour party in 1923. The common interest between the two incongruous allies was the protection of white, predominantly Afrikaner, workers. In its election campaign the Pact alliance not only promised to secure 'civilized labour' in the form of job reservation for whites, but also undertook to subsidise local manufacturing and agricultural interests which made up the second part of its support base. All this was built around a polemical campaign against 'British' and 'Jewish' capital, centred on a mythical man called Hoggenheimer, caricatured in press cartoons as a fat, hook-nosed businessman trampling white Afrikaner workers underfoot in relentless pursuit of profit.[33]

These promises of direct state intervention in the economy contrasted markedly with the traditions established by Botha and Smuts – the SAP had made little effort to utilise state resources directly on behalf of their supporters. After narrowly winning the 1924 election, however, the new government soon passed extensive legislation to reward its constituents. The Industrial Conciliation Act of 1924, the Wage Act of 1925 and the Mines and Works Amendment Act of 1926 were all aimed at securing the position of white labour and giving it state protection against capitalist employers. In addition, the Pact started providing large-scale subsidies for South African agriculture, the only sector of the South African economy dominated by Afrikaners. Meanwhile, the Customs Tariff Act of 1925 marked the beginnings of an import substitution policy that favoured manufacturing over mining.[34] Hertzog also sought to use the state to provide jobs for his supporters. He passed legislation requiring new civil servants to be bilingual in an attempt to disqualify the predominantly Anglophone bureaucrats that Milner had introduced. Despite such efforts, however, the stubborn resilience of the Anglophone bureaucrats continued throughout the UP administrations. While increasing numbers of Afrikaners were brought into the lower end of the civil service, the upper ranks of the state bureaucracy were still overwhelmingly English-speaking until 1948.[35]

Hertzog's policies of subsidising local manufacturing and agriculture led both sectors to become increasingly reliant on state support. More importantly, through the creation of ISCOR (the state-owned iron and steel corporation) and a massive increase in white employment on the railways, thousands more jobs for poorer Afrikaners were provided. This in turn served to create expectations of state assistance amongst many newly urbanised whites. Hein Grosskopf, one of the authors of the Carnegie Commission of 1932–33, which was established to document white poverty, observed this change:

> The Committee put this question to people: 'Well, what in your opinion is the solution of your troubles?' and in almost every case the reply was 'The government must do this or that', until the matter became almost ludicrous.... So conspicuous is this habit of expecting too much from the state that even visitors from other countries have been struck by it. A well-known sociologist from America after a visit of some months to our country expresses himself as follows: 'With the possible exception of Russia, I know of no other country whose dependence on the government is greater than in South Africa.'[36]

The official findings of the Commission revealed the existence of some 300 000 such poverty-stricken whites, the overwhelming majority of them rural or newly urbanised Afrikaners. Nationalists were horrified and resolved to find ways to solve 'the poor white problem', focusing, as the Commission suggested, on the creation of jobs by the state through such policies as import substitution.

Economic Mobilisation and the Trade Unions

While for Hertzog, the aim of this struggle 'was not to obtain domination but equality' the significance of his policies and the populist attitudes they had engendered was not lost on the Broederbond. During the 1920s, the group had explicitly endorsed the notion that members should give each other direct assistance, both political and financial.[37] As a result of Pact policies, Afrikaner nationalists in the Broederbond began to look at the state not only as a means of protecting existing Afrikaner interests, but also as a key vehicle to build up Afrikaner economic power. In concert with the drive to take control of the state on an exclusive ethnic basis the nationalist movement sought to appeal to this new expectation of material support from the state.

Although Afrikaners controlled nearly 90 per cent of agriculture in the country at the beginning of the 1930s, they owned less than 5 per cent of commercial and industrial interests – and that was largely the result of financial investments by wealthy Cape farmers.[38] Recognising this, the Broederbond called a first *Ekonomiese Volkskongres* in 1934 (the year Hertzog 'sold out' by forming the UP with Smuts) at which it resolved to start building Afrikaner influence in the economic sphere. Shortly after, the Broederbond formed the first Afrikaner bank, Volkskas, which was intended to serve both as an institution at which Afrikaners could deposit their savings and also as a vehicle to help promote Afrikaner business through loans and investment capital. By focusing on providing material support on an ethnic basis, this marked the beginning of a major new strand of the Broederbond policies.

To complement the programme, the Broederbond, fearing the attraction of Marxist, class-based philosophies among Afrikaner workers, sought to submerge Afrikaner class differences beneath a common nationalist umbrella. Failing to form its own trade unions in the face of industrial closed-shop agreements it resolved to try to take over existing unions from within. Its earliest and most conspicuous success came on the railways. After forming a Language and Culture Society for the railways, the *Afrikaanse Taal en Kultuurvereniging* (ATKV) which soon recruited 18 000 members, the Broederbond began to exert considerable influence on the largest employer of white labour in the country. Through the ATKV the Bond managed to put its members in leadership positions in the *Spoorbond*, the railway workers union. Offering many of the benefits of other unions such as pension schemes and insurance policies, the *Spoorbond* spearheaded the spread of nationalist ideology among Afrikaner workers, thus linking the notions of national culture and material benefit in the minds of the workers.

Hoping to build on this success, in 1936 the Broederbond formed the National Council of Trustees (NRT), specifically to cultivate Christian National ideas within the broader white labour movement. Driving this campaign was the knowledge that some 80 per cent of a total 223 000 white union members in 1937 were Afrikaners.[39] But outside the railways the response was at best lukewarm. As Iris Berger has shown, in the case of the staunchly socialist, non-racial Garment Workers Union, when a union fulfilled most of the material needs of its Afrikaner members, nationalist appeals were largely ineffective.[40] While the ethno-cultural dimension of the nationalist movement held some independent attraction for Afrikaner workers, without the promise of genuine material benefits as well as ethnic security it could not count on their political support.

The *Eeufees* and *Volkskapitalisme*

The poor white question had, however, become a potent political issue. As early as 1934, the National Party put forward a Programme of Action which incorporated demands for white social welfare and protection for agriculture and labourers, but did little to take this further. Its 1938 election manifesto focused on issues such as calling for a republic, removing 'God Save the Queen' and abolishing the remaining Native franchise but paid little attention to economic issues.[41] In the ensuing poll it won only 27 seats to the UP's 111, although its share of the Afrikaner vote had risen slightly despite five years of unparalleled prosperity that would under conventional circumstances have raised the ruling party's majority.[42] Encouraging though they were, the results fell well short of the overwhelming majority required for political victory.

Nevertheless, ethnic nationalism was making strides. This was dramatically demonstrated later that year during the Great Trek centenary celebrations, or *Eeufees*. Organised by the FAK, a symbolic oxwagon trek was launched to stir up patriotic feelings among Afrikaners. The results exceeded wildest expectations. The trek set out from Cape Town in August and slowly traversed the country, releasing an

unprecedented outburst of emotion. Streets were renamed after Afrikaner heroes while men and women started wearing trekker clothing
and men began growing beards to emulate their hardy ancestors. The
climax came on 16 December, the Day of the Covenant, when an
estimated 100 000 people, nearly 10 per cent of the entire Afrikaner
population, was present for the final celebrations outside Pretoria.[43]
This marked a crucial breakthrough in the spread of the nationalist
ideology. The Broederbond, through the FAK and its other community
organisations, was largely responsible, helping use the occasion to
portray the GNP as the keeper of the nationalist flame.

In the wake of the celebrations, in a speech at Blood River – site of
the most famous Boer victory over the Zulus in 1838 – Malan shifted
the party's strategic focus to what he called the 'The New Great Trek' –
the movement of Afrikaners into the cities and the need to alleviate
their economic plight.[44] Economic succour of Afrikaners was added to
the political and cultural demands for national self-determination. As
another prominent leader argued:

> The legend of a strict division between culture, economics and
> politics has fallen away. We will no longer be blinded by it. The
> volk is an organic whole.[45]

By the end of the decade, therefore, the National Party and, more
importantly, the Broederbond, were following a similar plan to that
articulated in Ireland by Arthur Griffith nearly thirty years earlier.
Unlike Sinn Fein, however, from the start, the Broederbond linked its
formation of capitalist ventures like a bank with a concerted attempt to
seize control of the trade unions. Griffith on the other hand left worker
mobilisation to Connolly's Socialist party, thereby creating a rift where
an alliance would probably have proved more fruitful. Also, South
Africa was, by virtue of its mining sector, a more advanced industrial
state while rural concerns focused not on land, as in Ireland, but on
state protection for commercial agriculture.

Building on this foundation, in 1939, the Broederbond, through the
FAK, called a second *Ekonomiese Volkskongres* to articulate its new
policy of *volkskapitalisme* – people's capitalism. The painful effects that
the growth of capitalism had on Afrikaners, it argued, lay not in the
doctrine itself but rather in the ownership of capital by 'foreign' and
'Jewish' interests while 'communists' were subverting workers. The
solution to this uncomfortable situation lay in Afrikaner control of
capital and labour. As L.J. du Plessis, the primary architect of the idea,
asserted:

[We must] mobilise the volk to conquer the capitalist system and to alter it so that it fits our ethnic nature.[46]

the state was seen as the main vehicle for this process and the very first resolution passed by the Congress called on the government to provide business training and support for Afrikaner cooperatives. As the official history of the economic movement shows, this was made explicit time and again, most strikingly by Verwoerd who asked:

What weapon can Afrikanerdom use in this great [economic] struggle? There is that of state power. If we can take control of it public credit could be used *inter alia* for the founding of mutual banks and properly established Afrikaner initiatives, especially in industry.[47]

Until that was achieved, however, the Broederbond aimed more practically at encouraging Afrikaner control of the means of production so that workers and businessmen could work together under the banner of ethnic solidarity and thus avoid the perils of class conflict. To further this aim, they formed *Federale Volksbeleggings* (FVB) as a holding company through which Afrikaners could make inroads into industry. By 1942, FVB had already diversified into 12 industries ranging from fishing to coal-mining. An Afrikaner equivalent to the Anglophone Chamber of Commerce, the *Afrikaanse Handelsinstituut* (AHI) was formed, bringing together a group of around 80 Afrikaner companies to 'provide guidance, direction and cooperation between Afrikaner businessmen'.[48]

In addition to these capitalist ventures, the *Reddingsdaadbond* (RDB) was formed as a charity to alleviate the seemingly intractable poor white problem. Derived in part from the mystical nationalist writing of preacher J.D. Kestell (which had echoes of Patrick Pearse's romantic nationalist economics in Ireland), it called for the spiritual upliftment of Afrikaners while tapping funds that could be used to help the community's poorest members. Under the broad slogan ''n volk red homself' (a people must rescue itself) it aimed at 'freeing Afrikaners from economic bondage'. In practice, however, the bulk of funds collected went towards the promotion of Afrikaner business. For the first time, Afrikaners, including both workers and farmers, were being persuaded in large numbers to put their savings into exclusively Afrikaner enterprises and financial organisations as investment capital. Using this money, the Afrikaner share of the private sector rose from 5 to 11 per cent between 1939–50 and some 25 000–30 000 new

Afrikaner jobs were created.[49] Even more important was the mass nature of the RDB. By 1946, membership peaked at 64 771, while its 381 branches were used to sponsor activities relating to all aspects of daily life.[50] Again, this was similar but more comprehensive than Sinn Fein's attempts to link its nascent Irish industrial initiatives with social and cultural nationalist initiatives made by other groupings in the Gaelic League.

Although support was uneven, these events immersed the urban community in exclusively Afrikaner activities, stimulating cultural awareness and at the same time suggesting that only in a broader ethnic nationalist framework would their economic needs be fully addressed. Once in place, the economic groupings provided another vital link in the formation of a powerful organisational infrastructure for the broader Christian National movement. The RDB in particular, in a similar but much more direct way than the FAK, was able to promote and foster an Afrikaner cultural and economic identity while vigorously developing a nationalist political agenda. In addition, the capital it amassed successfully built up Afrikaner private enterprise, creating thousands of jobs for poorer Afrikaners in the process. The underlying premise was that if the nationalists were to take over the state, they would employ its resources in a similar but more comprehensive manner, both protecting and supporting the Afrikaner's position in the economy.

Conclusions

During the course of the 1930s the Broederbond and the GNP set up satellite organisations in virtually every sphere of society. The resulting institutionalisation of Afrikaans culture, history and language within a set of new bureaucracies provided the foundation for a unified Afrikaner front which could mount a political challenge against the state. The common leadership of these groups, consisting predominantly of elites within the Broederbond and GNP, was able to use this new organisational infrastructure to propagate the demand that the Afrikaner nation should control the South African state. In order to succeed, however, the movement was dependent not simply on psychological appeals to an alienated populace. The interventionist state pioneered by Hertzog had promised to use the state to uplift Afrikaners. Poorer Afrikaners looked to government for economic succour. Responding to this, the Broederbond and the National Party established a wide variety of groups through which they sought to persuade

Afrikaners that ethnic nationalism could secure material benefits for them as well as political and cultural security.

At the same time, the Broederbond began to build up a pool of resources for ethnic patronage outside the state to complement its goal of converting the state into an instrument for Afrikaner economic protection. The RDB, *volkskapitalisme*, and the Trade Union movement all illustrated how the Afrikaner nationalist movement worked at creating extra-statal patronage networks focused on economic issues. These activities combined with the cultural mobilisation orchestrated by the FAK and its affiliates in supporting the creation of an Afrikaner nationalist movement ultimately aimed at gaining political power. The overall campaign was explicitly focused on the state and fuelled by the belief that an exclusive Afrikaner republic would be in a better position to reward and support Afrikaner workers and farmers. Together with the nationalist movement's ethno-cultural and political initiatives, the economic campaign sought to persuade all Afrikaners that their needs could best be addressed within an all-embracing ethnic movement focused on the state. Although the movement was not yet able to challenge the existing government, an exclusive Afrikaner nationalism was gaining increasing ground on three fronts: the social, the economic and the political.

THE ZIONISTS

For the Zionists any economic strategies linked to the state had to await the creation of suitable political conditions to establish a formal administrative structure in Palestine – a problem that was never faced by the Irish and disappeared for the Afrikaners after Union in 1910. This section shows how in the wake of the 1917 Balfour declaration, the Zionist movement within Palestine created the structural foundations for such a state by establishing a range of semi-autonomous cultural, political and economic institutions. It argues that these initiatives allowed for critical economic development which provided the wherewithal to attract and retain new immigrants.

The section opens by examining the political negotiations with Britain and other countries that led to the establishment of a Jewish homeland in Palestine and the political institutions which were subsequently established there during the 1920s. It then looks at the broader attempts by the Zionist movement within Palestine to set up a viable economy capable of providing jobs and welfare for new waves of Jewish immigrants. Finally it details the effect these structural changes had on the administrative structure of the Zionist movement and the broader distribution of political power within the WZO during the early 1930s.

Political Foundations

Although Weizmann's initial diplomatic initiatives had met with a tepid reception, he continued to attempt to persuade the British of the potential value of Zionism for their own designs in the Middle East. As the broader geopolitical situation in the region shifted during the First World War, these suggestions began to converge with British strategic interest. The Ottoman entry into the war on Germany's side meant that a fundamental rearrangement of the political map of the Middle East, whichever side triumphed, was very likely. Weizmann sought to capitalise on these prospective changes.

The British were conducting policy on a number of different levels, simultaneously planning to divide the region with France while conducting negotiations with both the Jews and the Arabs for support in the war effort. Weizmann held extensive discussions with many prominent politicians, most notably Sir Mark Sykes, a member of parliament heavily involved in the formulation of Middle-Eastern policy. He sought to persuade the British of the need to support a new wave of Jewish immigrants. This, he argued, would give them a loyal and stable population in a strategically important area. In addition, he suggested, a statement of support would pre-empt a similar declaration from the Germans and help persuade Jews in America to urge President Woodrow Wilson to enter the war. Domestically, too, Weizmann asserted, a pro-Zionist stance would retain electoral support for the government within the East End of London which had a substantial Jewish population.

In David Lloyd George's new cabinet, established in December 1916, there were at least three members with Zionist sympathies: the South African general Jan Smuts, Lloyd George himself and Arthur Balfour, the new Foreign Secretary. Following the First Russian revolution of 1917, it was also believed that Jews were very influential in the new government and would lobby to keep Russia in the war if Britain endorsed Zionism. More importantly, Weizmann despatched his colleague, Nahum Sokolow, to Paris in a successful attempt to persuade the French to leave Palestine in British hands, thereby providing tangible proof of the strategic utility of the Zionist movement to Britain.[51] The combination of these short- and long-term considerations resulted in the Balfour Declaration of March 1917, a Cabinet-approved document which stated that

> His Majesty's Government view with favour the establishment in Palestine of a national home for the Jewish people, and will use their best endeavours to facilitate the achievement of this object...

Political Zionism's aims of seeking external support to combine with the practical task of setting up national institutions had finally proved successful. For the first time, the Zionists had secured international recognition for their claim to Palestine.

To establish the compatibility of Zionism with the broader force of Arab nationalism, Weizmann met with the Hashemite Prince Feisal and each agreed to help the other attain their aims. Then, through extensive bilateral negotiations, the Zionist leadership secured the official endorsement of the rest of the 'Big Four' – France, the United States, and Italy – for the Balfour Declaration at the Paris peace talks in 1919.[52] After further negotiations, Palestine became a formal mandate under British guardianship to be monitored by the League of Nations. However there was still a strong anti-Zionist element in the British administration. In 1922, after responsibility for Palestine was transferred to the Colonial Office, a new White Paper modified the terms of the Mandate to permit only as much immigration as the 'economic absorptive capacity' of Palestine would allow. The same year, Britain formally divided Palestine into two parts, creating the new state of Transjordan on the east bank of the Jordan River under the Hashemite King Abdullah.

Despite his inability to rein in these pro-Arab compromises, Weizmann's influence in Britain remained high. In 1920 the WZO formally moved its headquarters to London and elected him its President. Through the course of the 1920s and early 1930s, Weizmann used this position to good effect, carrying out a broad international campaign to consolidate support for Zionism.[53] After further diplomatic maneouvring, the WZO managed to secure the appointment of the Zionist Liberal politician, Sir Herbert Samuel, as the Mandate's first High Commissioner.[54] From 1925 onwards the WZO maintained a special office at the Permanent Mandates Commission so as to be able to short-circuit any Palestinian grievances that might be brought to the League's attention. Meanwhile, given Zionism's new official status Palestine became an increasingly attractive destination for Jews and membership of the WZO soared. By the end of 1920 it had reached 750 000 worldwide, and continued to grow, albeit more slowly, during the course of the decade.[55] A complex diplomatic strategy that had combined nationalist demands for self-determination with strategic lobbying for great power support had opened the political space necessary to expand the process of practical development of the Jewish settlement in Palestine.

With a political base secured, the Zionists were able to turn their attention to the task of boosting immigration and building up new Jewish institutions. While South Africa had its own parliament, and Ireland (prior to 1922) was part of Westminster, Palestine had no indigenous representative institutions. Under the auspices of the British Colonial Office new structures were set out to govern the development of the *Yishuv*. Initially, Samuel hoped to create a binational legislative assembly but this was turned down by the Palestinians. The result was a *de facto* political separation of Palestine's two ethnic groups. In 1928, the British formally promulgated new legislation that endorsed a separate Jewish legislature and executive. In this way, the *Yishuv* itself, and not merely the Jewish presence in Palestine, was given legal status.

The new Jewish administration consisted of a two-tiered government. The legislature, which was known as the *Knesset* had two parts. First, a legislative assembly, the *Asefat Hanihavrim*, was established under a universal franchise. It was given the power to approve budgets and collect local taxes, both subject to the approval of the mandatory government. These budgets involved local concerns specific to the Jewish community, such as housing and education. The Assembly was supplemented by a second organ, the *Vaad Leumi*, or National Council, which was to serve as its executive branch. In theory, Jewish settlers were allowed to 'opt out' of membership of the Jewish community and if they did so would only be liable for taxation to the Mandate, and not their 'national' government. In practice, however, the vast majority of Jews chose to participate in the new structures. For the first time, the governing body of the *Yishuv* was constituted in a legally sanctioned manner, an important step on the path to independent statehood. It also demonstrated the extent to which the Jews now thought of themselves as a national community. Having to declare their citizenship within the Jewish community was a self-conscious, nationalist decision.

A second layer of government for the Jews involved the WZO. Initially, the organisation was represented by the Zionist Commission in Palestine, which had been set up in 1918. Article 4 of the Mandate called for the provision of a Jewish Agency in Palestine to act as the official mouthpiece for the Jews in their dealings with the British. Although the WZO endorsed it in 1922, the Agency was only recognised by the British in 1928. It began operations at the beginning of 1929 under Weizmann's presidency. The Agency then took control of all dealings with the British in Palestine and with local Arab leaders, in effect conducting a foreign policy for the *Yishuv* and the WZO. Domestically, it assumed responsibility for immigration, the purchase of land for Jewish settlers through the WZO's land funds, and the continuation of agricultural development and colonisation through Jewish labour. The Agency also undertook the promotion of Hebrew language and culture, again demonstrating the constant link between the nation and state in Zionist activities.

Providing a central executive body that could link all three elements of the Zionist strategy was highly significant. First, the Agency's roots within the WZO meant that its strength derived directly from Zionists both in and out of Palestine. Second, its role in all political negotiations with other groups and states, meant that it now served as a central conduit for the campaign for international diplomatic support for the movement. Third, its location in Jerusalem for the first time linked the international diplomatic/executive arm of the Zionist movement with the local political/economic one, making it a much more state-like unit. By the start of the 1930s, therefore, the *Yishuv* had achieved legal standing, internal and external authority, and control over a wide range of domestic and international institutions and activities more commonly found under the purview of states. It was still far from achieving full sovereignty, but a formal bureaucratic infrastructure was now in place that carried out many of the functions of a state.

Population Growth and Political Change

Over the course of the Mandate, the population of the *Yishuv* expanded rapidly with the arrival of two new waves of immigration: the 3rd *Aliyah* of 1919–24 which brought in 40 000 people, most of them highly politicised Russian Jews inspired by the Balfour Declaration, and the 4th *Aliyah* of 1925–29 consisting of some 68 000 Polish settlers fleeing unfavourable political conditions. The latter group was the first to be affected by new United States restrictions on immigration that were instituted in 1924. The trickle of committed Zionists had in the past been dwarfed by the flood of Jewish emigrants to America. Now that that route was closed, eastern European Jews seeking an escape from domestic problems were forced to turn their attention to

Palestine. This became even more important in the 1930s with the arrival of the 5th *Aliyah,* largely German Jews who sought escape from the growing predations of Nazism. Between 1930–36 these refugees more than doubled the *Yishuv*'s population from 164 950 to 384 078. As few of these were committed to establishing a Jewish state before their arrival in Palestine, the Zionist movement had to ensure that its strategies of nation and state building could convince the newcomers that their future lay in Jewish nationalism.

During this period the movement itself underwent significant political changes. Most notable was the establishment of the Revisionist Party in 1925, a faction created by Vladimir Jabotinsky, a Polish Jew and a charismatic orator who believed in a more direct and forceful approach to pursuing Zionist aims. Jabotinsky was an unabashed territorial maximalist who held that the Jewish right to political control over greater Palestine, including Transjordan, was absolute and should be achieved by force, preferably with logistical assistance from Britain. This message attracted significant support within the WZO and by 1931, the Revisionists garnered 25 per cent of the vote in the body's elections, receiving the bulk of their support from the Polish Jewish community which comprised a hefty 250 000 out of a total WZO membership of 691 000.[56] The Zionist left-wing, however, was growing with similar speed. In 1919 *Poale Zion,* largely at Ben Gurion's urging, merged with a number of smaller left-wing parties to form *Achdut Haavodah,* which, in 1930, joined with *Ha'poel Hatzair* to form *Mapai.* This new labour-oriented grouping soon became the most powerful faction in the WZO, and in 1931 narrowly defeated the Revisionists before establishing a governing coalition of the WZO which explicitly excluded them.

After an attempted compromise between Jabotinsky and Ben Gurion fell through in 1934, Jabotinsky took the Revisionists out of the WZO in protest and formed the New Zionist Organisation (NZO). The NZO, however proved unable to marshal a fraction of the resources available to the WZO/*Yishuv* combination serving labour's interests. Its failure graphically demonstrated how ideology alone was unable to compete as a mobilising agent without a comprehensive bureaucratic network to sustain it. Although Jabotinsky's personal stature remained very high until his death in 1940, the right wing never mounted another serious political challenge to the labour movement until after independence. Nevertheless, the Revisionists did have an important effect on overall Zionist strategies. They forced the WZO to maintain its focus on the broader nationalist issues involving the state rather than narrower, class-centred preoccupations of the more radical labour elements. They also pushed the plan of developing a viable military force into greater prominence. These were key elements in consolidating the overall nation-building thrust that was central to WZO activities.

Economic Strategies

Despite the pro-labour rhetoric of the political parties during the first few years after the arrival of the 2nd *Aliyah*, many of the immigrant workers found it very difficult to find any sort of jobs at all. Largely unused to manual labour, the Russians were unable to work as efficiently as the Arab labourers hired by local Jewish landowners, mostly survivors of the 1st *Aliyah*. At the same time they were not prepared to compete directly with the Arabs whose wages were insufficient to secure the higher standard of living to which even ghettoised Jews of eastern Europe and Russia were accustomed. The result was that many workers – according to one estimate some 70 per cent of the supposedly super-ideological 2nd *Aliyah* – gave up on their Zionist dreams, leaving to seek a better economic situation either back in Russia or in the United States.[57] Thus even among its most committed proponents, ideological and ethnic solidarity without material reward was an ineffective mobilizing instrument. While Zionism, as a form of Jewish ethnic mobilisation, had been able to engender sufficient commitment in eastern Europe for Jews to emigrate, a combination of ideological and ethnic allegiance alone was unable to develop a viable national community in Palestine.

An initial solution to these problems was found in the agricultural cooperatives, or *kibbutzes*. The WZO purchased land, to be held in trust for the Jewish people, which was then given to Jewish workers to develop through the medium of the *kibbutz*. The experiment proved a great success and led to other similar ventures. By 1914 the Zionists had succeeded in establishing 44 Jewish agricultural settlements, of which 14 were WZO/labour cooperatives. They were supplemented by educational initiatives and other programmes including a mobile agricultural library, a health insurance scheme, and a labour exchange. The strength of the new institutions lay in their ability simultaneously to provide a living for Jews while excluding Palestinians. At the same time, they were places which continually reinforced the development of nationalist sentiment. Because they were self-contained, the *kibbutzes* organised all political, cultural and educational initiatives within their communities, allowing for the extension of Zionist precepts through all facets of daily life. The dynamic effect of this total ethnic immersion was to become increasingly evident in the disproportionately large number of *kibbutz*-dwellers in the political hierarchy of the Palestine-based Zionist movement up to and after independence.[58]

The labour parties decided to consolidate these initiatives and formed the *Histadrut* in 1920. This was an umbrella group designed to have control and authority over four broad areas: trade unions, cooperative economic enterprises (including the *kibbutzes*), social services (such as health insurance and pensions), and education and culture. Ben Gurion was elected secretary-general and charged with involving the new group in all 'economic and cultural issues affecting labour in Palestine'.[59] This dual focus confirmed the continuing nationalist foundation to the movement. Economic development was perceived to be inextricably connected with broader Zionist activities. Expanding the *Yishuv*'s economic power, an important part of domestic state-building, was linked directly to the educational and cultural focus of nation-building.

The organisation was an immediate success, and by 1922 had already enlisted half of the *Yishuv*'s workforce. With the arrival of the 4th *Aliyah* it gave the parties a framework within which to welcome and, in effect, co-opt new arrivals who might otherwise have chosen to follow different political avenues. The *Histadrut* became directly involved in finding jobs and houses for new immigrants as well as providing for health, education and general welfare. As a result, it became seen by many new arrivals as the most important institution within the *Yishuv*. They willingly pledged allegiance to it – and by extension (labour) Zionism – in exchange for material support. Under the stimulus of the new immigration waves, and in particular the assets that the wealthier Polish Jews were able to bring with them, the Palestinian economy boomed and the *Histadrut* flourished. In addition to expanding trade union activities, the group formed a Bureau for Public Works, a bank, and *Soleh Boneh*, a large construction company. Later, it expanded into interests as diverse as insurance, fisheries and textiles – a process almost identical to that undertaken by FVB in South Africa in the 1940s.

The Zionists realised that they needed to secure the material well-being of Jews in Palestine if they were ever to achieve statehood. This was best illustrated in 1926, when a crisis in the Polish economy cut off all remitted income to the Polish immigrants. The effects were catastrophic. *Soleh Boneh*, by then the country's single largest corporation, and many other companies, collapsed. Unemployment and inflation both rose rapidly with dire consequences for the Jewish community. Where 1925 had been a record year for immigration, with 34 000 arrivals, 1927 saw Palestine's first net emigration of Jews since the war, a loss of 10 000 people.[60] The *Histadrut*, however, with support from the Jewish Agency, behaved like a proto-welfare state. It began providing unemployment aid to Jews, and maintained healthcare and housing for people who had lost theirs. At the same time, a new fundraising drive by the WZO allowed for the resumption of capital inflows which successfully resurrected the economy.[61] Without this material support offered by the *Histadrut* and its member institutions, the effect of the slump would have been far more devastating to the Zionist cause. With the global economy moving into a massive downturn, soon to be the Great Depression, the collapse of the Jewish economy might have utterly destroyed Zionist dreams by making one of the doctrine's main aims, the continuation of Jewish immigration to Palestine, unfeasible. After the 1926 experience, however, the economic cushions put in place by the *Histadrut* and the Jewish Agency allowed the *Yishuv* to weather the global dislocations of the early 1930s with comparatively little difficulty. Even though Jewish immigration was further restricted by the British from 1929 onwards, leading to more moderate growth, a solid economic foundation to the *Yishuv* had been laid.

After 1933, through a controversial deal negotiated by officials in the Anglo-Palestine bank with the Nazis, Jewish emigrants from Germany were allowed to convert their assets into goods that could be exported to Palestine. Combined with new capital inflows through the WZO and other Zionist organisations, this provided the wherewithal for a new expansion of the Jewish economy that was more than enough to provide jobs for the newcomers.[62] The movement did not neglect its labour union obligations either. Under Ben Gurion's leadership it continued to fight for better wages and living conditions for Jewish labour which (using the identical term adopted in South Africa) was termed 'civilised labour' and used as justification for differential rates of pay between Jews and Palestinians, even on British enterprises such as the railways.[63] Membership of the *Histadrut* rose extremely rapidly, reflecting its leading role in meeting and providing for immigrants. By 1935, some 65 per cent of all new immigrants received direct assistance of some kind, ranging from temporary accommodation to loans to full-time jobs, from the organisation.[64] The *Histadrut*'s grip over the economy became immense as its subsidiaries comprised nearly half the *Yishuv's* total output by the mid-1930s and 63 per cent of all tax revenue to the Palestinian administration.[65] More than any other single institution, it comprised the backbone of the *Yishuv's* state-making activities.

Cultural and Security Issues

Because the organisation was directly connected with educational and cultural activities, running many schools and recreational groups, economic membership of the *Histadrut* necessarily meant immersion in Zionist principles. This reinforced nationalist sentiment among incoming Jews. At the same time, it indicated to Jewish immigrants that only under the Zionist banner would their economic livelihood be maintained. In the social and cultural spheres the *Histadrut* formed a Central Cultural Commission to monitor the promotion of Hebrew activities and took many of the various labour parties' schools under its control. It also published a daily Hebrew newspaper (by then one of many countrywide) and formed organisations to promote sports and Hebrew theatre. Through the *Histadrut*, therefore, the nation-building goals of Zionism were linked directly with economic interests. Combined with similar nation-building activities undertaken by the political parties, the Jewish Agency and other Zionist institutions, this reinforced a sense of national community. By 1928 there were already 220 Jewish schools in operation with over 20 000 pupils, all teaching Zionist ideals of one type or another.[66] Newspaper readership of Hebrew language dailies increased rapidly with *Ha'aretz* and *Davar*, the two largest, commanding circulations of 17 000 and 25 000 respectively.[67] All of this was focused on Hebrew which was now universally recognised as the 'mark of the unity of Judaism'.[68] In 1935, the Bialik Foundation, was established to coordinate all Hebrew cultural activities, establishing a grouping that worked in a similar manner to the Gaelic League in Ireland and the FAK in South Africa, although it never achieved the influence of its counterparts. Nevertheless, even the British were forced to conclude that, '[a]ll in all the cultural achievements of this little community of 400 000 people is one of the most remarkable achievements of the National Home'.[69]

Another vital institution under the *Histadrut's* control was the *Haganah*, a new, semi-secret military force that succeeded *Hashomer*. It was formed in 1920, partly in response to Arab riots that had led to the deaths of several Jews, and partly out of a generalised need for increased security. It marked the formal establishment of a separate military arm for the Jewish community and was given the mandate to begin training groups of settlers in informal paramilitary units that would be used in defence of Jewish settlers. Over the course of the decade it grew into a disciplined fighting force that remained under the control of the labour parties, although a small faction did break away in 1928, later to become the pro-Revisionist *Irgun*. Most importantly, the *Haganah*'s creation marked yet another function normally ascribed to independent states that the *Yishuv* was able to abrogate to itself under the auspices of the Mandate.

A large part of the Labour Zionist political victory over the Revisionists was thus due to its much more powerful, economically oriented, organisational base. While the Revisionists had tried to implement similar initiatives to Labour by offering opportunities for new immigrants and developing new Zionist enterprises, neither proved particularly effective. Both groupings employed similar ideological platforms, extolling common religion, history and language to build up a Jewish national identity. But although the Revisionists took a much more hardline attitude to the Palestinian issue, their political platform was not the key reason behind their minority status in Zionist politics. Instead it was the labour movement's ability to link economic issues to the Zionist enterprise through the wide-ranging *Histradrut*, that allowed them to create a powerful, patronage-oriented organisation base that the Revisionists could not match.

Now in control over the political, economic and military matters for the *Yishuv*, *Mapai* was the dominant party in Zionist politics, and Ben Gurion, its leading exponent and a long-time political opponent of Weizmann, the most powerful politician. Although Weizmann's personal stature meant that he was still able to pursue his own diplomatic policies, domestic Palestinian matters were now largely out of his hands. As a result, while he was re-elected to the WZO Presidency at the 1935 Zionist Congress, Ben Gurion, who had left the *Histradrut*, was made chairman of the Jewish Agency, effectively becoming prime minister of Jewish Palestine. Significantly, this Congress was also the first to be conducted entirely in Hebrew, illustrating the new depth of national consciousness among all delegates, particularly those from the *Yishuv*.[70]

The move was in part a recognition by the labour movement of which institution was most important for the overall strategy of creating a state. The *Histradrut* had been the primary instrument for the first part of Zionist state-building, the establishment and consolidation of political, economic, military and cultural institutions. Now the Agency, the effective diplomatic arm of the *Yishuv*'s proto-state, was the key institution for the next stage of Zionist state-building: the further pursuit of political independence. *Mapai*, with Ben Gurion at its head, now constituted a *de facto*, elected government for the Jewish proto-state in Palestine. An emerging Jewish nation was assuming control of an emerging Jewish state after 'fifteen centuries of neglect and decay'.[71] As the WZO itself approvingly recorded, by 1935 the *Yishuv* had begun to show 'a gratifying appreciation of the implications of a political organisation and a mature sense of the quasi-civic responsibility of every member of the Zionist organisation towards the "state on the way"'.

Conclusions

By the mid-1930s the Zionists had managed to secure and maintain international support for their goals and to establish a viable institutional base in Palestine. The origins of this success lay in the Zionist diplomatic activities that secured the Balfour Declaration. Without having secured sponsorship from the British, the Zionists would not have had the political space needed to expand their presence within Palestine. In the 1920s, the *Yishuv* was still too weak to stand on its own as an independent state. Without the British protection secured by political Zionism, it would not have been able to withstand resistance from the Palestinians. Although the success of these diplomatic activities was dependent on favourable geopolitical factors following the First World War, the fact that the Zionists had an effective diplomatic campaign meant that it was they, and not the Palestinians, who were able to take full advantage of this structural shift.

The movement then made use of this opportunity to establish a complex set of institutions in the political, economic, social and military spheres, that were able to absorb and mould a vast expansion in the population of the *Yishuv*. Without any existing state institutions to use for the process of nation-building, the Zionists created their own. The labour faction skilfully manipulated the *Histadrut* by combining economic patronage and cultural activities to provide a base that would attract Jews to Palestine and capture the political allegiance of new immigrants. As a result, the tens of thousands of Jewish refugees who fled the Nazi threat in the 1930s were provided with jobs in an expanding community while simultaneously being immersed in a set of nationalist activities centred on the use of Hebrew.

This in turn led to increased power for the labour movement and, via its leadership in the economy, political administration, and the Jewish Agency, overall control over Zionist strategies for independence. In WZO voting, Labour's dominance was achieved due to its overwhelming strength within Palestine itself – the Revisionists' most powerful support groups were in the Russian and Polish Jewish communities. This was itself revealing: for those still outside Palestine, ideological appeals continued to have greater salience than those with an economic dimension, hence the growing support there for the Revisionists' combative vision of the future. For those on the ground in the *Yishuv*, however, the reality of having to find housing, jobs and food quickly brought people over to Labour's side. When, by the mid-1930s, Jews within Palestine became a numerical majority in the WZO, Labour, by dint of its organisational and economic dominance in the territory achieved a political majority in the council.

While not yet a sovereign state, therefore, the *Yishuv* was self-consciously becoming a state-in-the-making or proto-state, with the Jewish Agency as its effective government. It was, as Weizmann put it, being built up 'slowly, gradually, systematically and patiently'.[72] By the mid-1930s, the *Yishuv* conducted a great many of the functions of a state and exercised considerable political and administrative authority over the Jewish population in Palestine. Certainly from the perspective of most Zionists the legitimate government of Palestine was increasingly the Jewish Agency rather than the colonial administration. More importantly from the point of view of consolidating Zionism's nationalist base, it was a particular kind of state – a proto-welfare state that saw to the material needs of its citizens. Although the basis of the movement's legitimacy rested in its nationalist ideology, in order to keep its constituents in Palestine it needed to cater for their social and economic needs as well. Both the establishment of the Mandate and the institutions that the Jews created under it testified to the Zionists' multifaceted strategy to build a nation-state.

GENERAL CONCLUSIONS

In all three cases a key factor in building up a viable mass support base for an ethno-nationalist platform lay in combining earlier cultural and linguistic initiatives with newer political and economic ones through the agency of grass-roots organisations. The nationalist political parties were able to transform themselves from small coteries of

intellectuals propagating nationalist ideology into viable mass movements. In effect the focus of ethnic politics in each country was shifted
away from individual leaders to a set of institutions embracing the
common ideal of a national government. Analysing this process in
South Africa, F. Van Zyl Slabbert has described it as the 'bureau-
cratization of an ethos', with the ethos in question being an exclusive
Afrikaner nationalist ideology.[73] The same term is applicable to both
Irish nationalism and Zionism. In each case the organisational network
in effect created a new 'establishment' consisting of a set of bureaucracies focused on a common ideal – nationalism. The overlapping
membership and leadership of such organisations – the GNP, the FAK
and the RDB in South Africa, Sinn Fein, the IRB and the Gaelic
League in Ireland, the *Histadrut*, the Labour Parties and *Haganah* in
Palestine – greatly facilitated the formulation and execution of collective goals. Despite the wide range of these different bureaucracies, and
their differing short-term aims, they were always linked through their
common goal: control of the state.

In this process, the economic dimension of ethnic nationalism was
critical. All three movements explicitly sought to address the economic
concerns of their constituents as well as ethno-cultural ones. Nationalist leaders repeatedly asserted that control of the state would allow
them to provide important economic benefits for members of the
ethnic group. These arguments, were partly prompted by the development of a modern, centralised bureaucratic state structure that had
recently begun to use interventionist economic policies within each
territory. The growing presence of Catholics in the civil service in
Ireland mirrored the steady rise in the proportion of Afrikaners in
South Africa, while many Zionists got jobs as *de facto* bureaucrats who
came to operate the *Yishuv*'s proto-state. In many cases they were
more powerful than the civil servants running the small Palestinian
administration on behalf of the Colonial Office.

This process also helped focus attention on the potential utility of
state structures for ethnic benefit. Accordingly, Griffith's Sinn Fein
took note of Britain's limited state intervention in the land issue and
extended their demands to the fostering of state industries and
autarkic trade policies. Similarly, after Hertzog's experiments with
industrial interventionism in the 1920s and 30s, the Broederbond
began to complement its cultural initiatives with economic ones that
were to culminate in the articulation of *volkskapitalisme* at the end of
the decade. The Zionists had to await the establishment of a political
structure, in the shape of the Mandate, before setting out a formal

economic agenda. Once that was in place they too wasted little time setting up a linked set of economic and political institutions, in particular the *Histadrut*, aimed at indigenous economic development. State power was thus sought not only for reasons of political security but also for the potential benefits of ethnic patronage and general material security.

All three movements also set up separate organisations designed to provide tangible benefits for their supporters. The *Histadrut* proved an invaluable resource that provided substantial material benefits to the local community, thus cementing political loyalty to Zionist goals. The Broederbond's new organisations and industries, notably the RDB, and the various enterprises linked to the AHI, similarly provided concrete material support for Afrikaners and their businesses, with the promise of much more to come when the movement got its hands on the state. Sinn Fein, again given its limited resources, proved more ineffectual in its attempts to do the same thing, but nonetheless set a precedent for such ethnic patronage through its 'Irish Industry' programmes.

In each case, this process was reinforced by the activities of nationalist-oriented trade unions. In addition to its activities developing indigenous enterprises, the *Histadrut* became Palestine's dominant labour federation. In South Africa and Ireland, these campaigns proved less successful. Even there, however, the Broederbond's success in seizing control of the *Spoorbond* and the ITGWU's ability to launch successful strike action in Dublin under a nationalist banner, testified to the ability of each movement to attract workers to the nationalist cause. At root, however, even these promises were grounded in ethnic arguments. The message was that people would be rewarded for becoming members of an ethnic alliance not a class alliance. At the same time, those rewards would be not only economic but political and cultural as well.

4 Ethnic Conflict and State-Making

INTRODUCTION

By definition, nationalism is anti-cosmopolitan: its central premise is that different nationalities should live in different polities. Unsurprisingly, therefore, its articulation and dissemination frequently results in severe friction between two or more different ethnic groups occupying a single geographic area. A wide range of cultural and material issues, ranging from competition over scarce economic resources to demands for mother-tongue education, can result in vocal demonstrations against ethnic opponents. These in turn can often lead to sustained, violent campaigns on behalf of the paramount nationalist goal of constructing an ethnicity-based nation-state. As we have already seen, struggles of this nature combine with, and provide extra impetus for, the process of national mobilisation. What is rarely recognised, however, is how this process is directly linked to the nationalist movement's administrative and military organisational capacity. Ethnic competition played a critical role in the three movements under discussion. For the Irish, Afrikaners and Zionists alike, the nationalist struggle was waged simultaneously against two different 'others' – the British on one side and, respectively, the Protestants, Palestinians and blacks in the other three. How these relationships impacted on each movement and its strategies for statehood will be the focus of this chapter.

IRELAND

The use of force in Ireland in pursuit of ostensibly nationalist goals had a long pedigree. The quickly quashed uprisings of 1798, 1803, 1848 and 1867 are routinely cited by committed nationalists, however historically tenuous the claim, as evidence of the consistent nature of their nationalist struggle. This section argues, however, that attitudes to force amongst Irish Catholics changed qualitatively in the period immediately prior to the First World War. Influenced by the exclusive ideologies being propagated by the Gaelic movement, the emotional fervour surrounding the impending passage of Home Rule and, most important, the steadily growing hostility between Protestants and Catholics, Ireland was becoming increasingly militarised and politically unstable. With the advent of the First World War these forces helped precipitate the Easter Revolt of 1916 and laid the groundwork for the spectacular political resurgence of Sinn Fein and the nationalist movement that followed in its aftermath.

The section opens by briefly reviewing the historical attitudes to force by Irish nationalists during the nineteenth century. It then examines the history of the Protestant community in Ireland with particular reference to the effect that the Home Rule debates had on Ulster politics. Following this, it looks at the Catholic response to these activities and the formation of an armed ethnic nationalist militia, the Irish Volunteers. It further shows how the First World War indirectly precipitated the Easter Rebellion of 1916 and the growing nationalist sentiment in Ireland that followed in its wake. Finally the section looks at the burgeoning military struggle of the IRB against British rule and assesses the political campaign that resulted in Sinn Fein's triumph at the polls in 1918.

The Roots of Violence

Particularly among the more radical elements of the nationalist movement, violence was always seen as the best means of overthrowing English rule. The IRB's 1873 constitution asserted bluntly that the organisation's chief task was 'labouring to prepare Ireland for the task of recovering her independence by force of arms'.[1] Nevertheless, apart from the spontaneous violence that occurred as part of the Land War (most of which was anti-landlordism) as late as the start of the twentieth century relatively few Irishmen were, or had ever been, willing to take up arms in support of the national struggle. Indeed even among those in favour of severing the British connection, the vast majority would almost certainly have supported the resolution taken by O'Connell's Repeal Association in 1844 that independence should be sought 'solely by moral and legal means and without spilling of blood or the infliction of injury by any means'.[2] The rebellions of 1848 and 1867 were on a very small scale, involving hundreds rather than thousands of participants – hence their ignominious failures. But by the time of the Easter Rebellion in 1916, and certainly in its aftermath, the situation had altered dramatically. Relatively large numbers of Irishmen now proclaimed themselves willing to fight both for (and against) the cause of Irish independence, marking a fundamental change in the nature and power of the broader Irish nationalist movement. The key to this shift lay in the increasingly conflictual relationship between Protestants, particularly those in Ulster, and Catholics.

In 1861, Catholics made up 77.7 per cent of Ireland's population of 5.8m. Protestants, who comprised virtually all of the remaining 22.3 per cent were divided between 693 000 Anglicans and 523 000 Presbyterians. Although the total population declined steadily due to emigration, this ratio remained largely unaltered and of the 4.4m resident in the country in 1911, Catholics still made up 73.9 per cent of the total.[3] Outside Ulster, where numbers of Protestants and Catholics were fairly even, their demographic dominance was even more pronounced. Although divided into two major sects, the Protestants had for most of the nineteenth century been steadily developing a broad, independent political culture premised on their separation from the indigenous Catholic community. The militant and evangelical Orange Order claimed 135 000 members as early as 1835.[4] Over the next few decades, it was followed by a long series of Protestant clubs and societies, big and small, which nurtured this sense of separateness and superiority.

This process of mobilisation took place concurrently with the relatively rapid industrialisation of the North-East. As the regional economy expanded, Protestants predominated amongst both owners and workers, and the process provided a steady supply of patronage for the nascent Protestant political movement. Leaders were able to procure jobs and houses for their followers in exchange for political support – a fact which also fuelled the widespread belief that loss of political power to Catholics would mean loss of material rewards.[5] There were repeated Catholic–Protestant clashes throughout the century most notably when the erection of the O'Connell monument in 1864 led to 18 days of rioting in Belfast and 12 deaths. While the popularity of individual movements rose and fell, the broader sense of a separate Protestant identity became increasingly entrenched. It remained, however, an inchoate movement with little central ethos other than asserting a positive sense of Protestant identity. With the ascendancy of Parnell and the establishment of a powerful Irish Parliamentary Party fighting for Home Rule at Westminster during the 1880s, panic set in. Many Protestants feared being left a powerless minority in the hands of a predominantly Catholic government. The prospect aroused two mutually reinforcing fears within the community: concern over an ethno-cultural attack on its religious beliefs and way of life, and growing nervousness that a Catholic-dominated legislature would drastically over-tax the comparatively prosperous North-East to promote development elsewhere on the island.

In response, a number of local political groupings came together in the Ulster Coalition, an umbrella body set up to coordinate opposition to the bill. Together with the Orange Lodge the new body used mass marches, songs and their own glorified Protestant history of Ireland which extolled the community's military prowess and economic success to attract new supporters. Working with Tory allies at Westminster, this protest was enough to see off Home Rule. The same tactics of calling on political allies in Britain while mobilising grassroots support in Ulster were again successful in securing the overwhelming defeat of the Second Home Rule bill in the House of Lords in 1893. Not only had the Ulster Coalition managed to obtain substantial public support, but it set in place a powerful organisational framework, led by a committed leadership, that could readily mobilise constituents when necessary. As F.S. Lyons puts it Ulster became 'institutionally transformed' by the Home Rule Debate.[6] Although the sense of urgency stimulating the campaign faded away, a solid foundation had been laid for future resistance to any attempts to whittle away the connection with Britain. A group of militant, Protestant organisations deeply opposed to Irish nationalism was firmly entrenched in Ulster.[7]

Following a decade of relative quiescence, Protestant resistance resurfaced in the wake of the imposition of representative local government in 1903 and the devolution crisis of 1904. In 1905 a new body, the Ulster Unionist Council, was created to serve as a focus for this opposition. This was a broad-based movement encompassing Unionist MPs, the Orange Order, local Unionist Associations and a number of smaller, militant Protestant groups. From 1910 onwards, under the leadership of the indefatigable lawyer Sir Edward Carson, the UUC enjoyed growing status and power as it came to lead opposition to the new Home Rule Bill in 1912. That year, 100 000 people came together to sign the 'Solemn League and Covenant' of allegiance to Ulster, many reputedly using their own blood to charge that Home Rule would mark the 'subversion of our civil and religious freedom, destruction of our citizenship and [would be] perilous to the unity of empire'.[8]

As the Bill made its way through Parliament the new Conservative leader, Bonar Law exacerbated matters by endorsing the hard-line, anti-Home Rule coalition, saying that he could 'imagine no length of resistance to which Ulster can go in which I should not be prepared to support them'.[9]

Shortly afterwards the UUC proclaimed a provisional government, intended to provide an independent administrative structure for the province to serve as a base from which to resist any attempt to implement Home Rule. It also established the Ulster Volunteers, a local militia ostensibly recruited to help defend all Ireland, but in practice serving as an ominous warning to the nationalists not to push their demands too hard. By 1913, the new body, armed with the help of British sympathisers, had recruited over 100 000 members, although only around a quarter of these were mobilised for potential combat. Within a year it had made concrete plans for a *coup d'etat* in Ulster, estimating that the 1000 soldiers in the province could be quickly defeated if necessary.[10] Although neither the Liberals nor the Irish nationalists took these threats very seriously, they represented a major hardening of the Protestant position.

In early 1914, during the so-called Curragh mutiny, British officers suggested they might disobey orders to suppress Protestant unrest in Belfast. Asquith's Liberal government began to waver, seeking a compromise that would allow for Ulster to opt out of Home Rule Ireland for six years. Although accepted by a reluctant Redmond, the proposal was flatly rejected by Carson. With the Unionists insisting that they were more than prepared to resist with force, it was becoming increasingly clear that a united and independent Ireland would never be created through peaceful political negotiations. This realisation was to prompt a fundamental shift in strategy by the Irish nationalist movement.

The Catholic Response

While the Protestants savoured their victory over the first two Home Rule bills, Irish nationalism became steadily more sectarian and militant. In contrast to the attempts of most early movements to unite Catholics and Protestants behind a single banner, opposition to Protestantism and the perceived process of 'Anglicisation' of which it was implicitly regarded as the vanguard, was fundamental to the Gaelic movement. Indeed, the nationalist struggle became described in some radical quarters as nothing less than the 'Battle of Two Civilizations', an irreconcilable conflict between the oppressive force of Anglo-Protestantism and the liberating one of Gaelic-Catholicism.[11] Even the Parliamentary Party was not above using anti-Protestant rhetoric to further its ostensibly non-sectarian cause.[12] In such a confrontational context it was scarcely surprising that a new militancy began to emerge.

In Ulster itself, plans to adopt guerrilla tactics against the growing Protestant militia had been bandied around as early as 1905. Following the great Dublin strike of 1913 the increasingly nationalistic labour leader, James Connolly, formed a self-styled workers' brigade – the Citizens Army – to fight for socialism and 'Irish nationhood' although it was able to recruit only a few hundred members.[13] The same year, however, responding to formation of the Ulster Volunteers, Eoin MacNeill wrote a widely read article entitled 'The North Began'. In it, he charged that the growing propensity to violence by Protestants needed to be met with a considered Catholic response and suggested that the nationalist movement should not hesitate to consider using force itself. In November, together with a small coterie of other IRB representatives, MacNeill formed the Irish Volunteers, a Catholic militia deliberately set up as a counterpoint to the Ulster Volunteers. Initially the response was limited, but as the tone of Ulster objections to Home Rule increased, so did the prominence of the new grouping and more and more recruits joined up. The vast majority of these were not traditional IRB supporters but moderate Home Rulers.[14] Sensing the importance of the movement, Redmond and the Parliamentary Party then stepped in and used their overwhelming political influence effectively to assume control over a force which by early 1914 numbered 100 000 men and was continuing to expand.[15]

While the traditionally revolutionary IRB might have provided the initiative for the new force, therefore, the Volunteers' genuine mass base and the Parliamentary Party's willingness to participate signalled a change in mainstream Catholic attitudes to force. MacNeill's original proposals had a somewhat romantic air but the response, even if the new recruits were mostly unarmed and untrained, was striking. And although the Parliamentary Party remained firmly in the political ascendancy, the IRB had demonstrated that it remained a powerful force in Irish politics. Despite its low profile, the Brotherhood was not the moribund organisation many contemporaries considered it to be but was rapidly becoming a source of dynamic, elite leadership for the broader nationalist movement. The Volunteers, like the GAA, the League and even Sinn Fein were dominated at a leadership level by people who were members of, or had close links to, the IRB.[16] A major psychological shift was taking place within the broader nationalist movement.

7The impetus for this was in large part derived from the elements of nationalist ideology that had been introduced by the Gaelic League and its associates extolling the martial process of ancient Gaels. It also became increasingly apparent in the writings and speeches of others in the Volunteers, most notably those of Patrick Pearse, the increasingly radical schoolteacher who had joined the IRB in 1913 and was prone to such statements as describing bloodshed as a 'cleansing and sanctifying thing'.[17] Nevertheless, the chief reason for the establishment of the Volunteers was not the love of battle but the growing militancy of the Protestants. The founding manifesto of the Volunteers explicitly blamed the British, and by extension Ulster, for 'the display of military force and the message of armed violence'.[18] The creation of the Ulster Volunteers had indirectly led to the formation of a major armed grouping that had recruited more supporters than the IRB had managed to mobilise over the previous 40 years. More importantly, it was a movement that had been developed in the ideological context of ethnic nationalism – it was an exclusive, overwhelmingly Catholic force prepared, in principle, to carry out violent acts in support of Irish nationalism.

War and Rebellion

Important though it was, the establishment of the Volunteers did not have an immediate impact on political debate. The political focus remained firmly on the Parliamentary Party, then busy ushering the Home Rule Bill through further readings in the House of Commons. Even Griffith and Sinn Fein largely refrained from criticism of the ascendant Redmond (at least until mid-1914 when the Parliamentary Party was forced by the British government publicly to accept the temporary exclusion of six Ulster counties from the provisions of the Act). But even if the matter of the North remained unresolved, some kind of self-government for Ireland now appeared inevitable, and the parameters offered by Home Rule seemed broadly acceptable to the Irish public. With the advent of the crisis that was to become the First World War, however, the situation altered dramatically and permanently. Following the declaration of war on Germany by Britain in August, the UUC immediately and unconditionally offered full support for the war effort. Redmond had little choice but to do like-wise. He managed to persuade the government to put Home Rule on the statute books but agreed to an accompanying bill delaying its implementation until after the conclusion of the war.

At the time it seemed a fairly safe gamble. The conflict was expected to be over in a matter of months and Irish support would help reassure nervous British parliamentarians that permitting Home Rule would not mean having Ireland as an enemy in the international arena. Many party leaders also felt that joint military exercises with the Ulster Volunteers might ultimately ease the way to forging a new pan-Irish national spirit.[19] In September, however, Redmond made a critical error. In a speech at Woodenbridge he pledged the support of the Irish Volunteers to fight anywhere outside Ireland at Britain's behest. Even with the prospect of Home Rule, this was a commitment that radicals in the movement were not prepared to countenance. Within weeks Sinn Fein formed the Irish Neutrality League and approximately 10 000 men, led by a small group of IRB leaders including MacNeill and Pearse, split from the Volunteers, re-forming a separate Irish Volunteer army.[20]

Although much smaller than Redmond's forces, which were renamed the National Volunteers and numbered some 150 000, the establishment of the new group marked a major turning point for the broader ethno-nationalist movement. The fervour and ideological cohesion created by the Gaelic Revival were now, in the ferment of a global war, formally wedded to an organisation committed to the use of force and with the training and wherewithal to (at least partially) live up to that commitment. Its adherents were far from constituting a mainstream, even among Catholics, but, as with the rest of the Gaelic movement, a foundation had been laid that could be built on. Members of the new splinter group were publicly referred to as the 'Sinn Feiners'. Thus even though its establishment owed little to Griffith and his party, in practice the new Irish Volunteers became part of the broad, established infrastructure of the Irish ethno-nationalist movement, loosely under the direction of the Sinn Fein–IRB leadership axis.

With Home Rule suspended for the duration of the war, support for the National Volunteers dropped off sharply in 1915. Nevertheless, this was not immediately matched by a rise in ethnic nationalist involvement. The rural areas, where farmers were enjoying a mini-boom as a result of increased wartime demand for their products, were particularly calm. Membership of the IRB grew from 1660 in 1914 to 2000 in 1916, while the Irish Volunteers attracted a small number of new recruits.[21] Nevertheless, a new groundswell of support for the ethnic nationalist movement, and the use of force was growing. Within the Gaelic League, the Athletic Association and Sinn Fein itself, the notion of Home Rule was being increasingly criticised and a more confrontational attitude to the British and the Protestants emerging. By 1915, even Griffith, was making veiled calls to arms, telling Irishmen that they should emulate the Fenians of yore by creating 'another fighting and revolutionary generation'.[22] That year, Douglas

Hyde, the resolutely apolitical Protestant President of the League, resigned, charging that the body was now being used as a vehicle for national mobilisation and recruitment rather than the promotion of Irish culture.

As the mainstream movement radicalised, the radicals became even more militant, particularly as Britain placed restrictions on newspapers associated with the IRB and Sinn Fein. In late 1915 a secret Military Council, of which Pearse was a leader, began to make plans for a rebellion. With the possibility of logistical support from Germany, most of the Ulster Volunteers fighting in France, and only 6000 British troops and 10 000 armed policemen based in Ireland to contain a potential pool of around 18 000 Volunteers, the leaders hoped a well-organised uprising might be able to seize control of the country.[23] In practice, however, the Volunteers' lack of discipline and training made the odds against seasoned British soldiers very long and MacNeill vetoed any revolt. Undaunted, Pearse and his allies, including Connolly, pressed ahead with secret plans for a revolution over Easter weekend in 1916. Pearse managed to infuse several of his co-conspirators with his notion of making a blood sacrifice to the glory of Ireland and there was general consensus that it was time for a blow to be struck on behalf of the Irish nation.

Accordingly, despite explicit countermanding orders from MacNeill, failing even to inform Griffith and other Sinn Fein political leaders of their plans, and ignoring the non-arrival of promised German weapons, on 24 April 1916, a group of around 1300 Volunteers, together with 200 members of the Citizen's Army marched into central Dublin. After flying both Tone's Irish Harp flag and the Young Ireland tricolour from the General Post Office, Pearse melodramatically read a hastily scribed declaration of independence to a few dazed passers-by before seizing the building along with the courts and city hall. The British, regarding the operation as a grossly treasonous act during wartime, acted swiftly, calling in thousands of extra troops to combat the rebels. Following a week of bitter fighting, during which some 450 people were killed and 2600 wounded, the revolutionaries were comprehensively crushed and the survivors taken prisoner. Shortly afterwards, the army interned thousands more 'rebels', mostly members of Sinn Fein or the Volunteers, the two groupings which were perceived to be the driving forces behind the revolt.

The proclamation of the republic which was signed by Pearse and his co-conspirators provided clear evidence of the ethno-nationalist motivations behind the revolt. Invoking a proud Gaelic past and promising socially and economically radical policies, it drew together all of the strands that had emerged during the preceding two decades, combining cultural, historical, political and economic themes.[24] Although the rebellion itself seemed a small and unrepresentative event, it was the logical culmination of the forces that had been building in Ireland since Parnell's death. Those forces had had a far greater impact on Ireland than initially supposed.

Political Repercussions

The decisiveness displayed by the British in crushing the rebellion was replaced by vacillation on how to deal with its aftermath. In an excruciatingly drawn-out process, the government executed 15 of the surviving ringleaders, including Pearse, while indefinitely interning the other prisoners.[25] This proved the worst of all possible strategies. Although the Rising had initially been seen as a rather inconsequential affair by the Irish public, the manner of its suppression raised ire countrywide. In the weeks and months that followed, the portrayal of the rebellion in the newspapers shifted from one of derision to admiration combined with a staunch condemnation of Britain's high-handedness. With the country chafing under martial law imposed in the wake of the revolt, these sentiments steadily gathered force.[26] More important from the perspective of the ethnic nationalists was the fact that, despite the effective exclusion of Sinn Fein from the planning of the rebellion, in the public mind the Rising was inextricably associated with the party, particularly after Griffith's arrest. This connection was reinforced when Sinn Fein established an aid organisation to help the families of the dead and imprisoned. Support for Redmond and the parliamentarians had already begun to drain away. Now Sinn Fein's heightened profile combined with general disaffection with the British allowed the party to emerge as a major political player for the first time.

In 1917 in a critical series of by-elections Sinn Fein won its first seats at Westminster. One of them went to the imprisoned Eamonn de Valera, the highest-ranking survivor of the Rebellion. The Parliamentary Party steadily lost support as the political advantage shifted decisively to the ethnic nationalists. A protracted attempt by the British government through 1917 and 1918 to negotiate a compromise settlement via an Irish Convention was doomed from the start as Sinn Fein refused to participate. Meanwhile the party consolidated its new support base. By 1918 Sinn Fein had 1354 clubs in place countrywide with 112 080 members.[27] Combined with its many ancillary structures, the party was now openly campaigning for national independence. The organisational framework that it had so long nurtured was finally given an opportunity to prove itself.

Even with its rise to political favour, however, it is doubtful that the aftershocks of the rebellion alone would have been sufficient to push a majority of Irish Catholics into backing Sinn Fein had it not been for another political error by the British. In early 1918, Lloyd George decided to introduce conscription. In an unprecedented show of unity the Catholic Church, Sinn Fein, the IRB and the broad range of Irish nationalist organisations – including the Parliamentary Party – decried the move. For the first time nearly all the major institutions of Ireland were united behind a single issue with full public backing from the country's Catholics. Sinn Fein was seen as the major force behind the campaign, receiving the political credit from the public and implicitly emphasising the weakened state of its opponents. More than any other issue, this marked a shift in public perceptions about continued British rule. Acceptance of the government's right to call up its own citizens in time of war is perhaps the ultimate test of its public legitimacy. The fact that most Irishmen had been willing to heed a voluntary call to arms in 1914–15 but were now utterly unprepared to accept compulsory conscription, regarding it as tyranny, graphically demonstrated the extent to which public opinion had swung behind Sinn Fein and, by extension, its claim that the only acceptable form of government for Ireland was an independent Catholic state.

Just as important, and not often recognised, Sinn Fein continued to devote significant attention to economic issues. Industrial militancy across Ireland rose steadily as, in the wake of Connolly's participation in the Rebellion, the Socialists and labour movement found themselves more closely allied to the nationalists than ever before. Sinn Fein was able to persuade these groups (without having to endorse any communist proposals that might alienate conservative groups like the Church) that it was devoted to economic justice for the country's working classes. The hitherto urban party did not neglect land issues either. Taking advantage of rural discontent with the government's failure to enforce its own tillage regulations, the highly organised Sinn Fein clubs repeated the tactics that had helped the Land League 40 years previously, seizing unused land which they distributed to supporters.[28] Some of the more radical branches participated in cattle rustling which, despite the lack of any ideological connection to nationalism nonetheless further boosted the party's credibility.[29] For most rural dwellers the sentiments engendered by the Revival and the

Rebellion still needed to be reinforced with evidence of practical benefits before they could be translated into active political support.

In the wake of the war, Sinn Fein, under the leadership of De Valera and Griffith (the former still in jail) launched a vigorous campaign in the December 1918 election. Its platform had four parts: first, to follow the old Griffith strategy of withdrawing all elected representatives from Westminster; second, to resist Britain by any means including 'military force or otherwise'; third to establish a constituent assembly as the 'supreme national authority'; and fourth to make a formal appeal to the forthcoming Peace Conference at Versailles for recognition of Ireland's claims to independence.[30] The results confirmed the drastically altered political scene. Sinn Fein won 73 seats and 47 per cent of the total Irish vote, including 65 per cent outside the Protestant stronghold of Ulster. The Parliamentary Party retained only 6 seats while the Unionists held on to 22.[31] A few months later, this shift was confirmed when the party also won 98 out of 127 town corporations and 28 out of 33 county councils.

'The Nationalist Party Annihilated' is how the local newspapers reported the results, and so it was.[32] The party of Parnell and Redmond was no more while the ethnic nationalist movement that had so long been in the political wilderness had comprehensively triumphed. After 30 years, an exclusive ethnic nationalism, built around cultural identity and religion and demanding full political independence, was finally in the ascendant. While Sinn Fein's official line remained that the party 'regards as brothers Irishmen of every creed and class provided ... they place Ireland and her interests before those of any other nation', in practice it had campaigned on sectarian lines, emphasising issues like the right to denominational education.[33] These ideas not only pleased the Church, but also appealed to the public. The growing ethnic consciousness that had been steadily nurtured amongst the broader Catholic community over the previous 30 years through the work of the cultural nationalists had thrust itself into the mainstream.

In 1919 those Sinn Fein MPs who were not still imprisoned by the British duly boycotted Westminster and met in what came to be called the First Dail, named after the ancient Gaelic parliament. The new body passed resolutions confirming its support for the 1916 Proclamation of the Republic and pronounced itself the legislative assembly of an independent Ireland. De Valera was elected its first president while Griffith was made his deputy. Among its first acts, and testifying to the resonance of the Gaelic Revival among its membership, the Dail elevated Gaelic to the status of official language of Ireland. Frequently overlooked, however, is that it also placed a high priority on economic issues. The body officially adopted a socially radical agenda asserting that national sovereignty extended to 'material wealth and resources', that private property rights should be 'subordinated to...public welfare' and insisting that the 'first duty' of the republic would be 'food, clothing, shelter and the spiritual health of children'.[34] In addition, it called for wholesale land redistribution and the nationalisation of industry. With Britain still in administrative control of Ireland, the Dail had little way of effecting these declarations. Nonetheless, they proved an effective means of demonstrating the body's broader commitment to addressing popular grievances.

Conclusions

In just over two years Sinn Fein had emerged from being a fringe group on the perimeter of Irish politics to the dominant political force in the country. Just as important, it now had a military force at its disposal. The IRB and Volunteers were by 1918 fully prepared to use violence in support of their goals, even against the overwhelming might of the British army. The proximate causes of this new success had been the countrywide indignation and national pride aroused in the aftermath of the 1916 Rebellion and then the anti-conscription campaign two years later. But these two events would never have taken place were it not for two precipitating causes: the growing militancy of the Ulster Unionists in the face of impending Home Rule and the advent of the First World War itself.

The first of these, the dogged and powerful resistance by Protestants to any prospect of Catholic-led government, had, in the 1890s, helped precipitate the Gaelic Revival. In the context of the war-talk surrounding the Home Rule debate between 1912–14, Protestant Ulster's elaborate preparations for resistance led directly to the formation of the Irish Volunteers. In addition, the sense of insecurity, indignation and outright hostility from Catholics both inside and outside of Ulster led to a hardening of the exclusivist ethnic element in Irish nationalism. As a result, the response of the Irish public to the new force was far more favourable than it had been to any previous calls to arms in support of the national ideal. Among other civil and religious liberties, the proclamation of the republic praised the 'national and military spirit' of the new political order, showing how the two elements had become fused in the minds of the rebellion's leaders by 1916. Even so, the domestic political transformation that led to the Rebellion and the subsequent eclipse of the Parliamentary Party would not have taken place were it not for the First World War acting as a kind of *deus ex machina*, sweeping aside immediate Home Rule and ultimately pre-cipitating a new, violent uprising.

Understanding how a failed revolt could lay the foundation for a massive surge in support for ethnic nationalism over a relatively short time is a question that has preoccupied Irish historians for decades. Apart from the contingent episodes, such as the executions, the key lay in the fact that the 1916 Uprising was seen as Catholic in a way that the previous, abortive revolutions of Irish history were not. In terms of its leadership, ideology and its resolute anti-Protestantism the rebels were unabashed ethnic nationalists, seeking to secure (even though they would not publicly admit it) what would effectively be a Catholic state. The stunning effect that the Rebellion ultimately came to have in Ireland lay less in the event itself than in the popular outrage generated by the execution of the ringleaders. In the context of an unpopular war and within a Catholic population that, stimulated by both the Gaelic Revival from within and the forces of Ulster separat-ism without, was more aware of ethnic issues than ever before, anti-British feeling received an unprecedented boost just as the legitimacy of the existing order was called into question. Sinn Fein was perfectly placed to take advantage of such a shift in popular sentiments.

Accordingly, while at the time of the Rebellion, the IRB and Sinn Fein were still regarded by most Irish Catholics as marginal groups and the rebels themselves as radicals, within two years the First Dail could claim the support of a majority of those Catholics despite its lack of any real power. The fact that the nationalist movement had been able to take advantage of the structural crisis precipitated by the war helped create a legitimacy crisis to which the only solution they were prepared to accept was an independent Ireland. In this context, the British were forced to face the fact, decisively demonstrated by the failure of the Irish Convention, that the convoluted compromises offered by Home Rule were dead. By 1919, Sinn Fein had triumphed at the polls, the agitation had reached unprecedented levels, and the stakes were higher than ever.

THE AFRIKANERS

This section argues that the political structure of the South African state and its white franchise meant that, despite a more successful martial tradition than that of the Irish, an armed Afrikaner uprising was never likely to garner mass support during the twentieth century. It suggests, however, that the nationalist movement's efforts to secure its political victory over two groups of ethnic opponents – the British, represented locally by the Anglophone white community, and the indigenous black population – were to have a very powerful impact on its overall strategies. As a consequence of an extraneous international event, the Second World War, the deep-rooted Afrikaner aversion to British power and culture became manifest in the form of an exclusivist, militaristic form of Afrikaner nationalism entering the mainstream of South African politics. At the same time the political and economic threat posed by South Africa's black population in the context of a burgeoning industrial economy forced the movement to give particular attention to the race issue. This led to the combination of long-standing racist beliefs about the black population with contemporary nationalist ideology and economic demands from white labour, agriculture and the mines to restrict black labour through the policy of apartheid.

The section opens by reviewing Afrikaner attitudes to the use of force for political ends and the role such attitudes played in early Afrikaner politics, particularly during the First Word War. It then analyses the effect of the Second World War on South Africa. It details the resulting split in the United Party and looks at the activities of the *Ossewabrandwag* (OB), assessing that organisation's broader impact on the nationalist movement. From there the section turns to the issue of race, giving an overview of the cultural and economic attitudes of the Afrikaner nationalists to the black majority. Finally it looks at the origins of the apartheid doctrine and assesses its importance to the nationalist movement.

Military Force and Constitutional Politics

The early Afrikaner relationship with both the British and blacks was inextricably bound up with the use of force. During the nineteenth century, the Boers used their superior weaponry to carve out new farmsteads in the fragile states of the Transvaal and Orange Free State, dispossessing the various black tribes who already lived there. In many encounters, most notably the Battle of Blood River against the Zulus in 1838, Boer victories were extolled as proof of God's support for their enterprise. Fifty years later, the Battle of Majuba which successfully reclaimed Transvaal independence from the British seemed to provide further corroboration of both martial spirit and divine blessing. Despite the fact that it ended in defeat, the Anglo-Boer War confirmed the courage and skills of the Afrikaner people on the battlefield. More importantly, it provided the criticial, initial stimulus to the process of mobilisation that would lead to the establishment of an ethnically exclusive National Party.

It also, however, led to the establishment of a political structure within which further use of force by the Afrikaners in pursuit of their political goals was largely unnecessary. As Chapter 3 argued, given the limited franchise, a political victory over Anglophone whites in South Africa would, unlike a similar victory by Sinn Fein in Ireland, give nationalists control of the state. Accordingly, both Hertzog and Malan always felt that the Afrikaner struggle for political power should be a constitutional one. This is not, however, to suggest that the idea of military prowess and the threat of force played no part in nationalist strategies or the popular imagination. It was not coincidence that the country's first three prime ministers were all military men and through the 1930s many Afrikaners continued to vote for Smuts simply because he had been a Boer War hero.

Indeed, this military tradition reasserted itself when, following South Africa's declaration of war on Germany in 1914, a large number of Afrikaners refused to accept the fact that they were technically on the same side as the hated British. Several former Boer War leaders led nearly 10 000 Afrikaners in an armed rebellion against the Botha and Smuts government.[35] The rebels' stated aim was 'to trek to Pretoria, to pull down the British flag and to proclaim a free South African republic'.[36] Although numerically superior to the small force which undertook the Irish Easter Rebellion, the old soldiers were quickly crushed. Cleverly, the government used only Afrikaner troops, thereby managing to prevent the escalation of the conflict into open hatred between English and Afrikaners and the only major casualty was one old general (mistakenly shot at a roadblock looking for bank robbers). Although the government's treatment of the remaining rebels was relatively lenient, one officer, Jopie Fourie, was executed for treason having failed to resign his commission in the Union Defence Forces before embarking on the insurrection. Nevertheless, despite an upsurge in support for the National Party, the SAP government continued to command the allegiance of the white population.

There were several reasons why the Rebellion failed to ignite a mass shift in public perceptions in South Africa in the way that the Easter Rebellion was to in Ireland less than two years later. Most importantly, the National Party was a new political organisation. It lacked both Sinn Fein's ideological framework and bureaucratic infrastructure. Afrikaner nationalist histories of the type popularised during the Gaelic Revival did not become part of the public discourse until the 1920s and 1930s. Similarly, the wide-ranging set of organisations of the type able to mobilise large numbers of people were also not established until then. Fourie was later to be added to the nationalist canon as a martyr for the cause of Afrikanerdom, but the canon had to be established and popularised first – it was not simply a matter, as in Ireland, of adding the names of the rebels to a lengthy, existing honour roll. Also important was the fact that the offending power was an Afrikaner-led government of former war heroes leading predominantly Afrikaner soldiers. In consequence it was much more difficult to encourage popular resentment than if it had been the British Army re-entering South Africa to put down the rising.

But while the revolt and its suppression did not ultimately lead to mass popular protest along the lines of Ireland after the Rebellion, it did provide the means for the National Party to establish itself in the South African political firmament as the authentic political voice of Afrikanerdom. Nevertheless, as evidenced by the fact that the Broederbond made no attempt to form any military-type organisations to pursue their goals, force was never seen as a central weapon in the nationist struggle. Even after the GNP was formed following Malan's split from Hertzog, there was little serious debate over whether to try to establish an armed wing. There seemed no need for a militia when there was no armed internal force that would oppose the National Party were it to take control of the state legitimately through the ballot box.[37] For Malan in 1934 the equation remained the same as for Hertzog in 1914 – to achieve political control of the state all that was needed was to win the support of the vast majority of Afrikaners in a general election. Even in the midst of the patriotic fervour ignited by the Great Trek centenary celebration of 1938, that prospect still seemed very far away.

The Second World War and the *Ossewabrandwag*

The situation changed suddenly and permanently in September 1939 when, over Hertzog's violent objections, Smuts narrowly persuaded the government to declare war on Germany. The issue split the United Party irrevocably and Hertzog resigned in protest, charging that there was 'no doubt that nothing so quickly and tragically could lead to the

consolidation of Afrikaans-speaking Afrikanerdom'.[38] Shortly after, in
early 1940, he formally rejoined Malan in a new party dedicated to
Afrikaner ideals, the Reunited National Party (HNP). This was an
immensely important event as it united the two most important nationalist politicians under a nationalist banner for the first time since 1934.
However, the advances made by the ethno-nationalists over the previous decade meant that the overall tenor of the new party's policies
was far more ethnically exclusive than Hertzog's NP of the 1920s had
been, despite the fact that Hertzog himself had not changed his own
views. This inherent contradiction soon made itself evident in open
clashes between the two leaders. Once again, Hertzog's inclusive
nationalism, regarding 'unified Afrikanerdom' as composed of English
and Afrikaans speakers loyal to South Africa proved incompatible with
Malan's exclusive version. The new alliance quickly fell apart. A few
Hertzogites departed to form a low-key Afrikaner Party (AP) under
the leadership of Klasie Havenga, a former Hertzog minister, while
Hertzog himself retired from politics and died soon after. The vast
majority, however, stayed in the new fold under Malan. The old idea of
conciliation with Anglophones was destroyed for many Afrikaners who
would not support participation in an 'English' war against an enemy
many admired.

A second immensely important shift in nationalist politics indirectly
precipitated by the war was the transformation of the *Ossewabrandwag*
from a fringe cultural group to the most important mass political
movement in the country. Established in 1939 in the wake of the
Great Trek celebrations, the OB was ostensibly a cultural organisation
dedicated to preserving the cultural heritage of the Afrikaner nation.
In practice, however, the new body quickly became a forum within
which more militaristic nationalists could argue for the development of
a new extra-parliamentary forum built around Fascist principles.
Although there had been an upsurge in pro-Nazi activity during the
1930s with a number of small, sympathetic groups such as Louis
Weichardt's Greyshirts being established, the OB marked the first
broad-based organisation of this type.[39] With the advent of the war,
the organisation expanded very rapidly. Hans van Rensburg, a prominent Broederbond member, became its leader and argued that Afrikaners should reject democratic politics and join together as a united
volk to seize the state. Setting out a vision for the future he declared:

> I see the Ossewa Brandwag as mobilised Afrikanerdom. Mobilised
> for the struggle in the different task of our national life (*volkslewe*).

Mobilised economically, culturally and for protection....Democracy is not an end in itself. The end is the volk.[40]

Using uniforms, slogans and mass rallies, van Rensburg's message fell on fertile ground, particularly in urban areas. After the early Nazi military successes appeared to vindicate the power of Fascism, the movement had attracted close on 200 000 supporters by 1941.[41] Like the Irish Volunteers after 1914, moreover, the OB drew much of its support from what had previously been mainstream, non-militant Afrikaners.

Underlying the entire enterprise was a vision of exclusive ethnic-based control of the state. An OB publication stated explicitly in 1942 that

> [A mobilised nation] incorporated into a movement is the national movement [*volksbeweging*] which drives towards the formation of a unique state, a state with increased authority for the maintenance of the independence and assurance of the fullest and most far-reaching power of the unique volk.[42]

This rejection of democratic politics as a form of government became reflected in a different, more confrontational strategy than that endorsed by the National Party. Unlike Malan, van Rensburg rejected electoral participation and sought, at least in his rhetoric, to take over the state by force. Accordingly, the OB itself was run along paramilitary lines with marches, drills and uniforms, frequently carrying out random acts of mob violence or making physical attacks on political opponents. A radical offshoot called the *Stormjaers* sought to sabotage the war efforts and would bomb military installations and launch minor attacks on government buildings and installations, such as the electric systems in the towns of Krugersdorp, Delmas and Potchefstroom.[43] These activities were supplemented by a series of bank robberies and the money was used to finance further activities and provide aid for the families of jailed OB members.[44] However despite attempts by Nazi sympathisers to gain logistic support from Germany for an uprising, the Smuts government managed to keep the more radical elements under control, interning many of the leaders.

Nevertheless, while Afrikanerdom had largely broken with Hertzog's old ideals and was basically committed to an overtly ethno-nationalist platform, it was politically divided into two organisations. Despite ideological similarities, the OB's rejection of *partypolitiek*, or constitutional politics, in favour of extra-parliamentary *kultuurpolitiek* led to sharp divisions between it and the HNP. The two groups soon became locked in a bitter display of internecine *broedertwis* – struggle between brothers – arguing bitterly as to which of them should serve as standard bearer for Afrikaner nationalism. The situation was further complicated by the establishment of another pro-Nazi political party, *Nuwe Orde* (NO), created to participate in parliamentary politics, although it never achieved a large-scale following. With members prominent in all three organisations, the Broederbond tried to stay above the fray and promote unity, but was unable to do so.

Malan, meanwhile, remained bitterly opposed to the violent tactics of the OB and had severe misgivings about its totalitarian ideology.[45] He continued to campaign on ethnic issues, especially mother-tongue education, and railed against perceived threats from blacks and communists in the run-up to the 1943 elections. Despite the fervour raised by the war, Allied successes against Germany helped Smuts while a boycott by many OB supporters who staunchly rejected the concept of democracy hurt Malan, leading to a convincing victory for the UP. The government held onto 102 seats with the HNP managing 43, while the AP and NO elected not a single representative between them. Nevertheless, Smuts received only an estimated 32 per cent of the (boycott-reduced) Afrikaner vote, down from 40 per cent previously.[46]

Meanwhile, with the tide having turned against Hitler in Europe, the OB's fortunes began to wane along with those of the Nazis it had emulated. By 1945, both the OB and NO had effectively collapsed, leaving the National Party once again as the sole political representative of the Afrikaner nationalist movement. Later nationalists tended to disown the OB period as an aberration in an attempt to play down the discredited Nazi influences. In practice however, the OB played a crucial role in directly politicising a large number of Afrikaners and converting them to the ethnic nationalist cause. Indeed, the OB's very success, like that of Sinn Fein in the First World War, testified to the now widespread awareness of Christian National sentiments amongst the Afrikaner grassroots. It also demonstrated how the promotion and use of force as a strategy, even if not particularly effectively employed, could act as a powerful mobilising agent. As in Ireland, the extraneous event of a global war, and the issue of fighting on behalf of Britain, had helped to reshape dramatically the domestic political scene. Unlike Sinn Fein, however, to win a majority of seats, the National Party needed the support of an overwhelming majority of Afrikaner voters, not just a plurality.

Race and State

Underlying all the cultural, religious and racial arguments for Afrikaner hostility to South Africa's indigenous black community was a simple demographic fact. Given that they constituted an overwhelming majority of the population, enfranchised blacks could easily outvote whites, let alone just Afrikaners. This meant that race was always an important issue in white politics, as Hertzog's early election campaigns had demonstrated. Accordingly, the Broederbond and the GNP both gave prominence to the issue during the 1930s. At the party's 1937 conference, Malan warned repeatedly of the need to keep South Africa a 'white man's country' and the next year the party put out a 'Federal Plan of Action' aimed at comprehensive segregation. In both the 1938 and 1943 elections the party highlighted the issue. During the former campaign the party published a notorious poster of a black man, white woman and their mixed-race children, suggesting that such miscegenation would be the future under a UP government. Nonetheless, in both polls the Nationalists' performance was good but not overwhelming. In large part because the UP had never shown the slightest solicitousness towards blacks either, racism was not of enormous electoral appeal.[47]

But the race issue in South Africa was always an economic question as much as a political or cultural one. Blacks provided direct wage labour competition for poorer Afrikaners in the cities but were needed to run the flywheel of the South African economy, the goldmines. During the war, with the country cut off from many of its traditional sources of finished goods, the South African economy began a massive expansion, particularly in manufacturing, to try to make up the shortfall. The size of the urban labour force rose by 53 per cent amounting to the creation of 125 000 new jobs of which over 80 per cent went to blacks.[48] More significantly, for the first time in the country's history, the gap between black and white wage rates began to narrow substantially.[49] As a result of this increased employment, the black urban population soared by 652 000 between 1936–46. Pass law arrests, already exercising a tremendous burden on the state, became increasingly unmanageable. At the same time, powerful and increasingly militant black trade unions emerged, orchestrating a growing number of work stoppages that culminated in the miners' strike in August 1946 in which more than 70 000 black workers downed tools.[50]

The response of state and big business to this new wave of unrest was contradictory. Although the government had no hesitation in quashing the strike by force, state attitudes towards black labour became markedly more conciliatory. Smuts increased black education spending and introduced African unemployment insurance and old age pensions. As early as 1942, the Department of Native Affairs tentatively recommended the abolition of the pass system. In 1946, the state-run Social and Economic Planning Council signalled an official shift in policy by condemning the migrant labour system. Shortly after, the government appointed the Fagan Commission to investigate the issue. The body's final report recommended the creation of new, non-coercive labour bureaux to act as institutions for worker registration while suggesting that passes become voluntary cards to help guarantee security of employment. The government had clearly decided that state intervention to control black labour and prevent black urbanisation was both ineffective and unjust. As Smuts himself declared 'You might as well try and sweep the ocean back with a broom'.[51]

Several of the young ANS members who had studied in Germany during the 1930s turned their minds to these issues. In 1944, the FAK called a special Volkskongres on race which started to flesh out a policy of comprehensive segregation. These ideas were then developed and refined by G.J. Cronje in a book entitled *'n Tuiste vie die Nageslag* ('A Home for Posterity'). Promising the 'permanent solution to South Africa's racial problems', Cronje was the first explicitly to articulate apartheid, a policy of formal and permanent racial separation of black and whites into discrete and physically separate 'nations' inhabiting their own territories.[52] Shortly after, the Broederbond formed yet another organisation, the South African Bureau for Racial Affairs (SABRA) and charged it with developing the details of a policy based around the apartheid concept – the total separation of races except for the provision of black labour in white enterprises.

The new policy was influenced by both nationalist ideology and economic imperatives. On one level it represented an intellectualised form of white racism utilising a variant of Herderian nationalist ideology as a philosophical justification for segregation. It was an extension of the quasi-theological belief in the importance of separating different cultures that was an integral part of the Afrikaner political tradition. As a party statement on the issue put it: 'The party subscribes to the view that God has determined there will be a variety of races .... [with] each group having its own national character'.[53]

The NP in this way extended its own legitimating arguments concerning the independence of nations that had first been articulated in opposition to the British and applied them to blacks. If each race was divinely ordained to be separate, the Afrikaners were only following their own belief in the sanctity of nationhood by offering blacks 'independent' homelands.

On a second level, however, apartheid was predicated on the issue of the control of black labour. In the Sauer Report, published in 1946 following a three-year investigation, the NP set out its own vision of the position of black labour in the South African economy:

> Natives in the urban areas should be regarded as migratory citizens, not entitled to political and social rights equal to those of whites.... The entire migration of natives into and from the cities should be controlled by the state which will enlist the cooperation of municipal bodies.... Natives from the country areas shall be admitted to the urban areas or towns only as temporary employees obliged to return to their homes after the expiry of employment.[54]

Instead of relaxing state control over the labour market and phasing out migrant labour, as the UP now urged, the Sauer Report proposed its extension and permanent institutionalisation. In addition, the HNP remained committed to the policy that blacks should not be allowed to have permanent residence in white cities and towns.

For the movement's core constituency, apartheid proved a powerful adjunct to the nationalist movement's political platform. If an Afrikaner-run state could effect the permanent separation of blacks and whites, then white political security could be ensured indefinitely while traditional racist sentiments would be more than satisfied. It also attracted new supporters. In the agricultural sector, where Afrikaner farmers in the Transvaal remained loyal government supporters, the policy promised a permanent source of cheap rural labour that would bring an end to the dire shortages that had resulted from the war. At the same time, apartheid held tremendous appeal for Afrikaner workers to whom the narrowing wage gaps and rising skill levels of black workers posed an increasing threat. During the war both the OB and the HNP had sought to take advantage of these feelings by establishing competing labour arms: the former operating through the *Arbeidsfront* and the latter under the *BWBB* (White Workers Protection League). Although the first collapsed along with its parent, after the war the latter helped mount a strong campaign for control of the large Mine Workers Union. After a series of internal challenges, nationalist elements within the union were able to call a successful work stoppage, and force new union elections that brought Christian

National labour leaders to power. This gave the nationalist movement a critical new urban power base.

Conclusions

The aim of Afrikaner nationalism was always to shift Afrikaner political support away from the government and towards the nationalist movement. That this message generated substantial support before the articulation of apartheid or the advent of the Second World War is undeniable. Much of it was generated by hostility to the British. Opposition to any attempts at Anglicisation had been the driving force in the development of Afrikaner ethnic consciousness from the late nineteenth century. In the wake of the massive trauma resulting from the Boer War, these were reinforced by a deep sense of resentment that resulted in widespread popular outrage at the thought of South Africa's participation in both world wars against Germany. The Rebellion during the First World War pushed Hertzog's National Party into prominence and laid the foundation for its election victory a decade later. This process continued during the 1920s in the form of Malan's cultural initiatives in the Hertzog government and then in the 1930s with the work of the FAK and the GNP. In the wake of Afrikaner opposition to the Second World War, this changed dramatically as Hertzog left the UP, which became much more closely associated with the British empire, and many Afrikaners began to regard the existing order as illegitimate.

Largely because of the political structure of the racial franchise, however, the nationalist movement never felt the need to convert extra-parliamentary politics into outright rebellion or sustained guerrilla warfare. The few attempts at using force by Afrikaner nationalists – the Rebellion during the First World War and the OB's sabotage efforts in the Second – did not seriously damage the state even though they had a powerful psychological impact on the Afrikaner population. And although the OB gained mass support, it never came close to staging a successful coup or rebellion. Its demise marked the end of nationalist strategies to seize the state by force. But even though a majority of Afrikaners were now supporters of exclusive ethnic nationalism, the OB's fascist ideology caused many of its supporters to renounce parliamentary politics. This, combined with a drop in morale following Nazi defeats, led to a relatively weak showing by the HNP in the 1943 elections. Nevertheless, the OB had helped reinforce the notion that it was only by taking exclusive ethnic control of the state that Afrikaners could ensure their permanent protection from British influence.

It was also in the power of the state that the nationalist movement saw a solution to South Africa's racial conflict. Deeply held and long-standing religious and cultural fears about blacks created the necessary mindset for crafting a political ideology that left them permanently subordinated. Accordingly, the contention by Afrikaner intellectuals that each nation should have its own state was directly linked to the economic need to provide regular sources of cheap black labour for the farms, mines and industry and prevent urban black labourers from directly competing with whites for more highly skilled and better paid jobs through the emerging apartheid ideology. Grounded in the philosophical conviction that different races were fundamentally incompatible, it sought to present a future for South Africa which would also benefit the overall economy and, specifically, contribute to the process of Afrikaner economic upliftment. The policy was thus a prospective vote-winner amongst both farmers and white workers that neatly complemented traditional racist attitudes within the broader Afrikaner population. With this crucial addition to its policy arsenal, a wide-ranging bureaucratic apparatus in place, and the *broedertwis* of the war years a fading memory, the movement headed by the Broederbond and National Party were finally poised to make a serious bid for state power.

THE ZIONISTS

From its earliest beginnings, the unacknowledged dilemma at the heart of Zionist enterprise was the fact that the designated Jewish homeland, Palestine, was already occupied by another ethnic group. Although slower to organise, Palestinian nationalism became a genuine political force by the end of the First World War. This created an apparently unresolvable conundrum: how to accommodate two movements that both sought exclusive political control over the same state? The unspoken, but obvious conclusion was that such accommodation was impossible. A satisfactory solution implicitly entailed the subordination, elimination or expulsion of the opposing group. This section argues that Zionist strategies for independence in both the broader diplomatic sphere and within Palestine soon became focused on the Arab community and its own burgeoning nationalism. Internationally, it argues that the movement initially sought to accommodate Arabs and then, when compromise proved impossible, deliberately misled them by claiming that their goal was not necessarily a Jewish state. Domestically, it demonstrates how the *Yishuv* and particularly its military wing, became specifically directed at the exclusion of Palestinians.

The section opens with a brief discussion on the origins of the Palestinian and Arab nationalist movements. Next, it details Zionist relations with both Palestinians and the broader Arab community during the 1920s and 1930s and the impact this had on overall Zionist strategies. It then turns to the Arab Revolt of 1936–39 and British and Zionist reactions to it. The section concludes with a discussion of the London Conference in 1939 and its implications for the Zionists during the Second World War.

Arab Nationalism

After the Young Turk Revolution in 1908, Arab intellectuals within the Ottoman empire began calling for an independent Arab state. As with the Zionists, during the First World War the British sought to harness this nascent nationalist feeling in the war against the Turks. To that end, the British entered into a protracted series of written negotiations with King Husayn, guardian of Mecca, persuading him to raise troops in an internal rebellion against the Ottomans in exchange for independent Arab statehood. What remained unclear in the vaguely worded exchanges was whether the British promised Palestine to the Arabs at the same time that they had endorsed the call for a Jewish 'national home'.[55] Whatever the truth, in the peace talks after the war the British predictably followed their imperial interests. Under the system of mandates drawn up by the League of Nations, France was given Syria and the Levant while Britain gained control of Palestine and Iraq. The Hashemites were left with nominal independence in the underdeveloped Arab Gulf. Over the course of the decade, however, the status of these territories slowly altered. In 1921, the west bank of the Jordan was sliced off Palestine to create the new area of Transjordan, which was given nominal independence in 1928. Iraq was also given freer rein over internal politics, becoming a full member of the League in 1932. The same year Saudi Arabia was formally proclaimed as a new state, Ibn Saud having driven King Husayn from power. Egypt, Syria and Lebanon too were all granted increasing degrees of independence from their colonial masters.

These new Arab states were largely hostile to the Zionist presence in Palestine, and the Palestinians themselves began to resist the growing intrusions of the Jewish population by starting aggressively to pursue statehood. The Palestinian strength lay in numbers. In 1919 Palestine's Jewish population amounted to only 57 000 and owned just over 2 per cent of the land, compared with 530 000 Arabs who owned most of the rest. Although by 1930 this had increased to 156 840 compared to 744 250, and Jewish land ownership to 4.4 per cent of the total, Palestinian preponderance in the region remained overwhelming.[56] The Zionists, however, were not prepared to recognise Palestinian claims, asserting repeatedly that they sought merely to reunite the 'people without a land and the land without a people'.[57]

After the implementation of the Mandate, with its provisions for a Jewish national home, this hatred spilled over into violence. In 1920 and 1921 riots broke out, causing a number of Jewish deaths. Over the next few years, however, hostility subsided and Zionists attributed the trouble to 'mischief makers'.[58] Elements within the Zionist movement even attempted to seek reconciliation between the two communities. A group that acknowledged Palestinian rights and sought to effect a mutually satisfactory, binational state, *Brit Shalom*, was formed in 1925. Despite support from some prominent individuals, however, it was never able to gain any mass following. In 1929, new riots, arising from a dispute over the Wailing Wall, broke out, resulting in a number of deaths on both sides. The riots thus strengthened the notions of ethnic exclusivism that were so fundamental to the cohesiveness of the Zionist movement in its early development in Palestine. By reinforcing a security-related solidarity that complemented the ethno-cultural one being propagated by various Zionist organisations, the ethnic conflict contributed to the expanding sense of national community. It also made the population much more susceptible to hardline, militaristic appeals and led to a new determination on the part of the Zionists to end all attempts at mutual accommodation.

Orchestrating the expulsion of leftists who called for greater Arab reconciliation from the *Histadrut*, Ben Gurion formally withdrew support for joint Palestinian/Jewish trade unions.[59] The spread of these hardline, nationalist attitudes was symbolised by the collapse of *Brit Shalom* in 1933. The development of the proto-state thus became more than merely a means of consolidating the Jewish presence and insuring a political and economic foundation for the movement's diplomacy. It was a tool for the exclusion of a competing national group from power. As Chapter 3 noted, in the economic sphere the campaign for Jewish labour not only prevented competition from cheaper Palestinians – it led to the development of a separate, self-contained Jewish economy. Now, Jewish economic enterprises, particularly in the labour-intensive agricultural sector, accelerated their policy of replacing Arab labour with Jews so as to consolidate this ethnic base.[60] In the military arena the *Haganah* was crafted into a military instrument that could be utilised offensively as well as defensively if the occasion required. Hostility to the Palestinians had engendered a hardline Zionist policy of 'peace through strength'.

This ongoing conflict also had ramifications in the diplomatic sphere, where the Zionists followed two strategies. First, they offered financial aid to the Arabs in exchange for their recognition of Zionist aims.[61] Second, they publicly rejected the notion that the Palestinians had any legitimate nationalist claims, and argued that the Zionist presence had benefited them economically.[62] Nevertheless, Ben Gurion's diary of the 1920s, in which he refers repeatedly to a Palestinian 'national movement', shows clearly that the Zionist leaders' refusal to acknowledge the existence of Palestinian nationalism was deliberate.[63] In this strategy the Zionists were aided by the Palestinians themselves. Given the lack of any formal nationalist organisation, let alone the tightly knit infrastructure of the Jews, the Palestinian leadership largely comprised local landowners and was dominated by two families, the Hussaynis and the Nashashibis. A member of the former, Hajj Amin al-Hussayni, gained nominal leadership of the Palestinian Arabs when he was appointed Grand Mufti of Jerusalem in 1921. The Mufti firmly believed in the justice of the Arab position and the obligation of the British to grant the Palestinians statehood. Accordingly, he eschewed any compromise short of that goal and turned down such offers as Samuel's 1922 proposals for an elected bi-national Legislative Council, which would have had a solid Palestinian majority.

This proved a misguided stand that allowed the Zionist leaders to portray themselves as statesmanlike and peaceful. Because they knew of the Mufti's inflexibility, the Zionists were able to accept proposals (like that for the council) that they knew would be inimical to their overall strategy for creating a Jewish state in full confidence that they would never have to implement them. Given their substantial numerical inferiority, the Jews' greatest strength lay in a superior, diplomatic strategy to compensate for their inherent domestic weakness. The Zionists' ability to do this was most strikingly illustrated in 1930. Following the 1929 riots, the new Labour government in Britain sent an investigating commission to examine the causes. The resulting report pointed to the growing Jewish presence as the primary Arab irritant and in response Lord Passfield, the Colonial Secretary, issued a White Paper calling for a drastic curtailment of Jewish immigration. Insisting that 'we on our part contemplate no political domination [of Arabs]', Weizmann resigned his presidency of the WZO and mobilised his allies in Parliament and the House of Lords (including Lloyd George and Winston Churchill) against the bill.[64] Given the shaky foundation of Ramsay MacDonald's Labour government, this protest proved sufficient to prompt a personal letter from the Prime Minister to Weizmann re-endorsing Zionist goals. The bill was retracted before it even reached the floor.

Shifting Zionist Aims

By maintaining a duplicitous strategy about the Palestinians, therefore, the Zionists managed to retain the broad support of the British. This protection was necessary to give them the opportunity to develop the institutional framework that might one day become a state. The Zionists' international campaign and their domestic one interlocked to exclude a hostile nationalism from enlisting the support of the colonial government or gaining political control within Palestine. Following the furore over the White Paper, however, the Zionists realised that they could not rely on British protection indefinitely. In 1931, delegates from 12 Muslim countries met in Jerusalem to condemn Zionism.[65] The Zionist leadership had to develop a new strategy for dealing with the Arab challenge. Chaim Arlosoroff, the dynamic political secretary of the Jewish Agency, gave the matter particular thought. He observed in 1932 that while the *Yishuv* had entrenched itself sufficiently that the Palestinians were no longer strong enough to destroy it, neither were the Jews yet powerful enough to prevent the creation of a Palestinian state. Not trusting the British to hold to their promises of creating a Jewish national home, Arlosoroff argued that in order to assure the continued growth of the *Yishuv* through immigration and economic development, the Zionists needed to achieve a stage when 'the relation of real forces is such to preclude any possibility of the establishment of an Arab state in Palestine'.[66] Although Arlosoroff's solution of revolutionary minority rule was never officially endorsed by the Zionist movement (and he himself was assassinated in 1933, apparently by radical Revisionsts), his articulation of an Arab strategy implicitly underlay much of Zionist activity throughout the 1930s.

The Zionists first sought to achieve this through diplomacy. With the labour movement in political ascendancy, Ben Gurion and Moshe Sharrett, a *Mapai* Arab specialist, began a series of discussions with Arab leaders to find an arrangement whereby the Zionists and Arabs could come to a mutually satisfactory resolution of their differences. The preferred Zionist solution was to exchange resources to help the creation of a greater Arab state, of which the Palestinians would be part, in exchange for the establishment of Israel in Palestine. In 1933, in secret negotiations with King Abdullah of Transjordan, who hoped to offer the Zionists protection within a broader Palestinian state under his rule, they agreed to lease territory from him and develop it.[67] The same year they met several times with Musa Alami, a leading Palestinian spokesman with connections to the Mufti, for discussions about the possibility of creating a greater Jewish state that would be part of an Arab federation.[68] In 1934 Ben Gurion met with a high-level, joint Syro-Palestinian delegation in Geneva for similar discussions. Two years later, he held discussions with the Christian Arab nationalist George Antonius on three separate occasions.

While this dialogue appeared to indicate a new Zionist willingness towards compromise, in practice it was nothing of the sort. Throughout his discussions, Ben Gurion remained completely committed to the idea of a Jewish state and sought only to find ways of getting Arab acquiescence for that idea. The Arabs, by contrast, were prepared to discuss any solution short of the establishment of such a state. Nevertheless, by appearing publicly flexible while being privately obdurate, Ben Gurion managed to buy valuable time for the further development of the *Yishuv*. Despite appearing to acknowledge Palestinian claims, the Zionists were engaging, intentionally, in what has been accurately characterised as a period of 'futile diplomacy'.[69] It was, however, futile only insofar as it failed to achieve a mutually acceptable compromise. From 1930–35, which were the years of greatest population growth in the *Yishuv*, it managed to prevent any new riots. But, as the talks failed to produce tangible results, and the Jewish community expanded, Palestinian opposition hardened.

Despite the lack of a clear strategy such as that pursued by the Zionists, a growing fear of the real possibility of an exclusive, Jewish state accelerated the spread of nationalist sentiment among the Palestinians. Arab leaders became increasingly panicky, charging that continued immigration under the Mandate would 'end in overpowering [Palestine's] Arab inhabitants'.[70] Even the Mufti now realised the importance of checking Zionist expansion and in 1935 accepted a new British proposal for a unified legislative assembly. Given that the Palestinians still comprised 71 per cent of the population, this would almost certainly have led to Palestinian dominance of a binational legislature. This time, however, the Zionists were openly opposed to the plan, and they voted down the proposal in the 1935 WZO Congress. Whereas even in 1930 they had to rely on Weizmann's diplomatic skills to see off a political threat, five years later the leaders of the *Yishuv* now felt themselves in a strong enough position publicly to oppose a political plan that was inimical to their own interests. Although still far from constituting a real state, the development of the proto-state had now provided the Zionists with the structural wherewithal to resist encroachments on their ultimate goal.

The Arab Revolt

In the face of Zionist intransigence, in November 1935 the Palestinians gave a three-point ultimatum to the British: the introduction of a democratic parliament, the cessation of all land sales to the Zionists, and an end to Jewish immigration. By doing so, they hoped to take advantage of the uncertain international situation following Mussolini's invasion of Ethiopia that year, an event which raised British concerns about the security of Egypt. When concessions were not forthcoming, the traditionally fractured Palestinian leadership unified and formed the Arab Higher Committee (AHC) in 1936. For the first time, the forces of Palestinian nationalism had a coherent leadership and organisation to combat the Zionists. Inspired by the success of revolts in Syria and Egypt earlier that year that had resulted in major concessions towards both countries, they called for a general strike, a boycott of Jewish goods and the beginning of terrorist attacks against the Jews.[71]

After several months of heavy unrest, and under pressure from the English press which remained supportive of the Zionist cause, the British agreed to develop a new plan for the region. Following a long investigation, by the Peel Commission, a Royal Report of 1937, suggested a new possibility:

> An irrepressible conflict has arisen between two national communities within the narrow bounds of one small country.... Partition seems to offer at least a chance of ultimate peace. We can see none in any other plan.[72]

Despite reservations, Weizmann and Ben Gurion endorsed partition in principle while refusing to acknowledge the boundaries defined by the Commission. As Ben Gurion put it:

> A Jewish state in part of Palestine is not the end but the beginning. The establishment of such a Jewish state will serve as a means in our historical effort to redeem the country in its entirety.[73]

Since the proposed states involved the large-scale transfer of Arab land to the Jews as well as the displacement of some 296 000 Palestinians, the AHC refused to consider it, and entered into a new, more violent uprising. At little cost, therefore, the Zionists were able to regain the statesmanlike and conciliatory credentials necessary to pursue their campaign for international support that they had foregone by turning down the 1935 proposals. More importantly, the commission brought them closer to a formal international recognition of their right to a Jewish state. By accepting in principle a smaller state than it had traditionally demanded, the Zionists demonstrated their underlying pragmatism: half a loaf was certainly better than none and might one day grow larger.

Nevertheless, the new phase of the Arab Revolt was long and bloody. Although the British forced the Mufti into exile, he appealed for help from the neighbouring Arab states. Internal differences, such as continued rivalry between the Hashemites and Ibn Saud, prevented any concerted show of solidarity. However, a number of individual Arabs, under the leadership of a Lebanese, Fawzi al-Qawukji, volunteered to participate in the expanding operations against the British and the Jews. Together with the Palestinians they were able to carry out a wide-ranging and destructive campaign, orchestrating over 10 000 violent incidents over the course of the next two years. The mass nature of these protests provided dramatic illustration of the spread of disaffection among the Palestinian community. In response, the Jewish Agency insisted that Jews should be allowed 'the right to defend themselves'.[74] Due to the scale of the conflict, the British were forced to bring in 20 000 soldiers while deputising a similar number of Jews to help suppress the unrest.

In the end the Revolt proved devastating for both the Palestinian community and its cause. Between 1936–39, some 5000 Palestinians were killed, 15 000 were wounded and many more were detained out of a total population of only one million.[75] Their infant organisational and military infrastructure was destroyed and their leadership exiled. This significantly weakened the Zionists' primary competitor for control of Palestine. Palestinian nationalism had never been a coherent social movement, and now it had lost most of the little coherence it had.

Zionist Reactions

Meanwhile, the Jews had gone from strength to strength economically and militarily. When the Arab Revolt broke out, the *Yishuv* leadership adopted a policy of non-reprisal known as *Havlaga*. This allowed the Zionists to seem peaceful and non-threatening to the British. At the same time, they continued publicly to promote old theories about the benefits of Jewish settlement for the Arabs and the lack of Palestinian national sentiment. As Ben Gurion famously put it in 1936, the same year he held secret talks with Antonius: 'There is no conflict between Jewish and Palestinian nationalism because Jewish nationalism is not in Palestine and the Palestinians are not a nation.'[76]

He was, however, well aware of the opportunities presented by the revolt. Indeed, Ben Gurion realised that the Palestinians' own expression of force was but a forerunner of what the Jews themselves might one day choose to do. Accordingly, he felt the Zionists should seek whatever military advantage that they could from the situation. In a letter to his son in 1937 he made this point clearly:

> I do not doubt that our army will be among the world's finest and then it will not be beyond us to settle in the rest of the country, either by mutual agreement and understanding with our Arab neighbours or by some other way.... If we must resort to force – not to dispossess Arabs of the Negev or Transjordan, but to guarantee our own right to settle in those places – we shall rely on our force.[77]

The development of such a force was a direct by-product of Jewish policy during the Revolt. *Havlaga*'s chief dividend came in the form of the Jewish Settlement Police, a new body recruited by the British to help put down the revolt. This provided a vehicle through which the *Haganah* could operate openly. To help manage and coordinate its activities, a new High Command for the organisation was formed, technically separate from the *Histadrut* and political parties, but still under civilian control. By 1939, the *Haganah* comprised the nucleus of a viable, independent military force of over 20 000 men and 4000 women.[78]

Thus even though over 600 Jews lost their lives over the course of the unrest, the Zionists managed to put themselves in a far stronger position in Palestine than they had held previously. Also, a defensive 'tower and stockade' policy, led to the construction of some 52 new Zionist settlements between 1936–39, expanding and consolidating the Jewish presence in the territory.[79] Combined with the massive economic growth of the Jewish economy and the demographic shifts occasioned by the 5th *Aliyah*, the proto-state became even more powerful. Most importantly, while still a numerical majority, by 1939 the Palestinians were demoralised and weakened to such an extent that Arlosoroff's aim had largely been achieved. There was little chance that they would be able unilaterally to establish a state over Jewish objections. The proto-state of the *Yishuv* was now a self-sufficient political unit in almost all but name. It was also heavily militarised. This was primarily a consequence of political structure and demographics. Unlike the Afrikaners, who faced no real security threat from blacks, the Zionists were not fully protected by the existing state and for that reason worked hard to develop their coercive capacity.

War and State-making

Two obstacles to the fulfilment of Zionist aims remained: the neighbouring Arab countries and the British themselves. During the Revolt, the Arab states, while failing to unite in support of the Palestinians, were (publicly) unanimous in their hostility to Zionism. In the conflict's aftermath, therefore, Britain felt it strategically important to placate the Arabs in order to keep them in its sphere of influence, particularly given the increasing probability of war with the Fascist powers. These geopolitical factors meant that the British began to shift from their long-standing support of Zionist goals. After formally rejecting the Peel Commission's recommendations following a new study that pronounced partition unworkable, in February 1939 the British called another conference on the Palestinian issue at St James in London. In attendance were the Zionists, and representatives from Egypt, Saudi Arabia, Iraq, Yemen and Transjordan as well as a Palestinian delegation.

Although the Zionists put a brave face on matters, the fact was that their international leverage was now weaker than at any time since the fall of the Ottomans. Although the *Yishuv* might be strong enough to withstand coerced solutions, without great power backing it could not continue the process of state-building. With no possibility that the Jews would support the rabidly anti-semitic Nazis in the impending war,

Britain's priority was shoring up the support of vacillating Arab states. Aware of this the Zionists feared the worst, particularly in the wake of the Sudeten crisis in Czechoslovakia.[80] Shortly after, in what Weizmann described as an atmosphere of 'utter futility' talks broke down irrevocably.[81] In their wake, in May, the British published a new White Paper calling for a phased end to Jewish immigration over five years and the independence of Palestine, with a permanent Palestinian majority, within ten. Both sides rejected the plan – the Palestinians because it permitted some new immigration, the Jews because its implementation would mark the demise of the prospect of a Jewish state. Although the White Paper's official recommendations were suspended after the outbreak of war later that year, new Jewish immigration was reduced to a trickle and the Zionists were left operating under its Damoclean propositions while trying to help resist Hitler. Caught in a policy dilemma, Ben Gurion warned that the Zionists 'did not need any guarantor' in Palestine and insisted that 'both our immigration and our *Yishuv* will stand by virtue of their own strength and that of the Jewish people'.[82] Implicitly endorsing opposition to the British, he articulated a new strategy, declaring 'We must fight the war as if there were no White Paper and the White Paper as if there were no war.'

To do this, the Zionists embarked on a programme of illegal immigration to save some European Jews from Hitler. The Jewish Agency formed the *Mossad* as a secret organisation to coordinate the smuggling of new immigrants into Palestine. Despite British blockades, it was able to bring in some 92 000 new settlers over the course of the war.[83] The Agency also authorised the formation of *Palmach*, a new commando squad with offensive capabilities which was to become an elite section of the *Haganah*. At the same time, the *Irgun* started to follow a policy of active reprisal and terrorism against the British. An even more radical group, *Lehi*, known as the Stern Gang after its founder Avraham Stern, pursued a similar terrorist policy. In response, an infuriated Britain deducted all 'illegal' immigration from the official quotas. It also disbanded the special Jewish squads that it had used in the Arab Revolt and restricted land sales to Jews. In May 1941 Sir Anthony Eden, then Foreign Secretary, made a speech recognising the political, economic, and cultural rights of the Palestinians.

Despite these setbacks, Nazi Germany remained a far more serious threat for Jews everywhere. By 1944, 136 000 Palestinian Jews had volunteered for war service.[84] Of these, nearly 26 000 served in the

British Army, which formed a special Jewish Legion.[85] As an inadvertent, but important by-product of this struggle, many more Zionists gained access to formal military training and equipment. Unlike the Foreign Office, moreover, the Army was not firmly anti-Zionist. It happily gave supply contracts to the *Yishuv* for its Middle Eastern operations that provided a huge economic boost for Jewish industry and the *Histadrut*. In 1939 some 36 per cent of all Jews in Palestine, nearly 160 000 people, were already economically dependent on the *Histadrut* – a number greater than the total Jewish population of the *Yishuv* only a decade earlier.[86] This number continued to expand during the war as the industrial sector and agricultural sectors boomed under the influence of British demand.[87] By 1944, these factors, combined with the continued growth of the Jewish community, meant that the *Yishuv* itself, despite the withdrawal of official British favour, was even stronger than it had been at the start of the war. As Weizmann noted, the war had bred an unprecedented sense of self-reliance and Jewish Palestine now had reached an advanced state of technical development.[88]

Conclusions

In the early part of the twentieth century, Zionists tentatively embraced Arab nationalists as possible allies in the struggle to pry Palestine loose from the Ottomans. Once they realised that both Palestinian and Arab nationalists were fundamentally hostile to Zionist aims, however, a new strategy was required. In order to establish a functioning Jewish nation-state, Zionist leaders saw the achievement of a Jewish majority in Palestine as imperative. To achieve this goal, Zionist strategies aimed not only to establish a Jewish national presence in Palestine, but to exclude a Palestinian one – if possible by diplomacy, if necessary by force. To do this, the Zionists first had to shape the institutions of the proto-state in such a way that they explicitly excluded Palestinians from the *Yishuv*. In this way, the conflict with the Palestinians had a direct impact on the movement's domestic, state-building activities. Second, in order to prevent any new Arab riots, Ben Gurion entered into a deliberately misleading set of negotiations with various Arab leaders in which he duplicitously promised compromise in order to defuse immediate threats. Third, to maintain British support for immigration and the further development of the *Yishuv*, Zionist leaders continued to deny that a legitimate Palestinian nationalist movement existed. When Palestinian frustrations finally erupted in the Arab Revolt, the Zionists exploited the situation to expand their overall strategy of nation and state-building, developing the *Yishuv*'s economy and, more importantly, its military capacity. At the same time, in the international sphere, the Zionists used their acceptance of the Peel Commission's recommendations to establish international legitimacy for their goal of independent statehood. Although the Commission's findings were later repudiated, the concept of partition and the prospect of a predominantly Jewish state had for the first time been publicly mooted. More importantly, throughout the 1930s, the *Yishuv* itself expanded steadily. The *Haganah* developed into a significant military force, new towns were built, and the Jewish population and economy both grew very rapidly.

The conflict with the Palestinians and the broader Arab community also served to reinforce the sense of nationalist solidarity that underpinned the entire Zionist enterprise. Incoming immigrants were not only quickly assimilated within the institutions of the proto-state – they were brought face to face with the unmitigated hostility of Palestine's dominant ethnic group. This helped boost the legitimacy of the *Yishuv* in the eyes of the Jewish population. In response, the Zionists became increasingly intolerant of Palestinian aspirations and any suggestion of a binational state, a trend symbolised by the decline and demise of *Brit Shalom*. It was in direct response to such threats that Zionist leaders like Ben Gurion promoted the establishment of a strong, military force that would ultimately be able to withstand resistance not just from the Palestinians as Arlosoroff had argued, but from the broader Arab community as well. Even after the advent of the Second World War, the burgeoning proto-state made use of the British Army's presence to generate income while at the same time, developing new organisations, notably *Mossad* and *Palmach* to help continue the process of immigration in defiance of British orders. As with its earlier initiatives, a complex, bureaucratic network underpinned the entire Zionist enterprise in Palestine and was the key factor in its continuing success.

GENERAL CONCLUSIONS

With Ireland formally part of the United Kingdom, Palestine under a British mandate and South Africa part of the British Commonwealth, a key focus of each nationalist struggle was inevitably the British Empire. For the Zionists between the wars, this was only rarely a conflictual relationship. Apart from specific debates over the size of

Jewish immigration and the 1930 White Paper débâcle, the British served as protector rather than foe of the movement up to 1939. For the Irish and Afrikaner nationalists, however, both of whom founded their ethno-nationalist ideologies on the principle of opposition to Anglicisation, the reverse was the case. Accordingly, while the broader public was prepared to support the limited nationalist campaigns of men such as Redmond and Hertzog to secure some cultural and political concessions during periods of relative political calm, this was not true when a political crisis impinged directly on that burgeoning sense of national identity.

Accordingly, when Britain, with the pre-war excitement over Home Rule rapidly disappearing and the 1916 Rebellion having precipitated a rapid escalation in anti-British sentiment, mooted introducing conscription in Ireland in 1918, this was met with unprecedented opposition from the country's Catholic community. Similarly, after Smuts forced South Africa into the Second World War against Germany, much of the United Party's Afrikaner support base disappeared virtually overnight. In each case the contradictions of having to support a British war with little local relevance proved too great for the moderate, centrist leadership to contain. In a slightly different way, the shift in Britain's strategic interests in the Middle East led to an abrupt cessation of its traditional role as protector of the *Yishuv*. This forced the Zionist leadership into an increasingly conflictual relationship with the Mandatory power over the issues of immigration and the new White Paper. Even though Hitler was regarded as the greater threat, it significantly increased domestic hostility to the British presence.

All three movements were also engaged in a pressing conflict against another, ethnic group – Protestants, blacks and Palestinians respectively. This conflict helped shape the strategies of the nationalist movements and conditioned the responses of their constituents to nationalist arguments. In South Africa, given the white franchise and a strongly interventionist state, the nationalists sought ethnic hegemony through which they could divide and dominate both Anglophones and the much more numerous black tribes of South Africa through apartheid. In Ireland the nationalists also sought such hegemony but, given their numerical superiority, felt that this could be achieved in a unified, nominally non-denominational state that would in practice be run by Catholics. By withdrawing from parliament and forming the Dail, they sought to establish a viable Catholic administration that would eventually be able to take power and force recalcitrant Protestants into accepting the reality of Catholic-dominated independent Ireland. The Zionists by contrast, like the Afrikaners numerically inferior to their opponents, were nevertheless dependent on an increasingly unreliable British protector to preserve them from Palestinian aggression. Accordingly, they focused on developing indigenous institutions that not only had sufficient coercive power to withstand attacks from increasingly hostile co-inhabitants but also excluded Palestinians from day-to-day life.

This in turn had a direct impact on the decision by each movement whether to establish an armed wing. The Irish Volunteers, formed in response to the Ulster Volunteers, marked the implicit spread of the doctrine of revolutionary violence beyond the narrow ranks of the IRB into the broader Catholic community. And while it was an unrepresentative coterie of IRB members – more preoccupied with the romantic elements of armed struggle than its practicality – who launched the Easter Rebellion, the Volunteers were later to transform themselves into a genuine guerrilla force. In South Africa, however, despite a strong martial tradition, the 1914 Rebellion proved a failure and during the Second World War neither the OB nor its *Stormjaers* ever managed more than a few acts of sabotage. This was largely because the lack of a genuine military threat from either blacks or Anglophones made the formation of a formal armed wing superfluous. Rather, building on a long racist tradition, and given the numerical superiority of blacks in South Africa, Afrikaner leaders eventually constructed an ideological solution to the racial problem: apartheid. This proposed social engineering project was premised on the permanent separation of black 'nations' from whites (and the *de facto* separation of Anglophones from Afrikaners) a separation that would be best implemented using the increasingly powerful existing state apparatus. In stark contrast, fear of the Palestinians' overwhelming numerical superiority and increasingly violent attacks on Jewish settlers precipitated the creation of a Zionist ideology that both denied the legitimacy of Arab aspirations and sought their functional exclusion from the administration of the territory. In consequence, the Jewish community in Palestine was compelled to establish a powerful military arm. Supplied and trained by the British during first the Arab Revolt and then the Second World War, *Haganah* soon became a highly effective force.

The strategies and ideology of mobilisation were also inextricably bound up with narrower economic interests. Irish Catholics, Afrikaners and Zionists were all preoccupied with ensuring increased economic power and access to jobs *vis-à-vis* opposing ethnic groups. This power could best be ensured by the nationalist movement finding the ability to redirect state resources to favour their constituents. It was this that lay behind Sinn Fein's emphasis on state-led redistributivist policies in its election platform in 1918 as well as the economically radical resolutions of the First Dail, and the party's acquiescence in land raids and cattle rustling in rural areas. More striking, in South Africa, the central thrust of apartheid ideology was the exclusion of blacks from skilled jobs or capital in the white economy while maintaining them as cheap labour. It was also designed to help Afrikaner farmers and workers by tightly regulating the black labour market and ensuring a constant pool of cheap, rural workers. Similarly, the entire edifice of the *Histadrut* was built up in order to exclude Palestinian labour and capital from the Jewish economy, which operated as a semi-autonomous enclave within Palestine, providing jobs for Jewish workers.

The need for physical and economic security from perceived ethnic rivals, therefore, not only contributed to feelings of solidarity within each ethnic group but sparked organisational responses that played a key role in mobilising new support for nationalists. It also provided the necessary impetus – and capacity – for using violence in pursuit of nationalist goals. By the end of the First World War, the Irish Volunteers, under the control of Sinn Fein, were more than willing to fight the British Army for independence. By the end of the Second, the *Haganah* and other offshoots such as the *Irgun* were equally prepared to do so in Palestine. For their part, Afrikaner nationalists were closer than ever to taking power following the emotions raised during the war, especially after the influential, if short-lived, activities of the OB in politicising Afrikanerdom along ethnic lines. In 1919 in Ireland and in 1945 in South Africa and Palestine, each nationalist movement was more powerful than it had ever been and ready to begin a final push to secure an ethnic state.

5 International Politics and State Power

INTRODUCTION

Nationalist movements are frequently studied as if, apart from external ideological influences, they remain insulated from global affairs. The dynamic of ethnic mobilisation is seen primarily as a phenomenon which occurs within state boundaries. In practice, however, such movements rarely – if ever – develop in complete isolation from the broader international arena. On one level international events, relations with other states or movements, and broader geopolitical shifts can all have direct repercussions on both the shape of nationalist strategies and their success or failure. On another, achieving independent statehood, the ultimate political objective of nationalism, necessarily implies securing international recognition as well as domestic sovereignty. As Chapter 4 suggested, extraneous geopolitical events strongly influenced the nature and outcome of the nationalist struggle in each of the case studies. In addition, nationalist leaders were painfully aware of the need to achieve both *de jure* recognition for their claims as well as *de facto* control over their respective states. This chapter examines the implications of the international dimension of national mobilisation, focusing particularly on the issue of sovereignty. It argues that in each case the movement's domestic strategies were linked directly to international ones and helped them to secure both internal and international legitimacy in the drive for state power.

IRELAND

This section argues that international influences had a sustained impact on national mobilisation in Ireland. In particular, it suggests that international diplomacy played a key part in gaining support for Irish claims to sovereignty, particularly from the United States. It shows how this resulted in the final push for power taking place at two levels. First, the nationalists pursued a domestic strategy of trying to set up a viable alternative government structure to supplant the existing state apparatus while carrying out a sustained insurrection against British rule. Second, they promoted an international campaign that succeeded in putting the Imperial government under heavy diplomatic pressure, particularly from the United States. This dual strategy forced the British to begin negotiations that resulted in the creation of an independent Ireland.

The section opens by briefly recapping the impact of international events, and in particular the First World War, on Ireland. It then looks in detail at the broader international strategies followed by the nationalist movement to secure international support, particularly in the United States. It examines how the Irish nationalists were gradually able to undermine the legitimacy of British rule between 1919–21 while setting up alternative structures of government and administration. Finally it looks at the Treaty that resulted in the establishment of the Irish Free State in 1922 and the civil war that followed. It concludes by assessing the reasons for the resilience and ultimate victory of the moderate provisional government of the Irish Free State over more radical nationalists.

International Influences on Irish Politics

The level of support for nominally nationalist policies of whatever kind throughout Irish history was frequently a reflection of, or reaction to, extraneous international events. During the nineteenth century this was true with regard to both economic issues (the Land War was, at least in part, a response to international economic downturn) and political ones (the 1848 rising was directly inspired by the wave of liberal revolutions in Europe that year). External geopolitical influences also had a critical effect on the establishment and spread of the broader ethno-nationalist movement in Irish politics. The fortunes of all broadly nationalist movements, especially those that were part of the Gaelic Revival, surged during the anti-British fervour generated by the Anglo-Boer War at the turn of the century. Most important of all, as the previous chapter argued, the First World War had an enormous impact on the later development of the nationalist movement. The domestic upheaval caused by an unpopular conflict laid the foundation for the ethnic resentment that would be translated into political support in the wake of the Easter Rebellion. Indeed it is fair to say that without the advent of war, neither the 1916 rebellion nor Sinn Fein's 1918 election victory would have happened.

But even with the war, and the sea-change it produced in Irish politics, the nationalists were unable to take power until Britain could be persuaded to relax its hold on the country. Although predicting the broader consequences of these powerful international events and their effects on Ireland was clearly beyond the ability of the leaders of the nationalist movement, they were always conscious of the international dimension of their struggle. As the long-standing nationalist dictum 'England's difficulty is Ireland's opportunity' testified, the Irish were always aware that one of their most promising sources of potential assistance was countries hoping to undermine, or at least embarrass, the British Empire. From the 1790s onwards, Britain's major rivals – France in the first part of the nineteenth century, Germany in the second and early twentieth – were regularly solicited for assistance by eager Irish nationalists, especially when Britain was preoccupied with events outside Ireland.[1] It was by using exactly those arguments that the IRB succeeded in persuading the German High Command to help supply arms and ammunition, albeit to little effect, for the prospective 1916 rebels.

As the tide of the war turned against Germany, Sinn Fein shifted its diplomatic focus to Britain's most important ally, the United States. With its enormous pool of Irish-born-and-descended immigrants, from the mid-nineteenth century onwards America was a mainstay of financial, political and ideological support for the struggle for Irish independence.[2] In the 1860s the Fenians had more members in the United States than in Ireland. The IRB too retained an American wing, *Clan na Gael*, which often ended up sustaining it during fallow periods rather than vice-versa. In the 1880s, Americans dug deep into their pockets to support Parnell and the Home Rulers and during the 1890s and early 1900s also became large-scale consumers of much of the literature of the Gaelic revival.

This had already had a substantial impact on US politics by the time of the First World War. In 1915 the British ambassador to Washington wrote to London emphasising the 'very great importance' of avoiding actions in Ireland which 'might arouse a strong anti-British sentiment here'.[3] Two years later, the execution of the 1916 rebels, which received widespread coverage in the American press, did just that. The well-organised Irish political machine in the big East Coast cities was able to secure the support of key local politicians in condemning British actions. Just as America entered the war against Germany in 1917, lobbying groups for Irish independence sprang up and the United States government was forced to warn the British that pressure from the 'organised Irish' was putting severe pressure on the alliance. Given America's growing importance as the world's leading financial and military power, it was a source of protest that the British found increasingly difficult to ignore.

In desperate need of political and financial support for the beleaguered Dail, following his escape from prison in 1919, De Valera left for the United States. As 'President of the Irish Republic' he spent the next 18 months touring the country to try to raise funds and secure formal American political backing. Early on, however, he clashed with local Irish leaders, many of whom were frequently more concerned with using proffered cash to grease the wheels of their own patronage-based political machines. To circumvent this, De Valera formed his own organisation, the Irish Victory Fund, which proved remarkably successful. By the end of 1920 it had raised over $1m and over the next two years a further $9m was forthcoming – resources that were critical in sustaining the nationalist enterprise through its guerrilla war stage.[4] At the same time, the growing importance of the Irish electorate soon gave him access to major political figures. Over 700 000 Americans joined various lobbying groups in support of the Irish struggle. Although De Valera failed to win the endorsement of President Wilson, after a strong campaign, both houses of Congress passed resolutions pledging American support for the Irish cause.[5]

The Treaty of Versailles

De Valera's appeals were greatly helped by the increasing international acceptability of nationalist arguments. As Patrick Pearse pointed out shortly before his execution, there was an obvious contradiction in Britain fighting the First World War 'for the freedom of Belgium and Serbia' while ignoring Irish pleas for the same liberties.[6] Now President Wilson, who had included the right to national self-determination among his famous Fourteen Points, stated explicitly that '[n]o people must be forced to live under a sovereignty under which it does not wish to live'. By the end of the war the concept had been elevated to one of the guiding principles of the new world order.[7] This seemed to supply legal and philosophical justification for Irish demands – especially when the notion was, in theory at least, also subscribed to by the British government. Accordingly, among its first official acts, the Dail approved two documents, 'Ireland's Case for Independence' and 'An Address to the Free Nations of the World', which were then distributed internationally to generate support.[8] Insisting that 'for over a thousand years, Ireland possessed and exercised sovereignty', they demanded that Britain be required to recognise the existence of an Irish republic.[9]

Sinn Fein also called for Ireland to have a full vote at the Versailles Peace Conference, claiming it possessed 'suppressed sovereignty' – a similar claim to Bulgaria.[10] Although this request was unsurprisingly turned down, the Dail nonetheless dispatched a delegation to France to argue the Irish case. But despite the groundswell of support in the United States behind the Irish cause, Wilson was unwilling to alienate the British and refused to endorse Sinn Fein's claims. The French meanwhile, although sympathetic, remained irritated at the fact that the Rebels had sought an alliance with Germany during the war and ignored Sinn Fein's demands. While international diplomacy provided critical funding and political leverage for the nationalist movement, the party could not achieve a breakthrough in the international arena alone. The focus of Sinn Fein's campaign had to be consolidating its domestic position in the face of continued British intransigence.

The First Republic

As De Valera himself acknowledged, Sinn Fein's first priority had to be 'practical remedies, not high sounding statements'.[11] Rather than relying on Wilsonian sentiment, the movement had to consolidate the administrative and organisational gains of the previous two years and keep the British government under continued pressure. Taking advantage of an eight-month hiatus before the launch of a British crackdown, Michael Collins, the Dail's new finance minister and a survivor of the Easter Rebellion, successfully floated two small loans. The money gave the Republic the financial wherewithal to operate in the months before the funds raised by De Valera in America appeared, allowing it to fund a growing alternative government.

While boycotting Westminster, Sinn Fein made plans to establish an executive as well as a legislature. In addition to Collins in Finance, it established other 'ministries' which, while lacking sufficient bureaucratic infrastructure to perform any major tasks, helped consolidate the broad Sinn Fein organisation and provided it with centralised leadership. The party also continued to run the local councils it had won control over in the 1919 elections. Over the next two years many more local government authorities placed themselves voluntarily under Sinn Fein's authority, significantly widening the party's administrative base and giving it direct access to grassroots supporters. Between 1919–20 the Dail also established a set of independent courts operating on 'Gaelic' principles, circumventing the existing crown court system. As most tended to rule in favour of small farmers and tenants on land issues they also served to bolster the party's rural support base. In this way, Sinn Fein gradually usurped many of the local administrative tasks of Irish society, extending the popular legitimacy of the Dail and gradually weakening that of the British government.

Even more important than these administrative and judicial initiatives, however, was the rapidly growing military dimension to the Irish struggle. In 1919 the Irish Volunteers renamed themselves the Irish Republican Army and began a concerted guerrilla campaign for liberation. The new force was expressly designated as the military arm of the emerging proto-state and from August 1920 all IRA members were required to take an oath of allegiance to the Dail.[12] Like the *Haganah* in Palestine, it provided a critical military dimension for the provisional government and attracted recruits from all sections of Irish society. Nevertheless, given the troops' limited training and lack of weapons, the IRA's leaders were well aware that they had little chance of taking on the full might of the British army. Their real campaign was to raise the costs of British occupation to unacceptably high levels while simultaneously seeking to win the support of the majority of the Catholic population to the cause of a politically independent republic.

The resultant conflict, which primarily involved attacks on policemen and soldiers, proved to be a much more vicious and violent confrontation than anything that had preceded it in the previous century. Predictably, the worst violence took place in Ulster. The all-Protestant force the 'B-Specials' ruthlessly stamped out Catholic unrest, committing atrocities that were soon emulated by the IRA in a vicious cycle of reprisal. The South also saw an upsurge in violence, particularly in the eastern and southern parts of the country and the British were forced to call in nearly 40 000 soldiers to crack down on the rebels. A further 7000 special policemen, known as the Black-and-Tans and 6000 Auxiliaries were also appointed to help the beleaguered police force.[13]

Despite this show of force, the army proved unable to snuff out the rebellion. In De Valera's absence Collins, who had been made President of the Supreme Council of the IRB and the IRA's Commander-in-Chief, emerged as the central figure in the nationalist movement. Under his leadership, the IRA became increasingly adept at guerrilla tactics against security forces and militant Protestant groups in Ulster. Between 1920–21 the Republicans killed some 525 people, and wounded more than 1000. Meanwhile public sentiment steadily hardened against the British as the general populace chafed under the restrictions of martial law, mass arrests and atrocities committed by government forces. Although clearly incapable of taking over the state by force of arms, the IRA and the Dail had been able to create a situation where government as usual was no longer possible.

The Dail, under the *de facto* leadership of Collins, was now effectively running the IRA, and Sinn Fein was increasingly regarded by Irish Catholics as their legitimate government. The new reality was overwhelmingly confirmed in August 1921, when Sinn Fein won a crushing victory in new elections. Soon after it established the Second Dail, giving further impetus to its insistence that it represented the rightful, legitimately elected government of Ireland. While less cohesive and economically independent than that constructed by the Zionists during the 1930s and 1940s, the Dail had essentially created its own proto-state with a semi-autonomous administrative, financial, judicial and military base that claimed the allegiance of the vast majority of people outside Ulster. Although patently unable to wrest control of Ireland by force of arms, it had created a state of affairs under which the British claim of sovereign power seemed increasingly hollow.

Recognising this, Lloyd George sought an acceptable political solution short of submitting to Sinn Fein's demands. In 1920 he pushed the Government of Ireland Act through parliament to try to defuse the situation. This at long last gave Home Rule to Ireland, providing for two legislatures, one in Dublin and another in Belfast to cater for the six counties of Ulster. But although the two administrations would theoretically be grouped together into an overarching Council of Ireland, accepting the permanent division of Ireland (not to mention the fact that Britain retained the right to interfere directly in Irish financial affairs) remained completely unacceptable to Sinn Fein and the IRA.

But Ireland was not the only corner of the Empire causing concern to the British government. In the two years since 1919, Lloyd George had to deal with a rebellion in the Punjab, riots in Palestine, unrest in west Afghanistan, a rebellion in Iraq and ongoing problems in Turkey and Egypt. In such an unstable environment the Empire, already financially and militarily drained by the First World War, was becoming seriously overstretched. As the Chief of General Staff lamented, '[o]ur small army is too scattered. In no single arena are we strong enough'.[14] With a large proportion of those soldiers bogged down in Ireland, finding a negotiated solution to the Irish problem would ease the pressure enormously.

The situation was further exacerbated by continued diplomatic pressure especially from the United States. President Warren Harding, who had succeeded Wilson, expressed full support for the Irish cause (despite the fact that De Valera inadvertently irritated him by briefly proposing a 'Cuban solution' to the Irish problem involving a 'British Monroe Doctrine' encompassing Ireland). This combination of strategic and diplomatic factors made it imperative for Britain to seek a feasible, long-term solution. Accordingly, after allowing the conflict to simmer for several more months, in December 1921 Lloyd George finally gave in, called for a truce and invited Sinn Fein representatives to London for talks. But although other international pressures had certainly contributed, the primary reason for the decision was the tenacity and unexpected (to the British) coherence of Irish resistance.

The Irish Free State and Civil War

Unlike the IRB which remained inflexibly republican from the time of its formation, Sinn Fein had always been prepared to consider possible constitutional arrangements that fell short of this idealistic goal. Griffith himself had favoured the implementation of a policy of 'national self-development' – a gradual loosening of the ties with the metropole in emulation of the processes that had taken place in Poland, Hungary and Austria during the nineteenth century.[15] Although Sinn Fein regarded the Home Rule proposal of 1912 as inadequate, the party was willing to honour an arrangement 'that provides [Britain and Ireland] retain each their independence and exist co-equal in power under the rule of a common sovereign'.[16] Following the Easter Rebellion, however, the party had necessarily adopted the language of republicanism that had been espoused by the rebels, declaring its goals to be 'securing international recognition of the Irish republic', after which 'the Irish people may, by referendum, freely choose their own form of government'.[17] Accordingly, when Sinn Fein accepted Lloyd George's invitation, an internationally recognised republic was the goal that most party leaders regarded as the *sine qua non* of any negotiations.

At De Valera's own insistence, he did not participate in the formal London talks. Instead he dispatched Collins and Griffith to lead a Sinn Fein team split between moderates and radicals. The issues under discussion were to resolve British defence and security interests, to decide on the status of Ulster (which had assumed political autonomy in terms of the 1920 Act and was already being run by its own legislature) and to negotiate an acceptable political dispensation for Ireland. Surprisingly the first two points were dealt with relatively easily. The Irish accepted that Britain could retain control of ports for naval purposes. They also agreed to defer the question of partition to a Boundary Commission that would be appointed later. On the last issue Lloyd George offered the Irish delegation circumscribed dominion status. This would effectively have granted Ireland far greater political autonomy than Home Rule but kept the country subordinate to Britain in all major matters.[18] From his base in Ireland, De Valera offered a counterproposal, termed 'external association', a clever concept that would have allowed Ireland to become a republic under the authority of the crown but which the British regarded as absolutely unacceptable. After much wrangling and arm-twisting by Lloyd George, the delegation approved a compromise Treaty that allowed fiscal autonomy, complete control over domestic affairs and full dominion status.

When presented with the Treaty terms, however, De Valera turned them down flat, declaring that 'the terms of agreement are in violent conflict with the wishes of the majority of the Nation'.[19] In particular, he objected to the oath of allegiance to the Crown that new members of the Dail would have to make. He insisted on an alternative wording that would mention the King as sovereign of the Commonwealth, but not Ireland itself. Collins, however, who had cast the deciding vote in favour of the document, used his own credentials as IRA leader to push for acceptance. Presaging Ben Gurion's pragmatic endorsement of the partition plan mooted in the 1937 Peel Commission report, he argued that '[the treaty] gives us freedom. Not the ultimate freedom that all nations desire and develop to, but the freedom to achieve it'.[20]

He also stressed the fact that, in the longer run, enjoying similar status with Canada and especially South Africa, would prove advantageous as the other two countries were already pushing for extended constitutional powers. These sentiments were echoed by Griffith who vehemently denied that the Treaty represented a 'final settlement' of the constitutional issue.[21]

The Treaty was approved 4 to 3 by the cabinet over De Valera's objections. It was then presented to the Dail for discussion and, after a prolonged and bitter debate, passed by the narrow margin of 64 votes to 51. For radical nationalists, for whom the notion of a republic had been elevated virtually to holy writ, this was unacceptable. De Valera promptly resigned as President and left the government. Most of his supporters, including nearly two-thirds of the IRA rank and file (but only one-third of its leadership), chose to follow.[22] In the 1922 elections for the new Irish Free State, however, the Treatyites won easily, garnering 239 193 votes compared to 133 864 for De Valera. Testifying to the continued relevance of economic issues Labour finished a very strong third with 132 511 votes while the rural Farmers party garnered a respectable 51 075 (both had also endorsed the terms of the Treaty).[23] Arthur Griffith was elected President although Collins, who continued to command the pro-Treatyite IRA, now the Free State army, was the driving force of the new government.

As the polls clearly demonstrated, while they might now have embraced the broad doctrine of ethnic nationalism, the issue of a republic *per se* was never of overwhelming importance to the greater Irish public. For the vast majority the Treaty was a more than acceptable compromise. Under the impetus of the war, martial law and the conscription debate, they had been prepared to back Sinn Fein in rejecting Home Rule and insisting on full independence. Now that appeared to have been achieved, they wanted the new government to devote its attention to preserving peace and finding jobs and houses for its citizens, not to waste time over esoteric issues like the wording of an oath. With practical autonomy guaranteed, the attainment of Pearse's mystical republic was of far less import than it had seemed just a year previously.

De Valera and his supporters, however, refused to let matters rest. Although his forces joined with those from the newly established Irish Free State to fight on behalf of Catholics in Ulster (who were at that time being subjected to repeated attacks from militant Protestants) they turned on each other South of the Border.[24] Although the ensuing civil war was ostensibly about the symbolism of the oath, it soon became exacerbated by local grievances. Many of De Valera's supporters were among the more depressed and marginalised rural tenants and farmers, particularly in the South and West. As with every previous Irish struggle, this meant that the war also served as a cover for further cattle drives and land seizures, largely organised by anti-Treatyites. Gaelic institutions such as the GAA sought vainly to act as a mediator between the two sides but failed to reach an acceptable compromise.

Despite this, the outcome of the struggle was never really in doubt. Within six weeks the new government managed to secure the towns, overcoming a group of IRA members who had occupied the Four Courts in Dublin, and executing the leaders. After that the rebels were largely restricted to rural bases while the fledgling government, boosting the total number of security forces to a hefty 55 000, took firm control of the country.[25] Crucially, there was little public sympathy for De Valera's stand. Even after the provisional government used draconian measures against rebels, including mass arrests and further summary executions, there was no outcry comparable to the one that followed in the wake of 1916. As the Afrikaner rebels had found in South Africa in 1914, it was much more difficult to sustain public outrage against heavy-handed military action when the perpetrators were not the British but fellow countrymen in an elected government.

A large part of the Free State's authority derived from the strength of the state apparatus and the capability of its leadership. By choosing not to dismiss most civil servants (many of whom were already Sinn Fein supporters) the new government was able to maintain important continuity. [26] In addition it kept on, and praised, the incumbent police officers, thereby ensuring support from the existing security forces. Sinn Fein's broader organisational structure allowed it to start using the state to deliver on promises of material support to its constituents – especially those individuals who had been directly involved in the broader nationalist movement. Because the state bureaucracy was already relatively well developed (not unlike the institutions Hertzog had available for intervening on behalf of white labour during the Pact government of the 1920s in South Africa), the government was able to exert considerable, interventionist control over the country. This included the institutionalisation of patronage, particularly at the local and regional levels.[27] As one pro-Treaty leader later recalled: 'It is a historical fact that most of those who voted for the Treaty were rewarded in some material way and there was an unseemly rise of friends and relatives for a share in the plums of office.'[28]

The new government also took economic policy seriously. In his book *Path to Freedom*, published in 1922, Collins drew up a detailed blueprint for how to husband and manage the country's resources. Although most of these plans would never be carried out, they served to placate the labour movement whose propensity to strike had contributed to the anti-British struggle of the 1919–21 period and whose growing influence had been demonstrated by Labour's electoral success. Even more important, the Church overwhelmingly lent its support to the new government, going so far as to excommunicate the republican rebels. Although he held out for two years and scored some notable successes (most strikingly the death of his chief rival Collins in an ambush), De Valera was ultimately forced to acknowledge that he had no chance of victory. In April 1923, with over 10 000 of his followers in jail (and he himself having been briefly imprisoned) he called a unilateral ceasefire. While he claimed his decision was a voluntary move made to save Irish lives, in practice, the republicans ended the war for military reasons. They had found it increasingly difficult to sustain the guerrilla campaign without public support and, given the Free State's growing resilience and institutional strength, increasingly pointless.

At the same time, despite attempts by Griffith to work out a constitutional compromise, the separation between North and South became institutionalised. By the time of the Border Commission of 1924, the division of Ireland was an uncomfortable fact. De Valera, continued to charge that the Free State lacked legitimacy because of what he called 'an oath of allegiance to a foreign power acquiesced in by the majority under the duress of an external threat of war'.[29] But only a minority agreed with him. The Irish Free State was a Catholic-dominated, independent state with full domestic sovereignty and growing international assertiveness. It supported the Catholic Church and made Gaelic and religious instruction compulsory in schools. At the same time, the state and economy were already being used for ethnic patronage, directly rewarding many of the leaders of the struggle. An exclusivist, ethno-nationalist government now ruled an independent, Catholic Irish state.

Conclusions

International events, most notably the First World War, had a major effect on the course of Irish nationalist politics and contributed to Sinn Fein's new popular support. Nevertheless, the key to the nationalist movement's success in founding, and consolidating, an independent Irish state in 1922 lay primarily in its political and diplomatic strategies. These comprised a simultaneous initiative to put international pressure on Great Britain while trying to destabilise the local administration. The first part of the strategy met with limited success. Although De Valera received warm wishes of support from major political figures in the United States, these failed to translate into American backing at the Paris Peace talks in 1919. Nevertheless, the United States government remained broadly sympathetic to Ireland and strongly opposed the British crack-down during the conflict of 1919–21.

Ultimately, however, it was the process of domestic state-making – partly underwritten by America's large Irish Catholic community – that proved crucial in undermining British rule. The success of the first Dail in establishing a quasi-government with its own ministries, courts, sources of revenue and an army marked the real turning point.

Without this institutional foundation, the emotional fervour generated in the 1916–18 period would almost certainly have petered out, or at least become sufficiently diluted that tough British tactics might have proved successful in snuffing out resistance. In practice, while the proto-state established by the Dail may not have been particularly cohesive, it did prove strong enough to sustain itself during the conflict.

In large part this was because it had been able to build on the organisational foundations established by the ethnic nationalist movement over the preceding 30 years. Just as important was the transfer of legitimacy to the Dail. This was not just a question of a short-term shift in political allegiances. The central ideological claim of Irish nationalism was that the only legitimate state was one with full domestic and international sovereignty. In the wake of the Rebellion and the War this belief started to gain increasing currency. By the time of the guerrilla campaign against British rule it was firmly entrenched in the popular consciousness. The repressive tactics adopted by the government, including martial law and mass arrests, together with the vicious tactics used by the Black-and-Tans to suppress unrest, all helped persuade the public of the illegitimacy of British rule.

Significantly, this shift in popular attitudes applied only to domestic sovereignty. While the public had now overwhelmingly endorsed the nationalist call for an internationally recognised Irish state rather than Home Rule, it did not matter particularly to most people exactly what constitutional form that state took. As a result, when the Treaty, with its non-recognition of the republic, was presented to the public, it was overwhelmingly endorsed. Thereafter the pro-Treaty faction which as the first government of the Free State had full access to and control over the various institutions of state, used this powerful bureaucratic base for their operations in the ensuing civil war. This gave it institutional and financial resources, that De Valera and the anti-Treatyites could not match.

Harnessing the civil service, the economy and the party apparatus, the Irish Free State was able to seize control of the country and force the anti-Treaty forces to fight a rural, guerrilla war in which they had no hope of military victory. With an Irish government in charge and an Irish war hero, Michael Collins, commanding the Free State forces there was little chance that the new government's harsh reaction would engender popular sympathy for the rebels. Indeed, when the new prime minister, William Cosgrave, used Collins's assassination as a pretext for taking even more draconian steps, including more executions, the public readily acquiesced. The republic was important, but it could wait. For the moment it was enough that Irish nationalists had succeeded in establishing an internationally recognised state of their own.

It is important to recognise, however, that this process was only made possible by a dramatic change in the formal political structure of Ireland. For all the nationalist chest-thumping on the Ulster issue, in practice it was only the self-government of the six counties accorded by the 1920 act, which allowed for Unionist exclusion from the negotiations of 1921–22, that created the necessary preconditions for a final deal to be struck. As had been clearly demonstrated before the war, Carson and the Unionists were not prepared to consider any deal, however carefully worded, that separated the province from Great Britain and put it under Irish administration. Although officially none of the nationalist leaders were prepared to countenance this, in practice after 1920 it became a *de facto* reality. The fact that even De Valera chose to fight the civil war over the issue of the constitutional oath, not partition, bears this out.[30] Although no nationalist leader would ever be prepared to admit it publicly, partition was a godsend to the fledgling Irish Free State, which would never have been capable of controlling both radical Protestants and IRA dissenters simultaneously.

SOUTH AFRICA

For Afrikaners, who could claim to have lived in independent states from the mid-nineteenth century onwards, the issue of sovereignty was always very important. This section shows how from the formation of the National Party in 1914 onwards, the issue of South Africa's constitutional status was always a central part of the nationalist platform. It suggests that the resonance of the issue amongst Afrikaner leaders pre-dated the formation of the ethno-nationalist movement but became closely intertwined with it from the early 1920s. By arguing that only a republic could be completely free from British interference and thus guarantee the political, cultural and ethnic rights of Afrikaners, nationalists sought to give an international dimension to their wide-ranging claims about the ethnic security that would result from a nationalist takeover of the state. This overarching vision provided a critical link in the ideological framework that connected the broad organisational infrastructure that had been put in place by Afrikaner nationalists by the end of the Second World War. Three years later, in 1948, it was to help propel the movement to power.

The section begins by assessing the importance of international politics to the rise of the nationalist movement. It argues that geopolitical factors had an important effect on its broader fortunes, but that direct diplomatic and political pressures were not particularly significant. It then examines the question of South Africa's constitutional status and shows that this issue, while esoteric, was of critical importance to the development of the nationalist movement throughout its history. Finally it examines how the National Party was able to unite the great majority of Afrikaners behind an exclusivist ethno-national doctrine to win the 1948 election.

Geopolitics and International Alliances

As Chapter 4 argued, the process of mobilising Afrikaners under the nationalist banner would have proved far less successful had it not been for the intervention of extraneous international events. The First World War, especially in the wake of the government suppression of the Rebellion, led to a groundswell of popular dissatisfaction with the Botha government among Afrikaners, leaving many more receptive to Hertzog's arguments in favour of the official recognition of Afrikaans linguistic and cultural identity. Similarly, the Great Depression helped push Hertzog into formal alliance with Smuts in the United Party, indirectly precipitating the establishment of Malan's Purified National Party. Most important of all, the Second World War broke that alliance apart and unleashed a powerful emotional backlash against the British, and by extension the Smuts government, that pushed many Afrikaners into the ethnic nationalist camp.

But while the international environment might have had an enormous impact on Afrikaner nationalists, the movement had relatively few direct dealings with groups or countries outside South Africa. During the First World War the leaders of the 1914 Rebellion sought help from Germany, but little was forthcoming. In any case, German troops in South West Africa and East Africa were soon defeated by the South African army under Smuts. Afterwards, like Sinn Fein, the National Party sent a 'freedom deputation' led by Hertzog and Malan, to the Peace Conference to plead the Afrikaner cause. There they argued vigorously for the 'rights of small nations' and demanded, rather half-heartedly, the restoration of the old Boer republics. 'Unless our status is recognised by foreign nations we simply do not exist as a nation', Hertzog admitted.[31] However with Smuts himself one of the main players at Versailles, the delegation failed even to receive a proper hearing from the Great Powers.

During the Second World War this process was repeated with much the same result. The OB and various pro-Nazi groups tried to solicit direct aid from Germany for use in destabilisation and sabotage activities, but with little success. Some radical right-wingers made elaborate plans for a full-scale revolt, involving the assassination of leading political figures and a military coup with German assistance, but the plot never got off the ground. The conspirators were soon uncovered and arrested by Smuts's sophisticated military intelligence operations. Unlike the Irish, moreover, the Afrikaners had no domestic lobbying groups of expatriates in international metropoles (indeed anywhere else in the world), so there was little scope for nationalists either to raise funds or mount political campaigns abroad.

Constitutional Debates

Virtually the only issue that caused Afrikaner nationalists to pay regular attention to the international sphere was the ongoing debate over the enormously emotive issue of South Africa's constitutional relationship with Britain. As in Ireland, intense argument over the issue of independence and what exactly it might comprise long pre-dated the formation of an expressly ethno-nationalist movement. As far back as the mid-nineteenth century, the British had granted the trekker states of the Transvaal and Orange Free State a degree of political freedom that would have been unthinkable in contemporary Ireland.[32] When, in 1910, the new Union of South Africa was given full domestic autonomy but made subordinate to the Crown, and thus the British government, on all matters of war and peace, this proved a highly divisive issue.[33] Even though Botha was able to wangle some concessions, such as the right to found an army in 1911, remaining in a tightly bound constitutional arrangement with an imperial power against whom they had fought a bitter war was unacceptable to many Afrikaners. The Rebellion in 1914 was launched over the issue of South Africa participating in a 'British' war, not cultural, religious or economic questions. Accordingly, from the time of the National Party's inception, Hertzog made republicanism a central tenet of his political platform.

Smuts too was well aware of these tensions and was a major proponent of increasing the autonomy of the Dominions. During the

Imperial Conferences of 1917 and 1921 (both very much influenced by the contemporaneous Irish struggle) he proposed a motion seeking 'the practical recognition of the equality of the statehood of the Dominions with the United Kingdom'. This required scrapping the Colonial Laws Validity Act of 1865, which gave Britain power to strike down domestic legislation in any of the Dominions. However, in the face of opposition from the more imperialist Australians and New Zealanders, the proposals were rejected. This in turn allowed Hertzog to make substantial political capital by calling for a republic ahead of the 1924 elections. Once in power, however, Hertzog took a more pragmatic view. He demanded the right to secession but freely admitted that to take advantage of such a right would in practice be 'a flagrant mistake and a national disaster'.[34] On this basis, at the 1926 Imperial conference he vigorously asserted South Africa's right to full international sovereignty *within* the Commonwealth. Strongly supported by the representative from the newly formed Irish Free State, Kevin O'Higgins, he forced the other dominions and the British government to accept what became known as the Balfour Declaration, granting a significant increase in Dominion autonomy.[35]

It took a protracted two-year battle to push the measure through the South African parliament. The debate was particularly sensitive for English-speaking whites because it coincided with Malan's proposals for a new flag and Afrikaans national anthem. But, against the advice of more radical nationalists, Hertzog proved willing to accept a similar compromise on both issues. South Africa would exercise its political autonomy within the Commonwealth, fly both the new South African flag and the Union Jack at state occasions, and sing both anthems. Shortly afterwards, the government embarked on its own foreign policy, sending ambassadors and trade commissioners abroad for the first time, and playing a more active part at the League of Nations. Hertzog acknowledged that accepting this was a retreat from his long-held republican agenda, but emphasised the practical utility of the deal he had struck. At one stage he suggested that it actually permitted South Africa a degree of freedom greater than that enjoyed by the old Boer republics.[36]

Five years later, in 1931, again at Hertzog's urging, the essence of the Balfour Declaration was formally recognised by the British parliament in the Statute of Westminster.[37] This declaration effectively recognised South Africa (and the other dominions, including Ireland) as a fully independent country with the right to make its own laws and conduct its own foreign policy. It thus cleared away the main political obstacle standing in the way of reconciliation between Smuts and Hertzog. As such it was a major contributing factor in allowing for the formation of the United Party. In 1934, the passage of the Status and Seals Act in Westminster confirmed the divisibility of the crown and hence South Africa's status as a 'sovereign independent state', an interpretation that was finally approved by the Privy Council in London in 1935.

Republicanism and Ethnic Nationalism

Even if Hertzog's National Party had stopped short of insisting on the establishment of a republic, it succeeded in establishing the link between issues of political and cultural nationalism and the question of international sovereignty. And while Hertzog himself may have been satisfied with these compromises, many other Afrikaners were not. It was the apparent rejection of republicanism by the National Party rather than any cultural or religious issue that prompted the Broederbond to make its fateful decision to take an active part in contemporary politics in 1927. Like De Valera's pro-Treatyites, for many in the Broederbond, the republican ideal had both a physical and mystical dimension. Its members felt an Afrikaner state would simultaneously cater for the practical demands of political independence and the spiritual needs of the Afrikaner people. As Broederbond chairman L. J. du Plessis noted in 1932:

> [n]ational culture and national welfare cannot unfold fully if the people of South Africa do not also constitutionally sever all foreign ties. After the cultural and economic needs, the Afrikaner will have to devote his attention to the constitutional needs of our people. Added to that objective must be an entirely independent genuine, Afrikaans form of government for South Africa ... a form of government which through its embodiment in our own personal head of state, bone of our bone, and flesh of our flesh, will inspire us to irresistible unity and strength.[38]

Although the radical wing of the National Party couched it in less strident terms, the issue of a republic was also fundamental to Malan and his supporters (and had been actively promoted within the party by the Broederbond's sponsorship of a republican faction). After Hertzog sought rapprochement with Smuts in 1933, Malan, who already felt uneasy about the Statute of Westminster, made the establishment of a South African republic under Afrikaner control one of the fundamental tenets of the GNP. As in Ireland in 1921, the prag-matic acceptance of a political compromise short of full-blown repub-licanism had prompted a radical breakaway spearheaded by a small group of more committed ethnic nationalists. Unlike in Ireland, how-ever, the existing government of moderates was not also exclusivist, patronage-oriented and committed to the primacy of ethnic language and culture. This key fact gave Malan and the Broederbond the political space to embark on their programme of cultural and eco-nomic mobilisation.

Despite this, throughout the 1930s republicanism remained a relat-ively minor issue. Nearly all English speakers and a large majority of Afrikaners appeared satisfied with the constitutional relationship under the Statute of Westminster and might have remained so were it not for the onset of the Second World War. Hertzog's proudest achievement was that the statute allowed South Africa to particip-ate in British wars. On this basis, in 1938 he got the cabinet, including Smuts, to agree to South Africa's neutrality in the event of war in Europe. Once conflict broke out a year later, however, this consensus was shattered. While Smuts acknowledged South Africa's constitu-tional right not to participate in the conflict, he argued that the country had a moral and political obligation to do so anyway. This conviction split the cabinet and then parliament, giving the impetus for the reuniting of Afrikanerdom.

In the early part of the war, the nationalist movement's republican-ism became even more unabashed. The small fascist movements and the far more significant OB, were all fervently republican, seeking a non-democratic, quasi-fascist state.[39] Inspired by German war suc-cesses, these groups reflected a growing feeling among Afrikaners that it was time to cut all ties with the British empire, however cleverly worded the existing constitutional compromise. Responding to this changing mood, Malan and the NP were forced to make increasingly explicit statements on the issue. In early 1942 the NP formally pub-lished a draft republican constitution for South Africa. It called for the severing of all ties with Britain, the elevation of Afrikaans to the status of 'first official language' and the reintroduction of the old Transvaal flag.[40]

In keeping with the times, it was also infused with the *führerprinzip*, and made provision for a very powerful leader. Replete with noble sounding declarations about support for God and the sanctity of the nation, the document proved a powerful rallying cry. Malan now called for a republic 'free and independent from any foreign power ... [and]

Christian National in deed and character', (prompting the Anglophone press to call him a 'negative and evil influence', on South African politics).[41] Nevertheless, coinciding as it did with the start of Hitler's military setbacks, the constitution itself never became a central element of the NP's political campaign. Given his personal distaste for violence and his commitment to organisational (rather than charismatic, leader-based) mobilisation, Malan was prepared to let the issue drop and the document was not brought up again.[42] Nevertheless, the republic question now was thrust firmly into the mainstream of political debate.

While it reaffirmed its commitment to (restricted) democracy, the National Party continued to insist that the republic issue was one of 'deep conviction'.[43] Not unlike the shift during the First World War in Ireland, where most people favoured limited Home Rule in 1914 but were no longer prepared to do so in 1918, the bulk of the Afrikaner population who had previously supported Smuts and Hertzog and the Statute of Westminster were now more receptive to the idea of an ethnically controlled domestic state that would be an internationally recognised republic. Republicanism was also closely linked to the notion of securing cultural and economic security. As Malan freely acknowledged, the Second World War had served as the critical catalyst 'to bring Afrikanerdom back on course'.[44] Now his task was, in conjunction with the Broederbond and its myriad organisations, to lead his people to their ultimate goal: control of the state.

Consolidation and Victory

Although the broader movement had been hampered by *broedertwis*, the Bond itself had gained increasing power and influence during the war. In 1943, Verwoerd charged members to

> help each other to become members of school committees, of village committees, town and city councils, in short the Afrikaner Broederbond must gain control over everything it can lay its hands on in every walk of life in South Africa, and must not refrain from putting its members into any key position whatsoever.[45]

By this time, Smuts was openly criticising the Broederbond, branding it 'dangerous'.[46] Through Military Intelligence activities during the war he also now had a list of Broederbond members which he could have used to suppress the organisation. However, he chose not to do so apparently because he feared damage to the DRC in light of the numbers of Churchmen who were members. Instead, he took a middle road, ordering all civil servants who were part of the Broederbond to resign either from the organisation or from government. In consequence 1090 bureaucrats, many of them quite senior, left the Broederbond (870 of whom rejoined after the 1948 election victory).[47] But Smuts's action served to inspire rather than deflate the organisation. It published a relatively mild set of principles to allay public fears and, because Smuts did not make full disclosure of Broederbond activities, the general perception was that he had overreacted.

Although it had lost some of its base within the state the Broederbond was in fact stronger than ever. It now loosely controlled nationalist organisations working on every major front to mobilise Afrikaners behind the nationalist banner. The one outstanding obstacle was political: despite the OB's collapse, many of its supporters were unwilling to vote for the National Party given the antipathy that had prevailed between the two groupings during the war. Accordingly, the Broederbond devised a plan under which OB supporters would vote for the old Hertzogite Afrikaner Party. Then, in 1947, again at the behest of the Broederbond, which now had members prominent in the leadership of both parties, the HNP and the AP announced an election pact. This gave Afrikaners the unified political front they had lacked in 1943.

The Broederbond, having provided the foundation for the re-establishment of unity among the Afrikaner volk, now operated in the manner Nico Diedrichs, a high-ranking member, had proposed in 1940:

> In a certain sense the Afrikaner Broederbond must be the axle around which turn different aspects of the volk; or rather the authority that stands above them with a view to a unity of direction and action.[48]

The ethnic mobilisation process spearheaded by the Bond had produced a dynamic, wide-ranging alliance of organisations all presaged on the notion of exclusive Afrikaner control of the state. Now 2500 members strong, most entrenched in senior posts in political, economic, educational and religious spheres, the Broederbond was preparing to lead the nationalist bureaucracy it had so painstakingly built up over the previous 20 years in a new assault on the state.

The notion of replacing the existing bureaucracy with one more supportive of Afrikaner interests was an important part of the NP's 1948 campaign. The party promised openly to 'purify our State and public services of Communists and Communist influence'[49] – a thinly veiled attack on the remaining English-speaking bureaucracy that played on the Smuts government's support of Stalin during the war. At the same time, the development of the apartheid ideology had helped bolster the legitimacy of the nationalist movement in the eyes of Afrikaner workers while simultaneously attracting the support of many Transvaal farmers who had previously been steadfast UP supporters. Meanwhile the government was acting complacently. Smuts himself, as the elder statesman in international peace councils, was much in demand abroad and spent large periods of time outside South Africa. This lessened his profile among domestic constituents who felt increasingly neglected.

Also, for the first time, South Africa was coming under substantial criticism overseas for its racial policies (much, ironically, directed from the new United Nations that Smuts had helped establish).[50] This uncomfortable fact had already contributed to Smuts's partial liberalisation of black labour restrictions, but was in practice helping to engender a more defensive and defiant attitude amongst most whites, especially Afrikaners. The NP whipped up fear of the impending *swartgevaar* and *oorstroming* (black danger and flooding of the cities by blacks) thus helping to build support for the new apartheid doctrine. To reassure marginal voters who were broadly supportive of the nationalist and racial elements of the platform but uncertain about the wisdom of a republic, Malan became publicly cautious about exactly how and when the republic might be achieved. In addition, the National Party fought a powerful conventional election campaign. In contrast to the UP's ungainly system of provincial and regional councils operating with volunteer workers, the NP relied on a small steering committee, employed paid political organisers and used an excellent cell system to mobilise support on the grassroots level. It also used the substantial resources of the broader nationalist movement, from churches to unions to cultural groups and ruthlessly exploited bread and butter issues such as a white housing shortage, rising food prices and the shortage of jobs for over 220 000 demobilised soldiers.

Every broadly nationalist organisation across business, labour, the arts, the universities and the Church was now mobilised behind the cause of Afrikaner nationalism and helped promote the concept of an Afrikaner-dominated state in a context where nearly all Afrikaners now consciously identified themselves as part of the same, discrete nation. Although even the NP itself did not anticipate victory yet, the movement was confident that it would consolidate its position.[51] But in the resulting general election the HNP/AP alliance narrowly defeated the UP by 79 seats to 74, garnering over 80 per cent of all Afrikaner votes cast – powerful testament to the importance of nationalist appeals in gaining the allegiance of the Afrikaner electorate.[52] The UP lost all 15 of its rural seats in the Transvaal – clear evidence of the importance of the apartheid doctrine in gaining agricultural support. In addition, the National Party's victory in six working-class mining constituencies was an indication of how the nationalist movement and the apartheid doctrine had successfully worked together in getting the political support of blue-collar workers. For marginal voters such as these, apartheid and promises of state patronage were far more important than the republic. Although the Nationalist establishment dutifully attributed the victory to divine blessing, in practice the widespread, bureaucratic mobilisation orchestrated by the multifaceted Afrikaner nationalist movement had achieved its goal of control over the South African state. Smuts's comment after the election (in which he lost his own seat in Parliament) was particularly revealing: 'To think that I have been beaten by Broederbond.'[53]

Conclusions

Exogenous geopolitical and economic influences – notably the two world wars and the Great Depression – had an enormous impact on the development of Afrikaner nationalism. All three of those events brought the emotive issue of South Africa's constitutional independence to the fore and precipitated major upheavals in the nationalist movement. Most important was the Second World War which provided the catalyst for the political re-establishment of a united nationalist front – at least once the dust had settled from the volatile *broedertwis* clashes of the war years. Despite this, an international diplomatic effort of the type pursued by the Irish was impossible, largely because of the Afrikaners' lack of political leverage in any country other than South Africa. Attempts to solicit help from Germany during both World Wars came to little.

More important, it was unnecessary. Although some Afrikaners still occasionally suggested re-establishing the old Boer republics, in practice the nationalist struggle was always about control of the existing South African state. As South Africa already enjoyed international recognition there was no real need for Afrikaner nationalists, like the Irish, to seek support from foreign allies. Nevertheless, both conflicts served to refocus attention on the one area in which the country's independence was curtailed: its international status and obligations within the Commonwealth. The nature of its constitutional links to Great Britain were a source of intense political debate from the time of Union onwards. The progress of this debate had an enormous impact on nationalist politics. Hertzog's acceptance of the Statute of Westminster proved to be his long-term undoing, although both the Broederbond and Malan's GNP were initially unable to make significant political capital out of the issue. With the advent of the Second World War, and Smuts's rejection of neutrality, this changed radically.

But while geopolitical events and the debate over the republic created the opportunity for Afrikaner nationalism to develop, it was the organisational and ideological foundations established during the 1930s and 1940s that gave the Broederbond/NP alliance the wherewithal to mount a victorious campaign for state power. Ultimately the election victory of 1948 was neither a simplistic triumph for white racism, as liberal historians suggest, nor a victory for Afrikaner capital in alliance with the mines, as some Marxists propose, nor a triumph of nationalist ideology, although all were important factors. Rather the final electoral triumph owed more to the movement's superb organisational capacity and adept political campaigning using all three of these issues overlaid with a promise of ethnic patronage of the type that had been successfully employed in the economic movement. In the immediate context of 1948, this victory was by no means inevitable. In the medium term, however, had the NP lost in 1948 it would almost certainly have won in 1953. With its wide-ranging organisations in cultural, political and economic spheres combined with nationalist ideology and apartheid, the Afrikaner nationalist movement had created a political juggernaut that claimed the overwhelming allegiance of the Afrikaner population. A fundamental shift in Afrikaner perceptions of what constituted a legitimate state had taken place and, as long as an all-white franchise persisted, so would Afrikaner control of the South African state.

ZIONISM

For the Zionists, international diplomacy was never just an adjunct to the nationalist enterprise. With no domestic foothold to speak of in Palestine, international backing was a prerequisite – hence the long diplomatic campaign for support in the Ottoman Empire, Russia, Germany, and then, more fruitfully, the United States and Great Britain, leading to the Balfour Declaration. Even after the *Yishuv* was established, this diplomatic activity continued in conjunction with domestic state-making. This section argues that the final establishment of the state of Israel was the result of a sustained domestic and international campaign to secure internal and international legitimacy. By the end of the war the *Yishuv* was strong enough to mount a sustained internal struggle against the British presence and continued restrictions on immigration. Taking advantage of a newly politicised Jewish population in the United States in the wake of the Holocaust, the Zionists were able to shift their base of international support across the Atlantic. That allowed Zionist diplomacy to secure international recognition for the new nation-state of Israel in 1948 while using its strong domestic institutions to withstand the Arab military attack that followed.

The section opens with a brief review of geopolitical influences on the Zionist movement before examining Palestine's international status as a Jewish homeland. It then turns to Zionist strategies during the Second World War, focusing in particular on the movement's activities in America. It follows this by discussing the Zionist campaign against the British presence in Palestine at the end of the war. It details how the movement was able to exert sufficient domestic and international pressure to force British withdrawal and the means by which Zionist campaigns were able to secure the passage of a United Nations resolution recognising the right of a Jewish state to independence. In conclusion, it discusses how the Zionist movement managed to withstand the violent Arab onslaught immediately before and after the declaration of the state of Israel.

Geopolitics and the National Home

Extraneous international events had a critical effect on the Zionist movement throughout its history. As Herzl and Weizmann's fruitless diplomatic manoeuvrings prior to the First World War had illustrated, until the Zionists could persuade one or more existing powers of the benefits of their cause, no real progress was possible. The Balfour Declaration would not have happened had the Ottoman empire not started to implode during the First World War, leading to a temporary congruence between British strategic interests and Zionist goals for a new post-war order. The diversion of Jewish immigrants to Palestine in the 1920s was only made possible by the United States' decision to restrict new immigration in 1924. Even more important, the huge influx of German Jews during the 1930s was a direct consequence of the Nazis coming to power in Germany. Finally, the build-up to the Second World War saw British strategic priorities shift to favour conciliation of Arabs rather than Jews, severing the political alliance between the British Empire and Zionism but inadvertently leading directly to the economic and military consolidation of the *Yishuv*.

Part of the difficulty came from the fact that the Balfour Declaration had been deliberately ambiguous as to what type of polity the Jewish community in Palestine would be. The reference to 'national home' rather than state was, as it had been in the Basle Programme, a deliberately vague phrase, designed to suggest that Jewish aspirations posed no threat to the local Palestinian community or their British patrons. In the context of the First World War, however, the word 'national' had clear implications of independent government, and was assumed to mean as much by both the Zionists themselves and the newspapers of the day. As Max Nordau, a prominent Zionist writer, observed a few years later, 'It was equivocal but we all understood what it meant . . . it signified *Judenstaat* . . .'.[54]

In seeking to justify their claims to Palestine at the Versailles peace negotiations, the Zionists managed to utilise the principle of self-determination more adeptly than either the Irish or Afrikaners (in part because they had secured the support rather than the enmity of the British). The demand for a Jewish national home, however, ran foul of granting the same right of self-determination to the Palestinians and the broader Arab community in the same territory. Weizmann made a cautious but well-received submission to the American delegation at Versailles arguing that

> [t]he Zionist Organisation did not want an autonomous Jewish government but merely to establish in Palestine, under a mandatory power, an administration, not necessarily Jewish, which would render it possible to send to Palestine 70–80,000 Jews annually. The Zionist Association would require to have permission at the same time to build Jewish schools, where Hebrew would be taught and in that way to build up gradually a nationality which would be as Jewish as the French nation is French and the British Nation British. Later on, when the Jews formed the large majority they would be ripe to establish such a Government as would answer to the state of the development of the country and to their ideals.[55]

This laid the foundations for the official Zionist policy of claiming that seeking a Jewish state did not involve denying a similar right to the Palestinians because they did not constitute a nation.

In August 1920 the San Remo Treaty endorsed the establishment of a Jewish homeland in Palestine. This was acknowledged in the Treaty of Sèvres with Turkey a year later and finally confirmed by the League of Nations. The basic tenets of the Balfour Declaration were firmly ensconced in Article 2 of the resulting mandatory provisions:

> The mandate shall be responsible for placing the country under such political, administrative and economic conditions as will serve the establishment of a Jewish national home ... and the development of self-governing institutions.[56]

The Mandate did, however, have an important qualification with regard to the Palestinian community. In Article 6 it called for the 'facilitation of Jewish immigration' only insofar as 'the rights and position of other sections of the population are not prejudiced'.[57] Nevertheless, despite the opposition of Cabinet members such as the new Foreign Secretary, Lord Curzon, as well as many of the Foreign Office staff, who retained strongly pro-Arab sympathies, general recognition of Jewish rights to Palestine had been achieved. The Mandate even referred explicitly to the Jews' 'historical connection' with the territory, legitimising the Zionist presence there.

Nevertheless, given the diplomatic and practical uncertainties surrounding the Zionist enterprise the movement always focused on creating the capacity for such an independent state without ever explicitly endorsing its establishment. This allowed the *Yishuv* to continue immigration and exploit the growing legislative and administrative freedoms permitted by the British administration. Up to 1939, in public statements Zionists declined to call for a Jewish state for fear of alienating the British or increasing the already considerable hostility from the Arabs. During the Second World War, however, an incremental programme of state-building would no longer suffice. Geopolitical pressures meant that Britain could no longer be counted on as a benevolent protector. As Malcolm MacDonald, the Colonial Secretary, noted, for Britain it was now 'out of the question that we should antagonise either the Muslims within the Empire or the Arab kingdoms of the Near East'.[58] In response, the Zionist leadership turned its attention across the Atlantic, to the United States.

Diplomacy in America

Lobbying in America was nothing new for the Zionists. Under the leadership of Supreme Court Justice Louis Brandeis, the WZO had been very active in drumming up support for Zionist claims during the First World War (at exactly the time that the Irish nationalists in the United States were doing the same). Special resolutions endorsing Zionism were passed in Congress by overwhelming majorities and President Wilson gave his blessing to the enterprise.[59] In the wake of the Versailles Peace Conference, however, the influence of American Jewry in the Zionist movement receded, except as a source of funds.[60] Indeed, Weizmann's new prominence led to the effective exclusion of Brandeis and much of the American wing. Over the next 20 years the centres of Zionist power were Poland, other European countries and, increasingly, the *Yishuv* itself.

Following the withdrawal of British support for the Zionists in 1939, Weizmann's influence, linked as it was to Britain, began to decline. Ben Gurion, however, seized the opportunity to change the WZO's diplomatic focus. As he later stated:

> I was convinced that the main arena for our efforts – outside Palestine – was not Britain but America. Aside from the *Yishuv* itself we had no more effective tool at our disposal than the American Jewish community and the Zionist movement.[61]

Although Zionism had made only small inroads in the large American Jewish community before the late 1930s, given increasing concern about the Nazi persecution of European Jewry, the movement was able substantially to expand its membership there. As in the case of the Irish campaign in the aftermath of the First World War, a plethora of different domestic Jewish organisations started to mobilise on behalf of the Zionist cause. These efforts met with considerable success, and even gained substantial support from non-Jews who sympathised with the Jewish plight. In 1939 the American Zionist Emergency Council was formed to coordinate this new diplomatic offensive.

Under Ben Gurion's guidance, in 1942 the Emergency Council organised a special Zionist conference at the Biltmore Hotel in New York. It was the first such conference to be held outside Europe. There, the Zionist movement made its first public endorsement of a Jewish state, as opposed to a national home, passing a resolution demanding that:

> the gates of Palestine be opened; that the Jewish Agency be vested with control of immigration ... and that Palestine be established as a Jewish commonwealth integrated into the structure of the democratic world.[62]

The Biltmore declaration marked a final break with the cautious diplomacy of the past. Weizmann, however, was incensed by Ben Gurion's increasing dominance of the Zionist movement, dismissing his rival as a 'petty dictator'. At the same time, some left-wingers, accusing Ben Gurion of deserting his socialist roots, formed a new, radical faction within the WZO. Both sources of opposition, however, were largely ineffectual. *Mapai* controlled the *Yishuv*, and Ben Gurion himself, with his American allies, now also dominated the WZO.

In the context of the Holocaust, the Zionist struggle for a fully constituted Jewish state took on unprecedented urgency. Following the meeting, Weizmann, who remained a much more persuasive diplomat than the abrasive Ben Gurion sought President Roosevelt's endorsement. The President, however, who already enjoyed the political support of the vast majority of American Jews, gave only a qualified approval to the endeavour.[63] Nevertheless, by 1944, the country's major trade union federations and both the Democratic and Republican parties openly supported the creation of a Jewish state in Palestine. The Emergency Council even managed to sign up 67 Senators and 143 Representatives on the American Palestine Committee, a body actively lobbying for Zionist goals.[64] Armed with this support, as the war drew to a close the Zionists readied for a new drive for independence.

The conflict had, however, fundamentally altered the context within which the Zionist movement operated. By killing six million Jews, the Nazis had effectively removed the original *raison d'être* of Zionism as a homeland for the persecuted Jews of Europe. At the same time, however, the Holocaust kindled an ethnic spark among Jews worldwide that became manifest in unprecedented support for Zionism – it had generated an emotional reaction similar to that among Irish and Afrikaners over participation in a 'British' war. The vast majority of Jews now agreed on the need to establish a Jewish state with the capability to defend itself against any external enemies.

By the 1946 WZO elections, despite the murder of over a third of world Jewry, membership reached a record high of two million, over 40 per cent of which was now American.[65] Unlike previous East European Zionists, however, the vast majority of American Jews had no intention of ever emigrating to Israel. As such they were not truly nationalists, in the sense that their highest political loyalties were not necessarily to the Jewish nation. As with the Irish expatriates who worked for the cause of Irish nationalism, their sympathies arose from a more generalised sense of ethnic solidarity, or what Anthony

Smith has described as 'vicarious nationalism'.[66] This was an important qualitative difference between Zionists in Palestine and those outside. The ethnic identity of the former group had been largely reshaped by the nation-building activities of the proto-state and national conflict with the Arabs, influences which Jews elsewhere could not share. The result was the creation of a specifically Palestinian-Jewish, or Israeli, nationalism, rather than simply a Jewish one. While the links between the two communities remained very strong, American and Palestinian Jews had a different sense of what Zionism meant in terms of their own loyalties and aims. American Jewry became a critical political and financial resource for the *Yishuv*, but not a major source of new immigrants.

Campaigns in Palestine

By 1945 the Zionists controlled a powerful set of institutions that increasingly resembled a fully functioning state apparatus. As Arthur Koestler, who visited the country during the war, declared:

> the Jewish Agency, by force of circumstance, had developed into a shadow government, a state within the state. It controlled the Jewish economic sector of the country, it had its own hospitals and social services, it ran its own schools, its own intelligence services... and controlled its own para-military organisation....[67]

It was, moreover, a vastly more complex and wealthier proto-state than it had been six years earlier. The Agency had expanded its military, administrative, economic and social spheres of influence. Its budget had grown from £800 000 in 1939 to £6.56 million in 1945.[68] Contributions to the two main Zionist funds rose from $2m in 1938 to $15m in 1945, with almost all the increase coming from America.[69] In essence, the first part of the Jewish strategy was largely complete. There was not yet a Jewish majority in Palestine, but the institutions of statehood had been created by the Zionists and were regarded as the legitimate government by almost the entire Jewish population of Palestine. International recognition was now required to give a Jewish state international legitimacy as well.

Although Churchill, a long-time pro-Zionist, had suggested that the 1939 White Paper might be repealed and a Jewish state endorsed in early 1944, the assassination of a British envoy, Lord Moyne, in 1944 at the hands of *Irgun*, delayed implementation of this decision. This prompted the Agency to establish its good faith by cracking down on

Irgun and *Lehi* in a sustained internal campaign that became known as 'the season', mirroring the pro-Treatyite crackdown on the De Valera rebels after the formation of the Irish Free State. In July 1945, the Labour Party won the British elections. Despite an explicit pro-Zionist platform, the party reneged on its promises in favour of shoring up Arab support as Clement Attlee's new government found itself presiding over a bankrupt country in danger of losing its imperial status.

British military planners stressed the need to placate the Arab states and retain Palestine as a strategic base from which to protect the Suez canal. Accordingly, Ernest Bevin, the new foreign minister, warned that the Jews 'must not try to get to the head of the queue'. He continued to enforce immigration restrictions, despite the presence of 100 000 Holocaust survivors left waiting in concentration camps in Europe. In response, the Zionists stepped up illegal immigration and Ben Gurion declared the establishment of the 'Hebrew Resistance Movement', for the first time officially sanctioning the use of force to pursue Zionist goals. This new offensive represented the logical practical extension to the Biltmore programme's new political demands for statehood.

Although the *Haganah* tended to target only buildings or infrastructure, the Revisionist *Irgun* continued to assassinate British personnel. With each successive attack, the British grew increasingly desperate, unwilling to begin a full-scale military campaign, but equally determined not to give in to the Zionists' campaign of terror. The British Army, meanwhile, continued to promise Attlee that a military solution to Jewish terrorism was possible and in June 1946, 17 000 British troops carried out a swoop on Zionist leaders, arresting some 2700 activists.[70] Weizmann then declared a moratorium on the fighting. The *Irgun*, however, ignored his pleas and in July blew up the King David Hotel, the British military headquarters in Jerusalem, killing many soldiers.

The British responded by bringing out more and more troops, until their military presence totalled 100 000 men, 10 per cent of the entire British Army.[71] Despite such overwhelming firepower, however, they remained unable to end the uprising. The events of Ireland in 1919–21 were being replayed almost to the letter. Even if they lacked the resources to expel the British, the Zionists were now too strong to be crushed and enjoyed widespread popular support within the Jewish community which now regarded the British administration as an illegitimate, repressive regime. At the same time, the nature of their cause – demanding their right as a nation to independence – guaranteed an intensity of purpose that the weary British soldiers were unable to match. The interlocking strategies of nation- and state-building had made the Zionists powerful enough to deny anyone else control in Palestine. In the face of continued British opposition, however, they were still unable to establish a state.

International Implications

Aware that this policy of active resistance needed to be reinforced by continual diplomatic support, the Zionists were also continuing with a high-profile international campaign, particularly in America. President Harry Truman, who succeeded Roosevelt in April 1945, was both personally horrified by the Holocaust and the plight of Jewish displaced persons and aware of the need to secure the Jewish vote for the Democrats. Within days of taking office, he wrote to Bevin asking that action be taken on the Jewish refugee problem. The US State Department, however, like the British Foreign Office, was firmly against the idea of a Jewish state, fearing it would jeopardise American relations with the Arabs. Nevertheless, many members of Congress remained vocal in support of the Jews, and even threatened to delay or water down a critically needed $3.75bn loan to Britain unless policy was altered. Combined with the increasing global awareness of the Holocaust and highly publicised Zionist attempts to break the blockade, this helped increase international pressure on the British to withdraw.

Meanwhile, by 1946 all the Arab countries were fully constituted independent states. In May that year, the first Arab summit was held and all participants confirmed their unequivocal hostility to Zionism. Soon after, the Arab League was created as a forum for this opposition. Under the League's influence, the Palestinians reformed the AHC, again under the Mufti's leadership. The Arabs were, for the first time, seeking a coordinated response to the Zionist issue. With their control over critical oil supplies in the emerging context of the Cold War, moreover, their leverage with Western countries increased significantly. To retain the support of the United States, the Zionists had to prove to the Americans that their cause justified flouting obvious strategic interests.

While the Arabs were mobilising, Attlee and Truman agreed to the establishment of an Anglo-American commission of enquiry into the Palestine question. To Bevin's surprise, the commission, while hedging on the question of statehood, suggested that 100 000 Jewish refugees should be allowed to enter Palestine. Truman immediately endorsed the proposals, but the British ignored them and called for a new London conference on the issue. At this stage, the Zionists' diplomatic strategy entered a state of flux. The movement continued to need great power support from some quarter as it could not alone forcibly evict the British and withstand the Arabs. The leadership was divided on whether to place greater emphasis on relations with America, as the world's new superpower, or to try to win back Britain, the country that still controlled the Mandate.

In August 1946, at Weizmann's urging, the Agency's executive (with Ben Gurion abstaining) voted to participate in the British Conference with the Arabs.[72] As in 1939, however, both sides found little room for manoeuvre or compromise. Despite Zionist flexibility on the issue of partition, the Arabs continued to demand a Palestinian state with control over the whole country. Differences between the two sides were so entrenched that no unified solution to the Palestine problem seemed feasible. The alternatives were either partition or conquest. Aware of this, the Zionists began to lobby for the former outcome while preparing for the latter.

But while discussions with Britain were again proving futile, the American campaign was increasingly successful. Under pressure to retain the Jewish vote for the Democrats in the 1946 elections, Truman, speaking on the Jewish holy day of Yom Kippur, for the first time endorsed the creation of a Jewish state in Palestine. With this diplomatic success, and in the face of the deadlock at the London talks, Ben Gurion's focus on America was vindicated. In the WZO conference in Geneva that December he wrested full control of the Agency from Weizmann by entering into an alliance with the American Zionist leader Rabbi Abba Hillel Silver. Meanwhile, American public antipathy to the British position reached such an extent that Bevin, on visiting New York, was roundly jeered by crowds.

By the end of 1946 the situation had become untenable for the British. Despite the presence of a sizeable military force, and the large number of arrests, no end to the revolt seemed imminent. The presence of so many troops in one small territory was a terrible strain on the Treasury, draining some £40 million per year from public coffers.[73] As with Ireland in 1921, the situation was also costing the country the support of its most important post-war ally, the United States. In addition, Bevin's intransigence on the refugee issue met with condemnation in Europe, particularly in France. Within Britain itself, public opinion was shifting against staying in Palestine. The prevailing mood, as the London *Sunday Express* summarised, was 'Govern or Get

Out'.[74] In the face of such broad-based opposition, Bevin and Attlee reconsidered. As in 1921, the government was under severe pressure from insurrections elsewhere in the Empire, and the decision to pull out of India set a precedent for similar action in Palestine. In January 1947, Britain formally handed the matter over to the United Nations.

Several historians have attributed this decision to a loss of will and power in the British metropole leading to an 'imperial failure'.[75] It would be more accurate, however, to say that the Zionists forced the British out of Palestine. As before, the movement had concentrated on the twin strategies of diplomatic pressure and domestic consolidation. Internationally, the Zionists exploited the changed geopolitical situation in the Middle East by securing the support of a newly active United States and pursuing a high-profile propaganda campaign against British immigration policies. Domestically, it successfully orchestrated a resistance movement based on the resilience of the *Yishuv*, which gave the movement a solid foundation for its military operations against the British (which the Palestinians had lacked a decade earlier). The new, explicit focus on a Jewish state following Biltmore marked the logical culmination of the synthetic Zionist strategies first articulated at the turn of the century. Together, these factors led to the withdrawal of the British and set the scene for a final round of diplomacy to secure full international recognition.

The United Nations

Once the matter came under its purview, the United Nations created a Special Committee on Palestine (UNSCOP) to report on the question. Despite being boycotted by the AHC, the Commission published its findings that September. Like the Peel Commission a decade earlier, it recommended partition with Jerusalem remaining an international enclave. At the time, Jews still controlled only some 7 per cent of the land of Palestine, and even the designated Jewish state would contain 509 780 Palestinians compared to 499 020 Jews.[76] Because it brought them closer to statehood, however, the Zionists accepted the committee's decision. The Palestinians unequivocally rejected it. The proposals then went to the UN General Assembly, where they required a two-thirds majority to be enacted. The Zionists embarked on a spirited campaign for support. The main thrust was to secure official American backing by putting pressure on Truman to overrule detractors in the State Department and Pentagon who wished to placate the Arabs. The President was later moved to comment that:

not only were the pressure movements around the United Nations unlike anything that had been seen before, but that the White House, too, was subjected to a constant barrage. I do not think I ever had as much pressure and propaganda aimed at the White House as I had in this instance.[77]

Nevertheless, it had a decisive impact. Persuaded that a Jewish state would not be detrimental to American strategic interests, and with his natural sympathies and political interests inclined towards supporting Zionism, Truman threw the United States' considerable political weight behind the plan. The Americans then exerted significant pressure on a large number of countries, including China, Chile, Paraguay and Costa Rica, to support partition. In the final vote, on 29 November 1947, the plan was approved by 33 to 13. For the first time the Zionists had received unambiguous international sanction to establish an independent state. The Basle programme's avowed aim of a 'national home secured by public law' was finally a reality. Political Zionism, following a sustained 50-year long diplomatic campaign, had triumphed.

Immediately after the UN vote, the Jewish Agency began steps to establish a viable domestic state apparatus. It combined the National Council with the Agency executive to form a new 37-member People's Council to act as a provisional government. A committee of 13 was formed to serve as a cabinet-in-waiting, with Ben Gurion as its head. Significantly, the new body endorsed the UN's partition plan, but did not specify boundaries, accepting only the existence of 'a Jewish state in Palestine, the state of Israel'.[78] Nevertheless, it formalised the dissolution of the mandate and allowed Israel to portray itself as a victim rather than aggressor. But this new-found legitimacy depended on the Zionists' ability to hold on to their designated territory. International recognition had been obtained for the principle of a state, but not its final boundaries – those, if any state survived at all, would be defined by the coming struggle with the Arabs.

Although the British announced that they would act only in self-defence until their withdrawal the following May, they continued to block Jewish immigration and arms imports. This hampered the Zionists while leaving the Arab states free to prepare for war. In December 1947, the Arab League created an Army of National Liberation, primarily with Syrian assistance, to fight the *Yishuv* directly. The force, again under Qawukji's leadership, comprised between 5000 and 7000 Arab volunteers who had infiltrated Palestine.[79] Over the next three months they met with considerable success, leaving the Zionists battered and in danger of military collapse. But diplomatic strategies had done as much as they could to provide a favourable context for a Jewish state. The final fate of Israel was now in the hands of the *Yishuv*, and its army.

In March, following the arrival of secret arms shipments from France and Czechoslovakia, the *Haganah* implemented a new offensive. The same month, the *Irgun* attacked an Arab village, Deir Yassein, killing all 250 inhabitants, including women and children. Although the brutal attack was officially condemned by the provisional government, it nevertheless considerably helped the Zionist cause. Fearing for their lives, hundreds of thousands of Palestinians fled their farms and villages for neighbouring countries, expecting to be restored to their land after the Arab armies conquered the Jews. This mass evacuation, a response to an atrocity, meant that the Jews, for the first time, came to comprise a numerical majority within the territory they hoped to claim as a state.

The War of Independence

On 14 May 1948, following the final British withdrawal, the state of Israel was proclaimed. Ben Gurion was installed as the country's first Prime Minister while Weizmann was given the ceremonial role of President. The new state was immediately granted *de facto* recognition by the Americans, with many Western countries following soon after. The first country to accord Israel *de jure* recognition was the Soviet Union.[80] But having shown its resilience to the British and the Palestinians, the *Yishuv* had to prove its durability to its Arab neighbours. One day after the declaration, the armies of Syria, Iraq, Transjordan, Egypt and Lebanon attacked.

Contrary to popular belief, this attack was not inevitable and the Arabs were not united in their belief that war was the only solution. In fact, Ben Gurion had been in consultation with King Abdullah since November 1947 in negotiations offering him control over the West Bank in exchange for withholding his forces from invasion.[81] Similarly, Egypt had failed to mobilise its army as late as April 1948 in the expectation that a negotiated solution to the problem could be found.[82] But after several decades of conflict, many Zionists believed that only when the Arabs were forced to realise that they could not destroy the Jewish presence in Palestine would they learn to accept the existence of an Israeli state. Given the nature of the two nationalist movements, and the incompatibility of their demands, Ben Gurion rebuffed efforts at reconciliation and dismissed suggestions by other Zionist leaders that the declaration of independence should be delayed to seek peaceful mediation. Instead, the *Yishuv* prepared for war.

All the Arab states then joined forces to invade and destroy Israel. Azzam Pasha, the Arab League Secretary-General warned on 15 May that the resulting conflict would be 'a war of extermination and a momentous massacre which will be spoken of like the Mongolian massacres and the Crusades'.[83] As the invasion began, the Zionist institutions that had been so carefully built up over the preceding decades made the transition into a real state with relatively little difficulty. Within days, Israel had a functioning political and economic structure. It was a state, moreover, that proved able to function in the most trying circumstances. In addition to fighting a war, the new administration had to admit and process thousands of new Jewish refugees, some coming from camps in Europe, others expelled from Arab countries in the period leading up to and immediately after the onset of war. The fact that Israel could undertake both these tasks and not only remain intact but expand testified to the fundamental importance of having built up all the institutions of the proto-state in the first place. If the Zionists had either had to take over institutions from the British, or establish new ones upon declaring independence, they would almost certainly have been crushed beneath the Arab onslaught.

Nowhere was this more evident than in the military sphere. The *Haganah* was immediately transformed into the Israeli Defense Force, incorporating the *Irgun* and *Lehi*. The new army comprised some 30 000 soldiers, although only half of these were fully armed and trained. The combined Arab armies consisted of 24 000 fully equipped men.[84] Nevertheless, the unified Israeli army benefited from superior tactics and leadership. Also, after decades of being moulded by the nationalist precepts of Zionism, and in the wake of the Holocaust, the battle meant national survival. The invading Arabs, by contrast, were hampered by different and often conflicting goals and strategies. Despite some initial successes, they were beaten back by the better organised Israelis. Zionists managed first to open up a corridor from Tel Aviv to Jerusalem and then to take control of the cities of Haifa, Tiberias and Safed. On 10 June the UN mediated the first of several ceasefires.

While this took place, Ben Gurion remained absolutely convinced that his movement towards exerting *de facto* Israeli statehood was the correct strategy. As he stated at the time:

[O]ur boundaries are set wider, our forces multiply, we are administering public services and daily new multitudes arrive...All that we have taken we shall hold. During the ceasefire, we shall organise administration with fiercer energy, strengthen our forces in town and city, speed up colonisation and *aliyah* and look to the Army.[85]

As the fighting resumed, the Zionists did just that. By month's end, Israel had 60 000 soldiers in the field, while renewed arms shipments gave it access to tanks, planes and artillery. The Arabs also regrouped, expanding their forces to 35 000, although they remained without a central high command and lacked a coordinated strategy.[86] Unlike the first phase of the war, in which the Zionists had been fighting for survival, the new battles involved expansionary Israeli offensives. As victory followed victory, the new state seized territory well outside the purview of the UN recommendations.

As their position strengthened, the Israelis rejected territorial compromises that were offered by the Arab states, insisting on their right to hold onto conquered land. Underlining this attitude, members of *Lehi* assassinated the chief UN peace negotiator, Count Bernadotte, who was perceived to be demanding excessive concessions from Israel. By the end of the year, some 700 000 Palestinians had left their homes. Combined with the new Jewish immigrants, this left Jews a substantial majority on the territory they had seized.[87] By December, the Israelis had established firm control over the country and in January the United States granted belated *de jure* recognition to the new state. The nation-state of Israel, complete with a Jewish majority, covered 77 per cent of what had been Palestine.

Conclusions

By 1949 the Zionist dream articulated by Herzl had been fulfilled and the strategies laid out in the Basle programme vindicated. In the international sphere, despite the withdrawal of official British support in 1939, the Zionists successfully found a new great power patron in the form of the United States. By mobilising the American Jewish community against the backdrop of the Holocaust, the Zionists were able to exert considerable pressure, first on Congress, and then on the Truman administration, for the endorsement of Zionist goals. This in turn provided the Zionists with diplomatic leverage against the British and contributed to Bevin's final decision to relinquish authority over Palestine. Similarly, in the final UN vote, diplomatic activity managed to sideline anti-Zionists within the State Department and Pentagon and successfully lobby other countries to vote in favour of the establishment of a Jewish state.

From the Balfour Declaration onwards, it was implicitly accepted within Zionist circles that the goal of a National Home meant a fully independent state and the terms of the Mandate suggested that Britain was to prepare Palestine for independence. It did not, however, define whether the resultant state was to be Jewish, Palestinian or binational. But while the Zionists might at one stage have been willing to accept partition for reasons of pragmatism, Ben Gurion and his supporters were in practice never prepared to settle for anything short of an exclusively Jewish state. This was, however, only explicitly recognised in the 1942 Biltmore Declaration. Significantly, moreover, both the Balfour and Biltmore Declarations took place in response to the changes wrought by extraneous international events, the two world wars: the First destroyed the Ottoman Empire, the Second led to the murder of Europe's Jewish population and the severing of the Zionist alliance with Britain.

Within Palestine, meanwhile, the Zionist movement had taken advantage of the opportunities offered by the war, and new investment and aid from American Jewry, to strengthen the economic and military arms of the *Yishuv* in preparation for statehood. When this was not forthcoming in 1945, the Zionists mobilised these resources in an unprecedented manner, staging a revolt that ultimately forced the British to hand the matter over to the United Nations for adjudication. Following the UN's formal endorsement of partition, the effectiveness of the proto-state was such that the Zionists were able to transform it into a viable administrative apparatus within days of formal independence. This gave the nascent state of Israel the wherewithal to withstand a furious onslaught from the neighbouring Arabs states and not only maintain, but significantly expand, its territorial base.

The Zionists had successfully combined a programme of state- and nation-building with an international diplomatic campaign to achieve their goals. Zionism's nationalist ideology was strengthened by the Holocaust and the urgency it lent to the demand for a Jewish state. In conjunction with the now well-established Zionist cultural and educational programmes, and the continued threat from Arab nationalism, they were able to build a committed national community that, by 1948, was willing and able to fight for its right to statehood. The newly independent state of Israel had been created by combining a domestic programme of constructing a proto-state with international diplomatic initiatives that exploited broad geopolitical shifts to gain international recognition. By linking nationalism with state-building and international diplomacy, the Zionist movement had created a new nation-state with both internal and international legitimacy.

GENERAL CONCLUSIONS

In all three movements, therefore, geopolitical factors played a key role in the growth and development of nationalism. The Boer War for the Irish and the First World War for the Zionists and Afrikaners all helped the nascent ethno-national movements to establish themselves and lay an organisational foundation for future growth. Later, a second international war – the First World War for the Irish, the Second for both the Zionists and Afrikaners – gave each movement the opportunity to establish critical political mass for a final push for power. In the absence of these exogenous events, the final result of all three struggles would have been very different. At the same time, however, without wide-ranging organisational movements in place capable of exploiting such openings, the political repercussions of such occurrences would most likely have had a much more limited impact.[88] Nevertheless, by 1918 in Ireland and by 1945 in South Africa the Sinn Fein and National Party-led coalitions had used their powerful bureaucracies to exploit the structural crises precipitated by war to harness the growing popular hostility to the existing regime that had resulted. Sinn Fein was able to achieve a crushing victory at the polls, thereby transforming itself into the dominant political movement in Ireland. The National Party, hampered by its *broedertwis* with the temporarily ascendant *Ossewa-brandwag* and continued opposition from an Anglophone population that was proportionately much larger than the Protestant community in Ireland, proved unable to take similar advantage of the change in national sentiment during the war. However, it too reached the end of the conflict with a much larger and more committed support base to launch a fresh challenge on the state. Although the Zionists chose, for their own reasons, to fight on behalf of the British in the Second World War, Britain's decision to renege on the National Home in 1939 had already united Jewish support in and out of the *Yishuv* against the mandatory power.

The exact nature of an acceptable constitutional status for their future state preoccupied the leadership of each movement throughout the period of national mobilisation. In each case, the focus was on the relationship of each movement with the British government: Ireland as part of the United Kingdom, South Africa through the Common-wealth, and Palestine as a mandatory trust under British supervision. For nationalist ideologues, however, the only acceptable political sta-tus of an independent nation-state is a republic, unencumbered by any constitutional obligations or restrictions to other states. Sinn Fein's endorsement of a republic and its rejection of the limited domestic autonomy offered by the Home Rule Bills helped the party consolidate its position as chief representative of Irish nationalism in the wake of the Rebellion. In South Africa, Hertzog and the early NP initially made much of the issue but were later prepared to settle for a prag-matic compromise that guaranteed the country's sovereignty within the Commonwealth. This stand, however, not only precipitated the Broe-derbond's formation of the FAK and Malan's break with Hertzog, but ultimately proved fatal for the notion of an inclusive, white South African nationalism. The advent of the Second World War stimulated the formation of a militant republicanism which became a key platform for the OB during the war and Malan and the National Party after it.

The Zionists, while carefully refusing to make this goal public until 1942, were always working towards Herzl's original vision of a fully independent, internationally recognised state. Acceptance first of the mandate and then, in principle at least, of partition were seen by the Zionist leadership as steps along the road to that goal, not ends in themselves. This pragmatic approach to constitutional issues in the short term while continuing to promise the longer-term implementa-tion of full independence also characterised the other two movements as they made their final bid for power. In both cases radicals took an uncompromising stance on the issue (leading to a messy and traumatic civil war in Ireland). But ultimately, Collins and Griffith's acceptance of the Treaty and Malan's willingness to put the republican issue on the backburner during the 1948 election campaign demonstrated a will-ingness to compromise (temporarily) on powerful symbolic issues to make short-term political gains. Nevertheless, the issue remained a central precept of each movement. Eventually nationalist governments in both countries were to make good on their promise to become republics – Ireland in 1949 and South Africa in 1961.

The international dimension of the nationalist programme, and in particular the struggle to gain recognition from other states was thus a central preoccupation of all three movements. Each developed a diplomatic strategy designed to seek international support for its goals. Most notably, in 1919, pinning their hopes on the doctrine of self-determination being promoted by President Wilson, all three sent a delegation to the Versailles peace conference to state their case. The differing outcomes to their petitions, however, graphically demonstrated the priority of strategic over moral interests in international politics. The Zionists, sponsored by Britain and with the explicit backing of the United States, had their goals fully endorsed by the victorious powers. By contrast, the Irish received a sympathetic hearing from the United States but failed to achieve formal international recognition in the face of British opposition and French ambivalence. The National Party delegation, without any international support at all, did not even manage to secure a hearing for Afrikaner grievances.

Given the lack of international interest in domestic South African affairs, however, this proved a temporary setback as the Afrikaners had no real need to seek support from great powers. Only during the Second World War when some radicals in the fascist-oriented OB rejected parliamentary politics and tried to effect a rebellion with German support, was international aid again sought (and again denied). By contrast, both the Irish and Zionists had a large pool of ethnic supporters in the United States. This gave them privileged access to and influence over American politicians who in turn put heavy diplomatic pressure on Britain. More importantly, these immigrant communities also came to provide each nationalist movement with critical funding for the final stages of its struggle for independence.

In both the latter cases, this struggle also came to include the use of force. When Britain refused to recognise either movement in the wake of the First and Second World Wars respectively, both the IRA and the *Haganah* conducted sustained guerrilla campaigns to force the government either to withdraw or enter peace negotiations. The ultimate success of this strategy in both cases resulted in large part because of the overwhelming popular support for each nationalist movement, making any imposed political solution unviable. It was also greatly helped by the fact that Britain was under severe financial and military strain due to conflicts elsewhere: in the Arab states in 1919–20 during the Irish insurrection, and in India, Burma and other colonial possessions in 1945–47 during the struggle with the Zionists in Palestine. Given South Africa's international legitimacy, such a military struggle proved to be superfluous which was why, with the exception of the 1914 Rebellion and the OB's limited sabotage during the Second World War, violence never became a significant part of Afrikaner strategies.

The most important single factor in each movement's victory, however, was the existence of a powerful organisational infrastructure that allowed them to challenge the existing order and consolidate their own power bases rapidly after taking power. Without the institutional foundations laid by the Dail and its nascent proto-state, the IRA would never have been as successful and the British would probably have been able to impose a (temporary) political solution on the country. In its final campaign in the 1948 elections, the Broederbond and National Party utilised their comprehensive bureaucratic network to attract new supporters and surge to power. In Israel, the proto-state so meticulously nurtured by the Zionist movement displayed its fettle immediately upon assuming power, proving able to set up a viable administration, fight a successful war on several fronts simultaneously and cope with thousands of new refugee immigrants. Had it lacked that administrative base, the new state would have been quickly crushed by the invading Arab armies. In all three cases, therefore, the focus was on state-making as much as state-taking. The nationalist bureaucracies came to be regarded as the legitimate controllers of the state by the vast majority of the ethnic groups they had sought to mobilise. This allowed them to wrest full political control, effectively transforming each country into internationally recognised states controlled by, and on behalf of, the ethnic 'nation'.

Conclusions

In their long rise to power, the Irish, Afrikaners and Zionists followed a broadly similar path. First, each movement undertook a process of nation-building: articulating and disseminating nationalist ideology by means of a wide-ranging organisational network. Second, they focused on state-making: the establishment of a bureaucratic infrastructure, strongly grounded in economic issues and premised on control of an internationally recognised state. Studying these processes in the context of the analytical framework laid out in Chapter 1 has demonstrated the powerful linkages between the ideological framework established by each movement, the conditioning power of the state structure within which they operated and the nature of the organisational framework they established. Just as important, however, it also showed how their accession to power was by no means inevitable. Ultimately, the proximate causes for the success of each movement were extraneous historical events over which they had no control: the two world wars. The conclusion will briefly reassess these processes and discuss their implications for the broader understanding of nationalism.

STRUCTURAL CHANGE AND THE STATE

This entire process of national mobilisation was always conditioned by domestic structural factors. These ranged from demographic issues to economic ones, but most important was the degree of political freedom permitted each nationalist movement. On the one hand, each movement's ability to set up founding organisations and recruit supporters, at least in the early phases of mobilisation, was dependent on the existing government allowing such activities to take place. On the other, the nature of the administration in each territory conditioned the type of political tactics employed by the nationalist movements. In Ireland, the fact that the expansion of the franchise in the late nineteenth century gave many Catholics the vote in Westminster meant that a moderate, constitutional approach to addressing grievances dominated the political debate in that country until it was discredited by an extraneous event – the First World War. And even then, Sinn Fein chose to fight in the Westminster elections, using them as a springboard to establish the First Dail. Similarly, in South Africa, the all-white franchise adopted in 1910 shaped the broadly constitutional strategies adopted by the Broederbond and the National Party that eventually led them to electoral victory in 1948. For the Zionists, the initial foothold in Palestine was made possible by the peculiar political freedoms that Jews enjoyed in the Ottoman empire, while the establishment of ethnically exclusive, elected legislative and administrative bodies during the Mandate rather than the binational legislature originally envisaged by the British gave the the *Yishuv* the political space to establish its administrative foundations. Nevertheless, while these factors set the context within which national mobilisation took place, they were not responsible for its ultimate success. The exact manner in which each movement managed to exploit these political opportunities to take power lay in the nature of the organisational networks they established, the ethnic and material appeals they crafted and their ability to take advantage of unexpected international events.

ETHNICITY AND IDEOLOGY

One of the most important factors in each movement's success was the resonance of nationalist ideology itself among the target population. In the terminology favoured by collective mobilisation theorists, nationalism became the key framing process for each movement, setting out the context within which the struggle for state power took place. That resonance arose from its ability to tap into a pre-existing ethnic consciousness, which was itself a function of the development of an educated middle class and a broadly literate population. In all three cases, a portion of the intelligentsia, prompted by perceived ethnic discrimination, began the process of national mobilisation by articulating an ideology built around issues of language, culture and religion. This involved the development of a distorted, nationalist history and the establishment of a distinctive iconography focused on symbols such as a flag and national anthem. In all three cases the progenitors of this nationalist ideology did not create a wholly artificial national identity but utilised aspects of a pre-existing ethnic culture. They raided the storehouse of ethnic history to build up a picture of a glorious past and used it to promise future political salvation through nationalism. Added to this potent brew in each case was the notion that the ethnic community had a privileged relationship with God by virtue of its shared religion – a relationship that was partially endorsed by ecclesiastical authorities in exchange for privileged political access and direct influence over education. Combined with a purportedly organic link with the ethnic group's 'historic' territory and a common linguistic heritage, these belief systems became the primary means of legitimising the nationalist movements' claims to each country.

Tellingly, however, these ideological arguments proved unable to attract a substantial mass following. Even after nationalist political claims had been articulated and widely disseminated in each case, Jews still went to America rather than Palestine, the Irish continued to support the moderate Parliamentary Party and most Afrikaners remained quite content with the limited cultural achievements of Hertzog's government. Nevertheless, a core group which came to comprise the bulk of the later nationalist leadership was directly inspired by this ideology and its promises of power and patronage. It was this group in each case – the early Gaelic Leaguers and Sinn Fein leaders in Ireland, the Broederbond and National Party in South Africa, and the left-wing labour leaders of the 2nd *Aliyah* in Palestine – who were primarily responsible for the later construction of a broad organisational infrastructure to promote the nationalist agenda, and ultimately became the dominant faction within each movement, leading it to power.

ECONOMY AND ORGANISATION

Another critically important aspect of national mobilisation was the manner in which each movement sought to link ethnic affinity with economic interests through the prism of the state. Concern over issues like land, jobs, and income was never far from the thoughts of most members of each ethnic group. In order to expand their support base, nationalist leaders had to incorporate these issues into the broader nationalist ideology and organisational structure. In each case this was done in part by focusing on the use that might be made of the state to develop the economy and provide material benefits to members of the ethnic community. Griffith's impassioned calls for the development of Irish industry through autarkic trade and investment policies, the Broederbond's demands that the state be used to protect and create Afrikaner jobs and businesses, and the Zionists' astute use of first the Kibbutz movement and then the labour-dominated *Histadrut* all helped generate much greater public support for each movement than ethno-cultural arguments alone.

Critical to this process was the manner in which nationalist leaders sought to establish an economic base that would provide jobs and income for members. Each movement set up small banks and other businesses dedicated to the development of national wealth. Although in the Irish case such policies proved relatively ineffective, in South Africa they had a significant impact resulting in steady growth in Afrikaner financial and manufacturing strength. Most successful of all was the *Histadrut* which came to control the bulk of non-agricultural industry in Palestine while at the same time providing a secure union base within which Jewish workers could receive material benefits such as healthcare, pensions and unemployment assistance. Connolly's Socialists and the ITGWU in Ireland, and the Broederbond, through the *Spoorbond*, the BWBB and the Mine Workers Union, in South Africa, also offered direct material benefits to workers within a nationalist context. All sought to address members' economic needs as well as mobilise them politically behind the nationalist cause.

This was reflected in the social composition of each movement. In each case, the exact makeup of the movement varied according to the class structure of each society. For example rural activists played a much more important role in Ireland where land issues dominated the political debate while Zionists were influenced by the peculiar nature of the kibbutz culture that fostered so many of its leaders. Nevertheless, their broad social structure was similar. Intellectuals and professionals tended to be the leaders, shopkeepers, traders and wealthier farmers comprised the bulk of the committed, early membership, and smaller farmers, agricultural labourers and industrial workers joined towards the end of each struggle, helping each movement take power.

ETHNIC CONFLICT AND STATE-MAKING

Important though ideological and material arguments were to national mobilisation, both were ultimately predicated on the establishment of a powerful, wide-ranging organisational network. Driven by a mixture of psychological and material incentives, this process can best be understood as the formation of linked bureaucracies. At the head of each movement stood a set of political groupings, directed by a small elite, which sought to create and entrench a broad administrative structure co-ordinating the various nationalist activities taking place in cultural, economic and political spheres. They in turn oversaw a vast range of organisations from trade unions to cultural groups, all dedicated to the advancement of nationalism. By offering constituents an all-embracing set of organisations within which to situate their lives, each movement not only reinforced the broader process of nation-building but used those organisations as a source of genuine infra-structural power.

This process was fuelled by conflict with opposing ethnic groups. Not only did the existence of an ethnic threat stimulate feelings of national solidarity in each community, but it fundamentally shaped the mechanisms by which national mobilisation was effected, particularly in the military sphere. In Ireland, Protestant mobilisation in opposition to Home Rule helped precipitate the establishment of an exclusive Gaelic-Catholic movement. Similarly, the creation of the Protestant Ulster Volunteers contributed directly to the establishment of the predominantly Catholic Irish Volunteers, which in turn became not only the agent of the 1916 Rebellion but also the base for the guerrilla movement which took up an armed struggle for independence after 1919. In Palestine this was even more pronounced. The *Haganah*, formed to provide security from Palestinian Arabs, grew into a power-ful military force able to comprise a fully-fledged army immediately upon Israel's declaration of independence. In South Africa, the numerical inferiority of Anglophone whites and the powerlessness of South African blacks meant that a military dimension was never required. Nevertheless, Afrikaner fear of and hostility to the country's indigenous majority led to the development of apartheid, an ambitious programme of social engineering premised on the coerced, permanent exclusion of the black population from wealth and power.

At the same time, each movement was also characterised by ende-mic factionalism and deep divisions over which strategies and object-ives were most appropriate at any given time. At their worst, such as in the disputes between the pro-Treaty and anti-Treaty factions in Ireland, the National Party and *Ossewabrandwag* in South Africa, and the Labour and Revisionist movements within the WZO, these divisions proved unbridgeable and were often violently expressed. Indeed, the term 'movement' should only be loosely applied to all three cases. At no time was there absolute consensus on strategy or policy amongst nationalist leaders and groups, merely a loosely shared vision of a politically independent, ethnically-controlled state. Nevertheless, when tracking their development over decades, it becomes possible to discern how, even when they fought amongst themselves, these myriad groups were contributing to nation-building and state-making. In each case, these processes proved extremely wide-ranging, cutting across cultural, political, economic and military spheres, both domestically and internationally.

THE INTERNATIONAL SYSTEM AND LEGITIMACY

In addition to their domestic activities, all three nationalist movements participated in international politics as independent actors, both proactively by engaging in diplomacy with existing states, and reactively, by opposing outside interference in internal matters. In particular, the need to secure domestic sovereignty and international legitimacy preoccupied nationalist leaders throughout their struggle for power. The continuing salience of the republican issue in both the Afrikaner and Irish cases, and the impassioned debate over whether to endorse publicly the Zionist *endziel* of a fully independent state, repeatedly caused ructions within each movement. Although never of pressing significance to most of the mass base, republicanism was an article of faith for committed nationalists, and of particular importance to many of the core leadership. In the final bid for power, however, short-term pragmatism invariably won out over long-term ideological purity: Collins and Griffith approved the Irish Treaty, Ben Gurion and Weizmann proved willing to contemplate partition, and Malan retreated from republicanism when it proved an electoral liability with moderates. In the final analysis, most nationalist leaders proved to be political opportunists rather than ideologues, choosing to focus their campaigns on more emotive issues of cultural, economic and political security to win over vacillating constituents.

At the same time, international diplomacy remained a critically important element of nationalist strategy. For the Zionists in particular, the diplomatic dimension was inextricable from the broader process of state-making. Given their political weakness, international recognition and support from at least one major power was vital. Without a powerful international arm, they would never have been able to secure the necessary great power support to develop the institutions of the *Yishuv*, encourage Jewish immigration, and so lay the groundwork for the Jewish state. This was partly true of the Irish as well. Like the Zionists, they were able to exploit the internal politics of another country, the United States, by making use of ethnic loyalties still held by large emigrant groups. Both movements were also able to access important financial backing and political support from this source.

South Africa, by contrast, was already an internationally recognised state from 1910 onwards. As a result, outside powers lacked direct interests in the country that were either directly threatened by, or would obviously benefit from, the establishment of an Afrikaner government. That meant foreign states had little role in domestic politics, with the notable exception of the constant debate over the country's constitutional relationship with Great Britain. However, the Irish and Zionist cases demonstrated that when a small nationalist movement is actively opposed by a Great Power and lacks other international allies, then the chances of that movement achieving international recognition are minimal. Had Britain chosen to maintain its large military presence in Ireland or Palestine rather than bowing to diplomatic and domestic pressures in 1921 and 1947 respectively, the nationalist movements would never have been able to evict them by force of arms alone.

Indeed, extraneous international events not only affected the strategies and success of each nationalist movement, but, as with the domestic political structure, actively conditioned them. On one level, unrelated events in other regions of the world had an impact on nationalist struggles by altering the geopolitical constraints acting on Great Britain. For both the Irish and the Zionists, Britain's final decision to compromise came about, at least in part, because of sustained international and domestic pressures on the British government in the post-war environment that had little to do with the nationalist movements themselves. Just as important, however, external political and economic events, most notably the two world wars, had a profound effect on the internal affairs of each country and led directly to a substantial increase in support for the nationalist movements in each case. Particularly striking was the depth of national feeling engendered despite the fact that none of the territories were at any time a theatre of conflict. Only the Zionists had any compelling reason to join the fight against Germany, and even for them Second World War marked a major turning point as, in the wake of the 1939 White Paper, they launched a campaign of resistance to the British presence in Palestine.

Even more important, for the Irish during the First World War and Afrikaners in the Second, the decision by Redmond and Smuts respectively to fight on behalf of Britain proved the key event in shifting popular legitimacy away from the existing order and towards the challenging nationalist movement. The earlier activities of the nationalist movements in other spheres of activity had already secured widespread awareness of ethnic nationalism as a potential alternative form of state government, but in the context of sustained domestic political and economic stability, this message had limited impact. In each case, however, an external war precipitated a legitimacy crisis as a result of which the majority of the ethnic population lost faith in the existing order. In South Africa and Ireland, despite years of campaigning, each nationalist movement had conspicuously failed to generate sufficient support to seize power using only their internal resources. Both ultimately proved dependent on external events precipitating a domestic crisis which, given their powerful bureaucratic networks, they were all well placed to exploit for political gain.

Despite their similar mobilising strategies, however, the final outcome of each nationalist struggle was very different. Sinn Fein took over a truncated Irish state that was overwhelmingly Catholic, the Zionists established one with a Jewish majority after effectively forcing the eviction of most indigenous Palestinians, and the Afrikaners became minority rulers of a multi-ethnic state. The primary reason for these divergent outcomes was the differing structural and demographic environment in which each nationalist movement was forced to confront its ethnic antagonists. Faced with a powerful, organised, geographically discrete Protestant minority, the Irish had little option but to accept the *de facto* partition of the island. Forced to defend themselves against a Palestinian majority internally and a phalanx of hostile Arab states externally, the Zionists needed to establish themselves as an unassailable majority in Palestine and ultimately did so through force of arms. By contrast, the Afrikaners, in a country where white rule was already well established, and the ethnic population was widely – and thinly – spread across the territory, did not seek an independent homeland, or even (apart from their half-hearted petition at Versailles), the re-establishment of the Boer republics. Instead, nationalist leaders realised that they needed only to use the electoral system to assume control over the existing state apparatus that they could then use to segregate South African society and regulate the black labour market. Similar strategies were responsible for the common nature of each movement's organisational foundation, but diverse structural contexts dictated the nature of the eventual outcome of each struggle.

BROADER IMPLICATIONS

In essence, therefore, each movement's rise to power shared six broad characteristics:

1. A pre-existing ethnic identity based on both a subjectively held common culture, language, religion and history and clashes with other ethnic groups.
2. Relatively widespread literacy within the ethnic group and an intelligentsia able to articulate a nationalist ideology and history.
3. A cohesive, organisational infrastructure encompassing a wide range of fields – political, cultural, economic and, when necessary, military – with centralised, overlapping leadership.
4. The provision and/or promise of material benefits and physical security for members as well as the promise or expectation of more comprehensive ethnic patronage once the state was under nationalist control.
5. A favourable geopolitical context in which the nationalist movement was at worst not directly in conflict with the interests of existing states, particularly great powers, and at best secured the active support of one or more existing states for its aims.
6. A legitimacy crisis within the existing regime precipitated by a combination of domestic and international upheavals that the nationalist movement was able to exploit to take power.

While these factors are drawn from what are generally regarded as relatively atypical cases of nationalism most of them are likely to appear to a significant degree in all successful ethnic nationalist movements. Nevertheless, it is important to stress that these are variables, not unchanging criteria for success or failure. Even though broadly similar factors can act as causes or catalysts in the process of national mobilisation, this study clearly demonstrates that the domestic and international structural constraints on nationalist movements can differ widely. As a result, the success or failure of a nationalist movement in achieving state power depends at least as much on contingent domestic and international events as its internal resources and strategies. This means, for example, that if a political, economic or military crisis has completely destroyed the legitimacy of the existing order, then a relatively weak nationalist organisation might well be able to take power anyway. By contrast even a movement with a relatively strong organisational infrastructure and widespread popular legitimacy that faces sustained and committed opposition from the existing government and one or more international allies (as with black African nationalism in South Africa between 1948–90 and Palestinian nationalism in the West Bank and Gaza over the same period) will find it much more difficult to succeed in its goals. Accordingly, seeking to develop a general causal theory to explain how and why some nation- alist movements are able to seize state power is an all but impossible task. There will always be too many exceptions to establish a compre- hensive set of universal causes. The best that can be achieved is to increase our understanding of the range of factors that condition the growth and development of nationalist struggles, and then analyse how they are played out in different cases.

List of Major Organisations

IRELAND

Dail: The self-styled Irish parliament. The First Dail comprised Sinn Fein MPs after the 1918 election who set up a nominally independent Irish administration in defiance of Westminster.

Gaelic Athletic Association: Movement established in 1884 to promote the revival of Gaelic sports, particularly Gaelic Football and Hurling.

Gaelic League: Cultural and literary group dedicated to the promotion of the Gaelic language and traditions formed in 1892.

Irish Republican Army: The name taken by the faction of the Irish Volunteers that supported the First *Dail*. Later appropriated by radicals opposed to the establishment of the Irish Free State in 1922.

Irish Republican Brotherhood: Semi-secret revolutionary body dedicated to the establishment of an Irish republic, founded in 1858 as an offshoot of an American expatriate group and popularly known as the Fenians. Reconstituted after the failed 1867 uprising as a smaller, secret organisation.

Irish Socialist Republican Party: Party with close links to the trade union movement, formed by James Connolly in 1896 to mobilise Irish workers under a banner that was both nationalist and socialist.

Irish Volunteers: Armed Catholic militia formed in 1914, nominally under the control of the Parliamentary Party. Following a split after the onset of the First World War, the name was retained by the smaller, radical faction which broke away in protest at the body's participation in the conflict. The remaining rump was renamed the National Volunteers.

Land League: Association formed in 1879, most closely associated with Michael Davitt, to campaign for Land Reform. Reconstituted under Parnell as the National Land League in 1886.

Parliamentary Party (also known as the Irish Party): Party formed to campaign for Home Rule at Westminster. Temporarily split after the disgrace and death of its leader Charles Stewart Parnell in 1891, later reunited under John Redmond.

Sinn Fein (Ourselves): Party formed in 1905 by Arthur Griffith to promote national self-sufficiency in all spheres of Irish life.

Ulster Unionist Council: Coalition of Protestant groups based in Ulster, founded in 1905 to campaign against the implementation of Home Rule for Ireland.

Ulster Volunteers: Protestant militia, founded in 1913 to campaign against Home Rule.

Young Ireland: Organisation active in the 1840s styled on contemporary European nationalist groups such as Mazzini's Young Italy.

SOUTH AFRICA

Note: In South African history and political discourse it is common to use acronyms rather than full names of organisations, a convention I have largely followed. Accordingly, except where the acronym was not used in the main body of the text, this section of the glossary is organised by acronym, followed by the title (if it appears in the text), or English translation, of the organisation.

AHI (Afrikaans Chamber of Commerce): Afrikaans business grouping, founded in 1939 to increase Afrikaner private sector involvement.

ATKV (Afrikaans Language and Culture Association): Cultural grouping formed by the Broederbond, used to get control of the *Spoorbond* railway union.

Afrikaner Bond: Afrikaner-oriented political party active in the nineteenth-century Cape Colony.

AP (Afrikaner Party): Political party formed in 1940 after split between Malan and Hertzog.

Broederbond (Brotherhood): Semi-secret nationalist grouping formed in 1918.

BWBB (White Workers Protection League): Workers grouping formed by the National Party during the Second World War.

DRC (Dutch Reformed Church): The Church to which nearly all Afrikaners belonged.

FAK (Federation of Afrikaans Culture): Umbrella grouping of cultural groups formed by the Broederbond in 1927.

Labour Party: White, socialist party, joined the National Party in the 'Pact' government after 1924.

NO (New Order): Pro-Nazi political party active during the Second World War.

NP (National Party): The NP from 1914–34, the GNP (Purified National Party) from 1934–40, and the HNP (Re-united National Party) from 1940–48 were all known as the National Party, or the

Nationalists, in South African politics. Of these, the GNP and HNP were essentially the same party with the same leadership and the same political platform. Accordingly, when I use either abbreviation, it refers to the same party at different periods in South African history.

OB (*Ossewabrandwag* or Oxwagon Sentry): Ostensibly cultural nationalist movement formed after Great Trek celebrations in 1938.

RDB (*Reddingsdaadbond* or Society for an Act of Rescue): Mass organisation, founded in 1939, designed to raise funds for poor whites.

SAP (South African Party): Party of government in South Africa from 1910–24, led by former Boer Generals Botha and Smuts.

UP (United Party): Party formed in 1934 from the fusion of the first National Party, under Hertzog, and the South African Party, under Smuts.

THE ZIONISTS

Achdut Ha'avoda (United Labour) Political party formed from the merger of *Poale Zion* and several smaller parties in 1920.

Asefat Hanihavrim (Legislative Assembly): The legislative body for the *Yishuv* during the Mandate.

Aliyah (Ascent): The term used to describe immigration to Israel by Jews. Different waves are treated chronologically as the 1st *Aliyah*, 2nd *Aliyah*, etc.

American Zionist Emergency Council: Body formed in 1939 to promote Zionist goals in the United States during the Second World War.

Arab Higher Committee (AHC): Palestinian body under the leadership of the Mufti. First formed in 1935, destroyed in the Arab Revolt, and re-formed in 1946.

Brit Shalom (Covenant of Peace): Group founded by liberal Jews to promote a binational state in 1925, dissolved in 1933.

Bund (General Jewish Workers' Union of Lithuania, Poland and Russia): Jewish socialist party at the turn of the century seeking autonomy in Russia, Poland and Lithuania.

General Zionists: Centrist faction of the WZO.

Haganah (Defence): The underground military organisation of the *Yishuv*, formed in 1920.

Hapoel Ha'tzair (Young Worker): Left-leaning political party formed in 1905 to promote the 'conquest of labour'.

Hashomer (Watchman): Successor defence group to *Bar Giora*, formed in 1909.

Histadrut (The General Federation of Labour in Israel): An umbrella group of organisations formed in 1920 under the control of the labour movement. It included trade unions, economic enterprises and cultural groups.

Hovevei Zion (Lovers of Zion): A Russian-Jewish group whose members organised the 1st *Aliyah*.

Irgun: Right-wing Zionist military organisation formed in 1931.

Jewish Agency: Executive body of the *Yishuv* and WZO in Palestine under the Mandate. Formed in 1929.

Kibbutz: An agricultural collective community. The first was formed in 1909.

Knesset (Assembly): The term for the combined Jewish legislative bodies.

Lehi: Underground radical, right-wing Jewish military force operating during and after the Second World War. Also known as the Stern Gang.

Mapai (Israel Labour Party): Political Party formed in 1930 from the merger of *Hapoel Ha'tzair* and *Achdut Ha'avodah*.

Mizrahi: Religious Zionist faction within the WZO.

Mossad: Underground Zionist organisation designed to facilitate illegal immigration to Palestine during the Second World War.

New Zionist Organisation (NZO): Alternative to the WZO formed by the Revisionists in 1935.

Palmach (Assault Companies): The main strike force of the *Haganah*, formed in 1941.

Poale Zion (Workers of Zion): Zionist socialist party established in Palestine in 1905.

Revisionists: Right-wing Zionist faction under the leadership of Vladimir Jabotinsky, formed in 1925.

Soleh Boneh: Construction company formed by the *Histadrut*. Collapsed in 1926, but was re-formed in 1934.

Vaad Leumi (National Council): The representative body of the Jews of the *Yishuv* during the Mandate, elected from the *Asefat Hanihavrim*.

World Zionist Organisation (WZO): The central body of the Zionist movement, formed in 1897 by Herzl.

Yishuv (Settlement): The term used to describe the Jewish community and its institutions within Palestine in the period leading up to independence in 1948.

Notes

INTRODUCTION

1 As will become clear I use the term 'movement' for convenience to refer to the wide range of nationalist organisations at work in each case study. It should not be seen as implying or endorsing the notion of a single, cohesive movement.
2 There are many definitions of nationalism. I use a political one for two reasons. First, it highlights the fact that the fundamental demand of a nationalist movement is political sovereignty. Second, it focuses on the state and is thus appropriate for a study of how a nationalist movement builds or takes over a state. This approach is broadly accepted by writers such as Breuilly (1985, p. 3), Gellner (1983, p. 1) and Hobsbawm (1990, p. 9). See Smith (1983, p. 21) and Hutchinson (1987, p. 15) for broader sociological definitions, and Berlin (1989, p. 338) for a philosophical one.
3 Weber (1978) p. 905. Again, there are many definitions of the state. The advantage of Weber's conception is that it recognises both the internal and external dimensions of statehood. As Skocpol (1981, p. 21) argues, it is particularly useful when examining the state's relationship to social movements.
4 A. Smith (1987) pp. 3–5.
5 This is clearly different in the case of civic nationalism.
6 For an analysis of the historiography of each movement see Suzman (1996) pp. 13–40.
7 Lee (1989) p. xiii. Similar sentiments have been expressed by analysts of the other two movements. See for example Hertzberg (1959, p. 16) on the distinctiveness of Zionism.
8 Giliomee (1990).
9 Akenson (1992) p. 6.
10 This has rarely been true of the study of nationalism. Classic works such as Kohn (1985) and Seton-Watson (1977) range over a large number of cases. Nevertheless, a few, notably Greenfeld (1992) and Hroch (1985) go over a more limited number in some detail. See Moore (1966, pp. xiii–xiv) and Frederickson (1981, p. xv) on the general utility of the comparative method and George (1979, p. 50) on the advantages of restricting the number of case studies. See Skocpol and Somers (1980) for a discussion on the methodology of comparative study.
11 Skocpol (1979) p. xiv.

1. AN ANALYTICAL FRAMEWORK

1 Seton-Watson (1977, p. 3), A. Smith (1987, p. 4). See also Alter (1985, pp. 28–37) for a widely adopted general typology of different

nationalisms within this basic division and Hall (1995, pp. 12–20) for a slightly different classification. More recently, Brubaker (1996, p. 7) has taken a different argument, drawing a distinction between nationalism as a category of practice and a category of analysis. I accept that division, but, as will become clear, think that the two are not incompatible provided care is taken to emphasise the contingency of national mobilisation.

2   See Symmons-Symonolewicz (1968, p. 43) on the need to adapt collective mobilisation theory to nationalism.

3   McCarthy, McAdam and Zald (1996) p. 2. I have paraphrased the three factors and changed their original order so as to frame better the questions they pose for nationalist movements.

4   McCarthy, McAdam and Zald (1996) p. 8.

5   McAdam (1987) pp. 36–60.

6   Gellner (1983). Other variants include Hechter (1975) and Nairn (1977) who take a more marxist approach, arguing that nationalism is conditioned by tensions between the dominant economic 'core' and the marginalised groups on the 'periphery'.

7   Skocpol (1981) pp. 23–7; See also Birnbaum (1980) and Shefter (1977) on the effect of state structure on diverse political activities.

8   Breuilly (1985) pp. 35–6.

9   McCarthy, McAdam and Zald (1996) p. 10.

10 Snow *et al.* (1986) cited in McAdam, McCarthy and Zald (1995) p. 4.

11 Herder (1992) developed the notion that the world was divided into nations defined by language. He saw the nation as both the key medium of political authenticity and the repository of the collective memory, and hence distinctive identity, of the group. He did not, however, draw any political conclusions from this philosophy and was quite happy to see nations as part of broader multinational states and empires.

12 Fichte (1968).

13 Kedourie (1993) p. 68.

14 See Berlin (1989) for a discourse on the philosophical foundations of nationalism. It is also an approach implicitly adopted by some of the most important historians of nationalism, including, Kohn (1946) and Seton-Watson (1977). A popular variant of this approach is to attribute the doctrine's resonance to the fact that it is in effect a modern, civil religion. Derived from the work of Emile Durkheim (1967) and in particular his argument that all religion is, at core, a manifestation of society worshipping itself, theorists such as Hayes (1968) and C. O'Brien (1988b and 1993) sought to demonstrate the importance of religion in the nationalist makeup while highlighting the doctrine's quasi-religious aspects. This is a point of view shared by several analysts of the case studies under review. Most notably, in his widely admired study of Afrikaner nationalism, Moodie (1975) has argued that the intelligentsia act as 'cultural entrepreneurs', creating an overarching ideological framework based on a reified version of Afrikaner historical myths.

15 Smith, A. (1987). The broader debate over ethnicity has been very contentious. Primordialists such as Clifford Geertz (1977) have argued

that it is inherent in all human societies throughout history. By contrast, instrumentalists like Leroy Vail have argued that ethnic consciousness is 'an ideological construct, usually of the twentieth century, and not an anachronistic cultural artifact of the past'. (Vail 1989, p. 3). For fuller discussion see Barth (1970), Glazer and Moynihan (1975) and Vail (1989). More recently, these concepts have been enriched by exposure to developments in evolutionary theory in the rapidly growing area of sociobiology. But while these studies contain important new insights as to humankind's inherent propensity to support nationalist ideologies they have limited relevance to the study of nationalist movements and will not be discussed here.

16   Several studies have revealed an imperfect correlation between those individuals deemed most likely to mobilise in response to such changes most affected by feelings of marginalisation and insecurity (such as the unemployed during periods of economic depression) and their participation in collective social movements. See McCarthy and Zald (1977).

17   Tilly (1978).

18   McAdam (1987).

19   Gamson (1990) analyses a wide-range of challenging goups in the US and concludes that those who used force, while often subject to short-term repression, were more likely to see their goals achieved in the long run.

20   McCarthy (1995) p. 142.

21   Carr (1945, pp. 190–92) has argued that there are close links between such economic nationalist competition and the use of force between competing nationalities.

22   Bell (1975).

23   Gellner (1983) p. 108 and Kedourie (1960) p. 115.

24   Tilly (1975). See also Mann (1993) on 'infrastructural power', which encompasses the ability to extract resources and govern citizens in all aspects of society rather than simply military prowess.

25   Hintze (1906) p. 183. See also his discussion on how the form of state is influenced by international changes in Hintze (1902, pp. 159–177). More recently, Gourevitch (1979) has made the same assertions, albeit in the specific area of the effects of such events on modern foreign policy making. Amongst theorists of nationalism A. Smith (1986, pp. 35–40; 1991, p. 165) has pointed to the importance of this relationship but made little direct use of it in his broader studies. See also Skocpol (1981, pp. 13–15) for its effect on revolutions.

26   See Premdas *et al.* (1990), Watson (1990), Samarasinghe (1990), Ra'anam *et al.* (1991), Da Silva and May (1991) and Midlarsky (1992). However, although Premdas (1991, pp. 14–16) does look at some broader issues, for the most part these examinations focus either on understanding the nature of ethnic conflict and nationalism within specific case studies or examine how to 'solve' such conflicts, or at least moderate their international repercussions.

27   Cobban (1969) p. 39. See Tilly's (1993) plea for more study of national self-determination.

28 Interestingly, international law, holds that 'the formation of a new state is a matter of fact and not of law'. (Oppenheim, cited in Crawford 1979, p. 4). As Mayall (1990, p. 122) points out, there are also 'states' which have legal standing but little or no control over their territories.

29 Crawford (1979) p. 74. Thus, 'states' with domestic control, but no recognition (like the Japanese puppet state of Manchukuo in Manchuria during the 1930s or the South African 'homelands' for black tribes set up under apartheid in the 1970s and 80s), cannot be regarded as fully independent.

30 I have adapted this concept from the work of Jurgen Habermas, who defines it as 'the withdrawal from the existing order of the support of the loyalty of the mass of the population as their motivational commitment to its normative base is broken', but use it in a very different context. Habermas's work emphasises the economic sphere and the inherent tension between the state's accumulation and legitimation imperatives. From the perspective of this study, however, the important point is that legitimacy has political, economic and social components and is necessary for a stable society. See Benhabib (1986, pp. 231–5) and Held (1982, pp. 230–36) for further analysis.

31 Held (1982) p. 189.

2. ETHNICITY AND IDEOLOGY

1 See MacIntyre (1975).
2 Duffy (1848) p. 7.
3 Davis (1914) pp. 256–67. For its Protestant precursors see Hutchinson (1987, pp. 79–97).
4 Foster (1988) p. 311.
5 *United Irishman*, 12 February 1848.
6 *United Irishman*, 12 April 1848.
7 Ultimately, some 3 million departed for the USA between 1845–91 (Ward, 1969, p. 3).
8 Cromerford (1981) p. 26. See also Lee (1966) who shows how Fenian meetings were used as excuses for pub visits and leisure time.
9 Kee (1972) p. 28.
10 Ryan (1960) p. 26.
11 Home Rule Association (1871) in Mitchell and O'Snodaigh (1989).
12 I am, of necessity, drastically abbreviating one of the most complex and interesting periods in Irish history. For further analysis see C. O'Brien (1957) and Kee (1993).
13 Moody (1967) p. 275.
14 See O'Connor (1925) which serves as a relatively early example of how the Parnellian myth fitted into nationalist historiography.
15 Duffy (1894) pp. 16; 58–60.
16 Hyde (1894) p. 124. See Dillon (1960) on Hyde's beliefs.
17 W. O'Brien (1892) p. 4.
18 Boyce (1982) p. 240.

19   McCartney (1967) p. 295.
20   Yeats (1955) p. 493; See Maltby (1990) on fine arts.
21   Garvin (1987) p. 24; Rumpf and Hepburn (1977) p. 8.
22   Garvin (1987) p. 24.
23   Hutchinson (1987) p. 179. Some estimates put the number at over 100 000 (Kee, 1972, p. 135).
24   Mandle (1987) pp. 35–6.
25   Ibid, p. 120.
26   Ibid, p. 154.
27   *Weekly Nation*, 10 February 1900.
28   See Bew (1987) p. 185.
29   Hutchinson (1987) p. 138. Between 1850–1900, the clergy expanded from 5000 to 14 000 while the Catholic population dropped from 6 to 3.5 million (Kennedy, 1978, p. 167).
30   See Corish (1961). It was not above railing against Jews and Freemasons as well (Bew, 1987, p. 186).
31   Moran (1905) p. 26.
32   Boyce (1982) p. 243.
33   Hoppen (1989) p. 131.
34   *Sinn Fein*, 4 March 1899.
35   Griffith (1906) p. 9.
36   De Blacam (1921) pp. xiii; xvi.
37   This mobility worked in several different directions. Michael Collins, for example, joined the GAA before becoming an IRB member in 1909 (Coogan, 1990, pp. 15–16) while Patrick Pearse was first a member of the Gaelic League in 1896 before becoming involved with the IRB in 1913 (R. Dudley Edwards, 1971, p. 19). Batt O'Connor, later to become one of Collins's closest associates, joined first the League, then the GAA and finally, after being inspired by Tone's centenary celebrations in 1898, the IRB. (O'Connor, 1929).
38   Garvin (1987) pp. 49–56.
39   Redmond (1900) in Redmond (1910) p. 97. See also Redmond (1902) p. 5.
40   Rumpf and Hepburn (1977) p. 8.
41   The Orange Free State did make several representations to the Transvaal during the 1880s and 1890s calling for closer cooperation between the two states based on their common background but received little response. Van Jaarsveld (1962, p. 187).
42   When Afrikaans came into being as a separate language is unclear. Upper-class Afrikaners continued to speak High Dutch, which was the language of schools, while Afrikaans was seen as a *kombuistaal* or kitchen language. Fascinating new research, most of it by Davids (1991) has uncovered the fact that the first newspaper in recognisable Afrikaans (as distinct from Dutch) was in fact published nearly twenty years earlier by the 'Coloured' community – the group of descendants of mixed-race and Malay slaves at the Cape. The first book in Afrikaans is a copy of the Koran, written in Arabic script, dating from the 1840s.
43   Hancock (1962) p. 23.
44   Afrikaner Bond (1885).

45 Hofmeyr (1913) p. 524. See also p. 234 where he talks of the 'close linking together of Dutch and English Africander'.
46 Davenport (1966) pp. 306–7.
47 There are many different arguments about the causes of the Boer War. Pakenham (1979) remains the best general history of the conflict. Marks and Trapido (1981) are particularly informative on the underlying causes of the War, especially economic dimensions. For a fascinating first-hand account see Reitz (1975).
48 Hancock (1962) p. 109.
49 Floyd (1977) p. 74.
50 Hofmeyr (1987) p. 102; Welsh (1989) pp. 74–6.
51 See Hexham (1981) for a detailed study of this period and the role of the Church. The DRC was split into three factions of which the Doppers were the smallest and most doctrinally conservative.
52 Thompson (1956) remains the best discussion of this lengthy and con- voluted process. The transition from four states to one was not as abrupt as it might seem and various forms of union and confederation had been discussed from the time of Lord Carnarvon in 1877. Customs union proposals and railway linkages had been encouraged, and many people already spoke of 'South Africa', which was also the designated entity for cricket and rugby matches against England (South African Yearbook 1979, p. 833).
53 See Lewsen (1982, p. 298) for a discussion of Merriman's view on race and reconciliation with the Afrikaners.
54 Thompson (1971) p. 353. It is difficult to assess whether or not a racial franchise was inevitable. The original British intention after the war had been to force the Boer Republics to accept limited black participation. Despite this, Milner regarded blacks as 'children, needing and appre- ciating just, paternal government' and willingly conceded to Boer demands that there be no black enfranchisement (Porter 1984, p. 180). During the 1880s in the Cape, the black electorate often held the balance of power in various constituencies, giving it substantial leverage with white political parties and muting Afrikaner racism. Such a situa- tion might have been created in South Africa. Nevertheless, by the beginning of the twentieth century, there had been a 'surge toward racial discrimination' leaving the Cape more willing to concede to the repub- lics' demands (Davenport, 1987, pp. 30–33).
55 Smuts (1952) p. 128; Pirow (1953) p. 60.
56 Malan (1964) pp. 250–52.
57 Floyd (1977) p. 80.
58 Dept. of Information (1952) p. 5.
59 Neame (1930) p. 272.
60 Harrison (1981) p. 87.
61 Serfontein (1978) p. 31.
62 O'Meara (1983) p. 64.
63 Wilkins and Strydom (1977) p. 42.
64 *Die Huisgenoot*, 9 January 1925. The magazine's ethno-linguistic line was quite overt, and it was clear that it regarded language more than religion or culture as the key to Afrikaner national identity. A representative

poem in its pages, exuding the motifs of politics, religion and education built around ethnic identity, declared:

Nothing can break it
The legislator loves it
The priest preaches it
Afrikaans
Schools teach it
The statesman honours it
Afrikaans
Live our dear language: the people will struggle
For a mother language
As trustworthy as steel
Afrikaans is for me (*Die Huisgenoot*, 19 June 1925).

65   Diedrichs (1936) pp. 23–5.
66   Meyer (1941) pp. 55–8.
67   Pelzer (1979) p. 32.
68   Harrison (1981) p. 100.
69   Hess (1952).
70   Pinsker (1881) p. 14.
71   Wolffsohn (1987) p. 121.
72   Shafir (1988) p. 84.
73   Herzl (1946) pp. 71–2.
74   Taylor (1959) p. 4.
75   Laqueur (1972) p. 106.
76   See Gonen (1975) p. 332 for a discussion of the *Hatikvah* and its psychological role in Zionism.
77   Ha'Am (1902) pp. 254–5.
78   Zionist Federation, Lecture I (1945) p. 21.
79   Weizmann (1969), Volume III, p. 81.
80   Patkin (1943) p. 20.
81   Simon (1944) pp. 3–11.
82   Simon (1912) pp. 33–4. See also Ben Gurion (1970) p. 128.
83   Weizmann (1969), vol. III, pp. 192–3.
84   Ben Gurion (1972) p. 36.
85   Gorny (1975) pp. 61–7.
86   Shafir (1989) p. 60.
87   These initiatives also helped the Zionists legitimate their presence in Palestine. On the School's 25th anniversary, it was acclaimed as a 'spiritual centre', proof that 'the country belongs to that people which made its mark on it and there can be only one mark – national culture'. (*Palestine Weekly*, 1 August 1930).
88   Lucas (1974) p. 64.
89   Weizmann (1949) p. 183.
90   Weizmann (1974), vol. V, pp. 335–40; Weizmann (1949) pp. 183, 295.
91   Ben Gurion (1970) p. 129.
92   Ibid., p. 27.
93   C. O'Brien (1988a) p. 118.

94   Lucas (1974) p. 42.
95   Safran (1978) p. 21.
96   Weizmann (1949) p. 159.

3. ECONOMY AND ORGANISATION

1   Vaughan and Fitzpatrick (1978) p. 27.
2   Hutchinson (1987) p. 167.
3   Garvin (1981) p. 193.
4   McDowell (1964) p. 261.
5   Lee (1973) p. 168.
6   Between 1845–51 the population of Ireland declined by 2.25m as 750 000 people died of starvation and 1.5m emigrated, mostly to America (Foster, 1988, pp. 318–22).
7   Clark (1975) p. 72.
8   Davis (1914) pp. 163, 199.
9   Gavan Duffy (1848) p. 12.
10   Redmond (1902) p. 6.
11   Moran (1905) pp. 18–20. See also Inglis (1960, p. 113) on Moran's support of Irish industry.
12   Lee (1973) p. 147.
13   Clark (1975) p. 68.
14   Feingold (1975) p. 84.
15   Clark (1975) p. 61.
16   See Lyons (1971, p. 20) and Lyons (1979, p. 52).
17   Bew (1987) pp. 126–39.
18   *Christian Science Monitor*, 5 May 1918.
19   Griffith (1906) p. 9.
20   *United Irishman*, 9 December 1905.
21   Griffith (1906, p. 32). See also De Blacam (1921, pp. 45, 149–214) who shows how Sinn Fein continually sought to link culture, industry and agriculture and explicitly addressed all these issues together in various drafts of its constitution.
22   See for example *Sinn Fein*, 28 Dec. 1907.
23   Garvin (1987) pp. 49–56.
24   For these particular examples see *Sinn Fein*, 5 December 1908.
25   The railway workers, who were also trade unionised, were the one substantial group of non-agricultural workers who operated throughout the country and contained similar numbers of Protestant and Catholic workers.
26   Macardle (1960) p. 188. See Connolly (1949) for a selection of his writings on the subject. See also Rumpf and Hepburn (1977, pp. 12–13) for a discussion of these influences.
27   Kee (1972) p. 198. The Union's membership grew steadily through the war and reached 70 000 by 1918 (Rumpf and Hepburn, 1977, p. 12).
28   Hutchinson (1987) p. 184.

29 Interestingly, part of the Parliamentary Party's new-found strength was also due to indirect organisational cohesion and patronage. The United Irish League, based around Cork, established a powerful grassroots network in support of the party and helped provide pressure for the reunification of the pro and anti-Parnell factions. Even more strikingly, the Ancient Order of Hibernians, led by the maverick Joseph Devlin, overtly used patronage around its Belfast stronghold and throughout Ulster. Members relied on each other and the organisation for money, jobs and party posts. As William O'Brien (1923, p. 30) notes, the group's ruling council, the Board of Erin, became 'the primary dispenser of power' in the North between 1906–16. It attracted as many as 180 000 members, one-third of whom served in a ladies auxiliary (Ward, 1969, p. 27). Thus Catholicism was linked, via a powerful, cohesive organisation explicitly predicated on the practice of economic patronage, to a broadly nationalist political platform. Nevertheless, its focus was more on Catholic self-help than Gaelic traditions and ideology and its leaders more interested in their own power base rather than the achievement of an Irish state – hence their links to the Parliamentary Party rather than Sinn Fein.

30 The substance of what would be acceptable as Home Rule was a subject of contentious debate throughout this 30-year period. Parnell had been prepared to accept membership for Ireland in a vaguely defined imperial federation, and, while he demanded control over Ireland's 'resources and revenues', he had no objection to retaining the Queen as head of state or delegating foreign policy to Westminster (C. O'Brien, 1957, p. 349) The Home Rule Bill presented to parliament in 1886 insisted that a self-governing Ireland have no international powers or standing whatsoever. Any matters concerning the British monarch, defence, international trade and treaties and the like would be retained by London. In addition the prospective Irish legislature would have had only limited control over its own fiscal policy – it would be allowed to collect direct tax but customs and excise revenues would remain under British control. It would also be required to make a substantial annual contribution to the Imperial Exchequer (Lee, 1989, p. 7; Marshall, 1982, pp. 63–5). The substance of this bill was repeated in the 1893 version while the 1912 version was even further circumscribed. In addition to the previous restrictions, Britain now reserved the right to change Imperial taxes and impose new ones (Watson, 1893; Foster, 1988, pp. 424–5; Kee, 1972, p. 118).

31 Milner himself left a copious legacy of his time in South Africa, most of which is available in the Milner Papers (1931) and (1933). The second volume, which deals with the post-war period, reveals the centrality of administrative efficiency among Milner's aims.

32 Marks and Trapido (1981) pp. 69–70.

33 *Die Burger*, 1 May 1926. The NP supporting newspaper was the main proponent of this stereotype, running an ongoing series of cartoons lampooning Hoggenheimer and introducing what was to become a well-established anti-semitic streak amongst Afrikaner nationalists.

34 Kaplan (1976, pp. 76–82). Research by David Yudelman (1983, pp. 191–233) has since revealed that neither of these activities had the desired effect, as white wages remained static and mining found loopholes for new legislation. Nevertheless, the perception was that an interventionist state was helping in these sectors and it was this perception that inspired the Broederbond.

35 It should nonetheless be noted that the absolute number of Afrikaners in the civil service rose steadily throughout this period and they filled 43% of government posts by 1939 and 54% of posts by 1948 (O'Meara, 1983, p. 24).

36 Magubane (1979) p. 184.

37 Serfontein (1978) p. 35.

38 Adam and Giliomee (1979) pp. 170–71. While small, these institutions were already highly influential within the nationalist movement. The linked insurance houses Sanlam and Santam, formed in 1918, had already been involved in bankrolling D.F. Malan and the Cape National Party.

39 Bloomberg (1990), p. 126.

40 Berger (1985) pp. 132–40.

41 Robins (1953) pp. 26–7.

42 Stultz (1974) p. 57.

43 Moodie (1975) p. 184. While this is the most commonly cited figure it is drawn from contemporary press accounts and is probably substantially exaggerated. Nevertheless, it is unquestionably true that the final turn-out was much larger than had been anticipated.

44 Malan (1938) in Malan (1964) pp. 121–30. The rate of Afrikaner urbanisation was prodigious and between 1936–51 250 000 streamed to the cities. (Hancock, 1968, p. 289).

45 Serfontein (1978) p. 50.

46 Du Plessis (1964) p. 104.

47 Ibid, p. 121.

48 O'Meara (1983) p. 190, p. 145.

49 Adam and Giliomee (1979) p. 159; Degenaar (1976) p. 29.

50 O'Meara (1983) p. 158.

51 Cabinet records show that this was particularly important in securing support for the Declaration (Stookey, 1986, p. 151). However, Weizmann himself later attributed the decision largely to a British 'sense of fair play'. (Weizmann, 1931, p. 6).

52 See Vital (1987, pp. 329–30), Taylor (1959, pp. 20–30) and Sankowitz (1947, pp. 88–91) for further discussion of this lobbying.

53 Interestingly, Weizmann had a tangential link to Afrikaner nationalism, travelling to South Africa in 1932 where he met with both Hertzog and Smuts (the latter having been a Zionist supporter in the British cabinet in 1917 and at Versailles in 1919) while drumming up support from the local Jewish community, which was very highly mobilised in support of Zionism. (Weizmann, 1949, p. 427).

54 As Wasserstein (1991) makes clear, Samuel was always a British administrator first and a Zionist second – although he worked hard to ensure there were as few incompatibilities between the two as possible.

55 Lucas (1974) p. 104.
56 Cohen, Mitchell (1987) p. 147 By contrast only 45 000 American Jews were voting members at that time (World Zionist Organisation, 1935, pp. 53–5).
57 Wolffsohn (1987), p. 132.
58 Ibid, p. 191.
59 *Encyclopedia of Zionism* (1971) p. 504.
60 Giladi (1975) pp. 171–7.
61 In many ways, the Zionists were developing the framework for a post-war welfare state a decade ahead of its time. Countercyclical 'government' spending, unemployment insurance, health and welfare provisions were all extremely unusual activities for a state at the time. As Gianfranco Poggi (1978, pp. 117–38) has argued, such patronage and focus on economic growth has a highly significant impact in establishing and maintaining the legitimacy of the modern state in the eyes of its citizens. The *Histadrut*/Agency joint economic initiatives had this effect on the Jewish populace in Palestine.
62 Official British calculations estimated that the amount of money invested in industry between 1929–37 grew from £2.5m to £8.5m (Palestine Royal Commission, 1937, p. 115). Total Jewish capital invested amounted to £80m in 1936 (UN Special Committee on Palestine, 1947, p. 15).
63 As in South Africa, this was justified as providing economic opportunities for Palestinians that would not have been available elsewhere. As Berl Katznelson (1937, p. 8) a prominent labour leader, observed: 'Never before has the white man undertaken colonisation with that sense of justice and social progress which fills the Jew'.
64 Jewish Agency (1937) p. 433.
65 See Muenzer (1947).
66 These covered a wide range of activities from the establishment of youth groups to theatre initiatives all linked to the conscious process of 'Hebraization'. (World Zionist Organisation, 1935, pp. 18–22; Zionist Federation, 1945, Lecture IV, p. 22).
67 Palestine Royal Commission (1937) p. 116; Jewish Agency (1937) p. 441.
68 *Palestine Weekly*, 7 March 1930, p. 153.
69 Palestine Royal Commission (1937) p. 118.
70 Sankowitz (1947) p. 155.
71 Jewish Agency (1937) p. 54.
72 Weizmann (1949) p. 253.
73 Van Zyl Slabbert (1975) p. 4.

4. ETHNIC CONFLICT AND STATE-MAKING

1 IRB Constitution (1873) in Mitchell and O'Snodaigh (1989) pp. 22–5.
2 See Boyce (1982, p. 167) and Moley (1974) for discussion of O'Connor's attitude to violence.
3 Lyons (1971) p. 6.
4 Hoppen (1989) p. 20.

5   See Akenson (1992, pp. 145–9) for a useful discussion of this, although he continues to see this movement as subordinate to what he describes as the 'adamantine immovability' of the Calvinist covenant.

6   Lyons (1971) p. 286.

7   Many commentators treat Ulster politics as a form of nationalism. It certainly did have many of the superficial marks of a genuine nationalist movement – use of history, cultural references, holy dates and the like (see Lyons 1979, pp. 132–44; Akenson 1988). But on the key distinguishing feature, the demand for political independence, the Protestant Irish community cannot be regarded as nationalist – its primary demand was always to remain part of the United Kingdom, not to seek a Protestant state.

8   Lee (1989) p. 9. It is interesting to note that all Protestant clergymen were made honorary members.

9   Hoppen (1989) p. 135.

10   Foster (1988) p. 470.

11   Moran (1905), ch. 6.

12   United Irish League (1903).

13   Constitution of the Irish Citizen Army (1913) in Mitchell and O'Snodaigh (1989).

14   Nearly all the recruits to the new militia were townspeople. Only a small minority of the farmers and labour tenants in the West and South, the shock troops of the Land War, seemed concerned by the developing Ulster crisis. Secure in their new-found agricultural prosperity most remained remarkably impervious to nationalist arguments. Townshend (1983) p. 237.

15   Kee (1972) p. 202.

16   Ibid, pp. 204–8.

17   Pearse (1913) p. 83. In one of his most famous speeches, at the grave of old Fenian O'Donovan Rossa in 1915, he declared that '[l]ife springs from death and from the graves of patriotic men and women spring living nations'. Pearse (1915) in Mitchell and O'Snodaigh (1989).

18   Manifesto of the Irish Volunteers (1913) in Mitchell and O'Snodaigh (1989).

19   Kee (1972) p. 220.

20   *Sinn Fein*, 8 August 1914.

21   Foster (1988) p. 475.

22   Henry (1920) p. 188.

23   Lee (1973) p. 154.

24   Proclamation of the Republic (1916) in Mitchell and O'Snodaigh (1989).

25   Fully a third of those executed had been members of the GAA, indicating the importance of that organisation in providing a recruitment pool for the IRB. Mandle (1987) p. 178.

26   Several papers made mention of the contrast between the lenient treatment offered the leaders of the contemporaneous Afrikaner rebellion in South Africa with the executions meted out by the British. See Lee (1989, pp. 29–35) for a fascinating account of exactly how the issue played through the local press over the six-month period following the rebellion.

27   Lee (1989) p. 40.

28   Rumpf and Hepburn (1977) p. 21.

29   Lee (1989) p. 40 and Townshend (1983) p. 318. See also Bew (1983, pp. 213–14) for a particularly interesting discussion of how the old United Irish League organisations in the rural heartland were defeated by Sinn Fein in large part because of such activities.

30   Lyons (1971) p. 396.

31   The real Sinn Fein vote was almost certainly larger as the party failed to contest 25 seats.

32   Weekly *Irish Times*, 4 Jan. 1919.

33   De Valera (1918).

34   Lyons (1971) p. 400.

35   Neame (1930) p. 172.

36   Hancock (1962) p. 357.

37   Given their qualified approval of Home Rule as a first step to full independence, both Sinn Fein and the IRB might well have followed a similar constitutional strategy had Home Rule come to pass before the First World War.

38   *Die Vaderland*, 5 September 1939.

39   See Furlong (1991, pp. 34–53) for a detailed discussion of early activity by pro-Nazi organisations and the role of anti-semitism in Afrikaner politics during that era.

40   *Die Vaderland*, 16 January 1942.

41   Although accurate numbers are hard to establish, and Malan himself stated in Parliament that the OB had 400 000 members, both Harrison (1981, p. 125) and Bloomberg (1990, p. 167) rely on this estimate.

42   Moodie (1972) p. 223.

43   Bloomberg (1990) p. 166.

44   Furlong (1991) pp. 142–3.

45   Robins (1953) p. 33; Thom (1980) p. 17.

46   Davenport (1991) p. 306.

47   In fact the UP worked hard to prove its own racial credentials. In 1936, Hertzog formally did away with the black franchise in the Cape and passed legislation explicitly denying blacks the right to purchase property outside certain designated areas.

48   Houghton (1971) p. 36.

49   Lipton (1985) p. 43.

50   Davies *et al.* (1976) p. 24.

51   Welsh (1971) p. 189.

52   Cronje (1945) pp. 25, 79. In addition to its social engineering theories, the book is riddled with cruder racist theories about the effects of miscegenation on the white race.

53   Greenberg (1987) p. 133.

54   O'Meara (1983) p. 237.

55   See Kedourie (1976).

56   All figures are from Khalidi (1971) pp. 841–2.

57   Taylor (1959) p. 31; see also Said (1992) p. 82.

58   *Palestine Weekly*, 14 April 1927.

59 These had operated on the railways, and in the post office where the British were the employer. Teveth (1985) pp. 63–5. Interestingly, these were the same two areas in which Protestant and Catholic workers had cooperated in Ireland.

60 Horowitz and Lissak (1978) pp. 35–6.

61 It was this offer that had put Weizmann on friendly terms with Feisal at Versailles. Under pressure from hostile Syrian nationalists upon his return home, Feisal was forced to disavow these sentiments and later denied ever having expressed them. Weizmann for his part publicly criticised the 'treacherous nature of the Arab'. C. Smith, 1992, p. 59).

62 Flapan (1979) p. 19.

63 Teveth (1985) p. 80.

64 Weizmann (1931) p. 27.

65 Mansfield (1985) p. 213.

66 Arlosoroff (1932) p. 246.

67 This deal later collapsed after being made public. Shlaim (1990) p. 49.

68 Landau (1971) p. 49.

69 Caplan (1986).

70 Arab Federation (1935) pp. 5–6.

71 Arab Higher Committee (1937a) and (1937b).

72 Palestine Royal Commission Report (1937).

73 C. O'Brien (1988a) p. 230.

74 Jewish Agency (1937) p. 54.

75 Khalidi (1971) p. xli.

76 Flapan (1979) p. 128. See Ben Gurion (1970, p. 82) for a later version of similar sentiments.

77 Teveth (1987) pp. 612–13.

78 Lucas (1974) p. 177.

79 Horowitz and Lissak (1978) p. 51.

80 Palestine *Post*, 16 March 1939.

81 Weizmann (1949), p. 494.

82 Teveth (1987) p. 60. See also Ben Gurion (1972) p. 53.

83 Halevi and Klinov-Malu (1968) p. 17.

84 Laqueur (1972) p. 135.

85 Lucas (1974) p. 200.

86 Ibid, p. 122.

87 Szreszewski (1968) p. 11.

88 Weizmann (1949) p. 538.

5. INTERNATIONAL POLITICS AND STATE POWER

1 Prill (1975) shows how German interest in Irish affairs was consistently high in the late nineteenth and early twentieth centuries, even if it was never translated into concrete action.

2 The entire phenomenon of Irish emigration during the nineteenth and twentieth century is a vast and fascinating topic which had a significant

impact on the domestic politics and economy in Australia, New Zealand and Great Britain itself. For an overview see Foster (1988, ch. 15). On the American phenomenon see Schrier (1958) and Miller (1985).

3   Mansergh (1940) p. 237.

4   Lyons (1971) p. 421; Foster (1988) p. 360.

5   McCartan (1932), who accompanied De Valera on his American sojourn, provides an illuminating discussion of this whole process, including the complicated local politics of Irish America.

6   Pearse (1980) p. 350.

7   See Mansergh (1940, p. 243) on the details of self-determination as understood by the Americans.

8   Dail (1919c).

9   Dail (1919a) and (1919b).

10   *Cork Examiner*, 26 October 1917.

11   *Christian Science Monitor*, 5 May 1918.

12   In practice the IRA always operated semi-autonomously. Most of its leaders were IRB members, and although there was strong overlap between the Sinn Fein and IRB components, the division of authority was never completely clarified.

13   Lee (1989) p. 43.

14   Porter (1984) p. 251.

15   Griffith (1906) pp. 1–5.

16   Kee (1972) p. 185.

17   Younger (1972) p. 47.

18   General Smuts, as a former rebel against the British empire himself, was called in to extol the virtues of such an arrangement to the Irish. He met with De Valera and told him that being part of the Commonwealth would offer 'more peace, more power, more security in such a statehood than in a small, nervous republic'.

19   Younger (1972) p. 264.

20   Ibid, p. 129.

21   *The Free State*, 24 June 1922.

22   Garvin (1987) p. 142; Younger (1972) p. 132.

23   Rumpf and Hepburn (1977) p. 32. See Gallagher (1980) on the failed attempt to forge a political compromise between Collins and De Valera prior to the elections.

24   Accusing the new government of ruling a 'slave state' the rebels self-consciously cloaked themselves in the rhetoric adopted by Pearse in 1916, claiming their blood sacrifice would open the door for the creation of the republic. See *The Plain People*, 21 May 1922; *Poblacht na-h-Eireann*, 1 September 1922.

25   Lee (1989) p. 63.

26   Boyce (1982) p. 345. Interestingly, however the socialisation of civil servants through the nationalist movement was a trend that became entrenched in Ireland – as many as 50% of all civil servants hired after 1921 were former Gaelic Leaguers. Foster (1988) p. 450.

27   Garvin (1981) p. 196.

28   Garvin (1987) p. 32.

29   De Valera (1926).

30   As his biographer Owen Dudley Edwards (1987, p. 118) asserts, 'Between sovereignty *de jure* (involving Northern Ireland) and sovereignty *de facto* (involving 26 counties) it was the latter he worked for, the former he talked about'.

31   Judd (1968) p. 328. Smuts's position was further reinforced because of the significant contribution by the Dominions in the war effort.

32   Gladstone recognised, '[t]he fullest right of the emigrant farmers beyond the Vaal River to manage their own affairs and govern themselves according to their own laws without any interference on the part of the British government'. (Davenport, 1991, p. 170; Judd, 1968, p. 151). Following their botched annexation in 1878 that had resulted in the British defeat at Majuba the two states regained political autonomy under the proviso that Britain retain 'suzerainty'. This was a deliberately vague term that Gladstone defined as those aspects of sovereignty 'which relate to the relations between the Transvaal community and foreign countries'. By 1884, even this had fallen away and Britain once again fully recognised the independence of the South African Republic and Free State – if only because the expense of reasserting British supremacy appeared far to outweigh any potential benefits.

33   Apart from Thompson (1962) whose work remains definitive, good discussions of this process from the perspectives of Britain and the Cape respectively can be seen in Judd (1968, pp. 208–17) and Lewsen (1982, pp. 315–24).

34   Davenport (1991) p. 261.

35   Judd (1968) p. 313. This should not to be confused with the earlier Balfour Declaration, announced by the same Arthur John Balfour, granting the Jewish homeland in 1917. Balfour was, through a sequence of historical coincidences, the individual on the British side with the greatest influence on all three nationalist movements under investigation. He was Secretary for Ireland in the 1880s, Prime Minister in the early 1900s after the Boer War, Foreign Secretary during the First World War when he drafted the first Balfour Declaration calling for a Zionist Homeland, and finally Lord President of the Council and Leader of the House of Lords at the time of the Imperial Conference.

36   Pirow (1957) p. 153.

37   At Irish and South African insistence, this encompassed 'complete sovereign rights'. Marshall (1952) p. 79.

38   *The Star*, 25 May 1948.

39   See for example Meyer (1942).

40   The constitution is published in full in *Die Transvaler* between 22–24 January 1942.

41   *The Star*, 12 January 1942; *The Star*, 24 January 1942.

42   Malan's biographer, H. B Thom (1980, pp. 17–19), tries to suggest that the NP always rejected the totalitarian experiment. In practice, many Nazi ideas remained part and parcel of the National Party, and in particular Broederbond thinking on the nature and role of the state, both during and after the war. See Furlong (1991, pp. 169–89) and Bloomberg (1990, pp. 138–55).

43   Malan (1942) p. 60.

44   Malan (1959) p. 233.
45   Bloomberg (1990) p. 51.
46   Wilkins and Strydom (1977) p. 89.
47   Serfontein (1987) pp. 43,74.
48   Harrison (1981) p. 138.
49   Heard (1974) p. 33.
50   The UN formally censured South Africa's racial policies in August 1946.
51   See *Die Burger*, 24 May 1948.
52   Despite losing power, Smuts actually received 620 682 votes to the NP's 462 332, or 53.49% compared to 39.85% (Hancock, 1968, pp. 501–2). The HNP was nevertheless able to win the elections because of a South African electoral law that allowed rural districts to be up to 20 per cent smaller than urban ones. As the HNP's support was largely based in smaller towns and the countryside while the UP's was concentrated in the big cities, Malan and the Nationalists were able to win an electoral majority in Parliament.
53   Hancock (1968) p. 506.
54   Hirst (1984) p. 19.
55   United Nations Special Committee on Palestine (1947) p. 3.
56   Khalidi (1971) p. xxxv.
57   Jones (1986) p. 3.
58   Lapping (1985) p. 113.
59   Zionist Organisation of America (1919).
60   World Zionist Organisation (1935) pp. 53–5. On tensions between himself and Brandeis see Weizmann (1949) pp. 333–6.
61   Ben Gurion (1964) p. 488.
62   Teveth (1987) p. 817.
63   See Grose (1986, pp. 35–8) for a discussion on Roosevelt's changing views on Palestine.
64   Taylor (1959) pp. 78–81; Roosevelt (1948) p. 577.
65   Laqueur (1972) p. 574.
66   Smith, A. (1987) pp. 151–2.
67   Koestler (1949) p. 12.
68   Horowitz and Lissak (1978) p. 60.
69   Khalidi (1971) p. liv.
70   Cohen, Michael J. (1988) p. 83.
71   Hirst (1984) p. 120.
72   Part of the reasoning behind this was that Bevin, for all his personal attitudes towards the Zionists, was outwardly committed to the speedy decolonisation of Britain's South Asian colonies, a commitment Weizmann felt could be played to the Zionists's advantage. Porter (1984) p. 312.
73   Louis (1986) p. 20.
74   Hirst (1984) p. 120.
75   See, for example, Jones (1986) p. 343.
76   Hirst (1984) p. 133.
77   Taylor (1959) p. 104.
78   Lucas (1974) p. 238.
79   Shlaim (1988) p. 129.

80   South Africa followed on 25 May. It was to be Smuts's last major act of foreign policy the day before the election that was to remove him from power.
81   See Shlaim (1988, pp. 93–100) for a discussion of these negotiations.
82   Flapan (1979) p. 341.
83   Landau (1971) p. 60.
84   Safran (1978) p. 50.
85   Hirst (1984) p. 142.
86   Safran (1978) p. 51.
87   Over the first three and a half years of its existence, Israel absorbed 320 000 immigrants from Europe, 325 000 from the Middle East and 125 000 from Iraq, which expelled its entire Jewish population. This effectively doubled its pre-independence population of 750 000. (Lucas, 1974, p. 272).
88   That is certainly what happened among Afrikaners in the wake of the 1914 rebellion. It is possible that, had the OB proved capable of launching a major revolt in South Africa in 1941, it might have had a similar effect within the Afrikaner community to that of 1916 for the Catholic population in Ireland. Given the existence of a well-established and wide-ranging nationalist movement capable of taking advantage of the situation and an Afrikaner public infatuated with Hitler and largely disillusioned with the Smuts government, the South African situation was at least as receptive to Afrikaner nationalism as Ireland was to Catholic nationalism in the wake of the Easter Rebellion.

Bibliography

THEORETICAL AND GENERAL WORKS

Akenson, Donald Harman (1992) *God's Peoples: Covenant and Land in South Africa, Israel and Ulster*, London: Cornell University Press.

Alter, Peter (1985) *Nationalism*, London: Edward Arnold.

Anderson, Benedict (1983) *Imagined Communities*, London: Verso.

Armstrong, John (1982) *Nations before Nationalism*, Durham: University of North Carolina Press.

Bell, Daniel (1975) 'Ethnicity and Social Change', in Nathan Glazer and Daniel P. Moynihan (eds), *Ethnicity*, Cambridge: Harvard University Press.

Benhabib, Seyla (1986) *Critique, Norm and Utopia*. New York: Columbia University Press.

Berlin, Isaiah (1989) *Against the Current: Essays in the History of Ideas*, Henry Hardy (ed.), Oxford: Clarendon Press.

Birnbaum, Pierre (1980) 'States, Ideologies and Collective Action in Western Europe', *Social Science Journal*, vol. XXXII, No. 4.

Bonnell, Victoria E. (1980) 'The Uses of Theory, Concepts and Comparisons in Historical Sociology', in *Comparative Studies in Society and History*, vol. 22.

Brass, Paul (1979) 'Elite Groups, Symbol Manipulation and Ethnic Identity among the Muslims of South Asia', in D. Taylor and M. Yapp (eds) *Political Identity in South Asia*, London: Curzon Press.

Breuilly, John (1985) *Nationalism and the State*, Chicago: University of Chicago Press.

Carr, E.H. (1945) *Nationalism and After*, London: Macmillan.

Chapman, Malcom (ed.) (1993) *Social and Biological Aspects of Ethnicity*, Oxford: Oxford University Press.

Cobban, Alfred (1969) *The Nation State and National Self-Determination*, London: Fontana Press.

Connor, Walker (1972) 'Nation Building or Nation Destroying' in *World Politics*, vol. 24, no. 3.

Connor, Walker (1990) 'Ethno-nationalism and Political Instability: An Overview' in Herman Giliomee and Jannie Gagiano (eds) *The Elusive Search for Peace*, Cape Town: Oxford University Press.

Crawford, James (1979) *The Creation of States in International Law*, Oxford: Clarendon Press.

De Silva, K.M. and May, R.J. (eds) (1991) *The Internationalization of Ethnic Conflict*, London: Pinter.

Dunleavy, Patrick and O'Leary, Brendan (1987) *Theories of the State: the Politics of Liberal Democracy*, London: Macmillan.

Durkheim, Emile (1965) *The Elementary Forms of the Religious Life*, New York: The Free Press.

Eddy, John and Schreuder, Deryck (1988) *The Rise of Colonial Nationalism*, Boston: Allen and Unwin.

Fichte, Johann Gottlieb (1968) [1807] *Addresses to the German Nation*, New York: Harper & Row.

Fishman, Joshua (ed.) (1985) *The Rise and Fall of Ethnic Revival: Perspectives on Language and Ethnicity*, New York: Mouton.

Frederickson, George (1981) *White Supremacy: A Comparative Study in American and South African History*, Oxford: Oxford University Press.

Gallagher, John (1982) *The Decline, Revival and Fall of the British Empire*, Cambridge: Cambridge University Press.

Gamson, William (1990) *The Strategy of Social Protest*, Belmont: Wadsworth.

Geertz, Clifford (1977) *The Interpretation of Cultures*, New York: Basic Books.

Gellner, Ernest (1983) *Nations and Nationalism*, New York: Cornell University Press.

George, Alexander (1979) 'Case Studies and Theory Development: The Method of Structured, Focused Comparison' in Paul Gordon Lawrence (ed.) *Diplomacy: New Approaches in History, Theory and Policy*, New York: Free Press.

Gerth, H.H. and Mills, C. Wright (eds) (1957) *From Max Weber: Essays in Sociology*, London: Routledge and Kegan Paul.

Giddens, Anthony (1985) *The Nation State and Violence*, Polity Press: Cambridge.

Giliomee, Herman (1990) 'Introduction' in Herman Giliomee and Jannie Gagiano (eds) *The Elusive Search for Peace: South Africa, Israel and Northern Ireland*, Cape Town: Oxford University Press.

Gilmour, David (1994) *Curzon*, London: John Murray.

Glazer, Nathan and Moynihan, Daniel P. (1975) 'Ethnicity: Theory and Experience' in N. Glazer and D.P. Moynihan (eds) *Ethnicity*. Cambridge: Harvard University Press.

Gourevitch, Peter (1978) 'The Second Image Reversed' in *International Organisation*, vol. 32, no. 4.

Greenberg, Stanley (1980) *Race and State in Capitalist Development: Comparative Perspectives*, New Haven: Yale University Press.

Greenfeld, Liah (1992) *Nationalism: Five Roads to Modernity*, Cambridge, Mass: Harvard University Press.

Haas, Ernst (1986) 'What is Nationalism and Why should we Study It?' in *International Organisation*, vol. 40, no. 3.

Habermas, Jurgen (1973) *Legitimation Crisis*, Cambridge: Polity Press.

Hall, John A. (1986) 'Introduction' in John A. Hall (ed.), *States in History*, Oxford: Basil Blackwell.

Hall, John A. (1993) 'Nationalisms Classified and Explained' in *Daedalus*, vol. 122, no. 3.

Hall, John A. and Ikenberry, G.J. (1989) *The State*, Milton Keynes: Open University Press.

Hayes, Carlton B. (1960) *Nationalism: A Religion*, New York: Macmillan.

Hechter, Michael (1975) *Internal Colonialism*, London: Routledge & Kegan Paul.

Held, David (1982) 'Crisis Tendencies, Legitimation and the State' in John B. Thompson and David Held (eds), *Habermas – Critical Debates*, Cambridge: The MIT Press.

Held, David (1983) 'Introduction: Central Perspectives on the Modern State' in David Held *et al.* (eds) *States and Societies*, Oxford: Basil Blackwell.

Herder, Johan Gottfried (1969) in F.M. Barnard (ed.), *J.G. Herder on Social and Political Culture*, Cambridge: Cambridge University Press.

Hinsley, E.H. (1973) *Nationalism and the International System*, London: Hodder and Stoughton.

Hintze, Otto (1975) [1902] 'The Formation of States and Constitutional Development: A Study in History and Politics' in F. Gilbert (ed.) *Historical Essays*, New York: Oxford University Press.

Hintze, Otto (1975) [1906] 'Military Organization and the Organization of the State' in F. Gilbert (ed.) *Historical Essays*, New York: Oxford University Press.

Hobsbawm, Eric (1992) *Nations and Nationalism since 1780*, Cambridge: Cambridge University Press.

Horowitz, Donald (1985) *Ethnic Groups in Conflict*, Berkeley: University of California Press.

Hroch, Miloslav (1985) *Social Preconditions of National Revival in Europe. A Comparative Analysis of the Social Composition of Patriotic Groups among the Smaller European Nations*, Cambridge: Cambridge University Press.

Hutchinson, John (1987) *The Dynamics of Cultural Nationalism*, London: Allen and Unwin.

Hutchinson, John and Smith, Anthony (1994) *Nationalism*, Oxford: Oxford University Press.

Judd, Denis (1968) *Balfour and the British Empire: A Study in Imperial Evolution, 1874–1932*, London: Macmillan.

Kedourie, Elie (1993) *Nationalism*, London: Hutchinson and Co.

Kedourie, Elie (1970) *Nationalism in Asia and Africa*, London: Weidenfeld and Nicolson.

Keeton, George W. (ed.) (1951–55) *The British Commonwealth: The Development of its Laws and Constitutions*, London: Stevens and Sons.

Kellas, James (1991) *The Politics of Nationalism and Ethnicity*, London: Macmillan.

Kohn, Hans (1946) *The Idea of Nationalism: A Study in its Origins and Background*, New York: Macmillan.

Lapping, Brian (1985) *End of Empire*, London: Granada.

Lloyd, T.O. (1984) *The British Empire 1558–1983*, Oxford: Oxford University Press.

Mann, Michael (1993) 'Nation-States in Europe and Other Countries: Diversifying, Developing or Dying' in *Daedalus*, vol. 122, no. 3.

Marshall, Geoffrey (1957) *Parliamentary Sovereignty and the Commonwealth*, Oxford: Clarendon Press.

Mayall, James (1990) *Nationalism and International Society*, Cambridge: Cambridge University Press.

McAdam, Doug (1987) *Political Process and the Development of Black Insurgency 1930–1970*, Chicago: University of Chicago.

McAdam, Doug, McCarthy, John D. and Zald, Mayer N. (1996) *Comparative Perspectives on Social Movements*, Cambridge: Cambridge University Press.

McCarthy, John D. (1996) 'Constraints and Opportunities in Adopting, Adapting and Inventing' in McAdam, D., McCarthy, J., and Zald, M. (1996)

Comparative Perspectives on Social Movements, Cambridge: Cambridge University Press.

McCarthy, John D. and Zald, Mayer N. 'Resource Mobilization and Social Movements: A Partial Theory', *American Journal of Sociology*, (82: 6).

Midlarsky, Manus I. (ed.) (1992) *The Internationalisation of Ethnic Conflict*, London: Routledge.

Moore, Barrington J. (1966) *Social Origins of Dictatorship and Democracy: Lord and Peasant in the Making of the Modern World*, Boston: Beacon Press.

Moynihan, Daniel Patrick (1993) *Pandaemonium: Ethnicity in International Politics*, Oxford: Oxford University Press.

Nairn, Tom (1977) *The Breakup of Britain: Crisis and Neo-Nationalism*, London: NLB.

Nordlinger, Eric (1987) 'Taking the State Seriously', in Myron Weiner and Samuel Huntington (eds), *Understanding Political Development*, Boston and Toronto: Little Brown.

O'Brien, Conor Cruise (1988b) *GodLand: Reflections on Religion and Nationalism*, Cambridge: Harvard University Press.

O'Brien, Conor Cruise (1993) 'The Wrath of Ages: Nationalism's Primordial Past' in *Foreign Affairs*, vol. 71, no. 5.

Orridge, Andrew (1982) 'Separatist and Autonomist Nationalisms: The Structure of Regional Loyalties in the Modern State' in C.Williams (ed.) *National Separatism*, Cardiff: University of Wales Press.

Poggi, Gianfranco (1978) *The Development of the Modern State*, Stanford: Stanford University Press.

Porter, Bernard (1984) *The Lion's Share*, London and New York: Longman.

Premdas, R., Samarasinghe, S.W.R., Anderson, A. (eds) (1990) *Secessionist Movements in Comparative Perspective*, London: Pinter.

Premdas, Ralph (1991) 'The Internationalization of Ethnic Conflict' in K.M. de Silva and R.J. May (eds) *The Internationalization of Ethnic Conflict*, London: Pinter.

Ra'anam, Uri, *et al.* (eds) (1991) *State and Nation in Multi-ethnic Societies*, Manchester: Manchester University Press.

Rejai, Mustafa and Enloe, Cynthia H. (1969) 'Nation-States and State-Nations' in *International Studies Quarterly*, vol. 13, no. 2.

Riggs, Fred W. (ed.) (1987) *The Sociobiology of Ethnocentrism, Evolutionary Dimensions of Xenophobia, Discrimination, Racism and Nationalism*, London: Croom Helm.

Rokkan, Stein (1975) 'Dimensions of State Formation and Nation-Building: A Possible Paradigm for Research on Variations within Europe' in C. Tilly (ed.) *The Formation of National States in Western Europe*, Princeton: Princeton University Press.

Rokkan, Stein and Urwin, Derek (1983) *Economy, Territory, Identity: Politics of Western European Identities*, London: Sage.

Ryan, Stephen (1990) *Ethnic Conflict and International Relations*, Aldershot: Dartmouth Publishing.

Samarasinghe, S.W.R. (1990) 'Introduction' in R. Premdas, S.W.R Samarasinghe and A. Anderson (eds) *Secessionist Movements in Comparative Perspective*, London: Pinter.

Seers, Dudley (1983) *The Political Economy of Nationalism*, Oxford: Oxford University Press.

Seton-Watson, Hugh (1977) *Nations and States*, London: Methuen Press.

Shefter, Martin (1977) 'Party and Patronage: Germany, England and Italy' in *Politics and Society* 7, no. 4.

Skocpol, Theda (1979) *States and Social Revolution: A Comparative Analysis of France, Russia and China*, Cambridge: Cambridge University Press.

Skocpol, Theda (1981) 'Bringing the State Back In', In Peter B. Evans, Dietrich Rueschmeyer and Theda Skocpol (eds) *Bringing the State Back in*, New York: Cambridge University Press.

Skocpol, Theda and Somers, Margaret (1980) 'The Uses of Comparative History in Macrosocial Inquiry' in *Comparative Studies in Society and History*, vol. 22.

Smelser, Neil A (1962) *Theory of Collective Behaviour*, New York: Free Press.

Smith, Anthony D. (1983) *Theories of Nationalism*, Ithaca: Cornell University Press.

Smith, Anthony D. (1987) *The Ethnic Origins of Nations*, Oxford: Basil Blackwell.

Smith, Anthony D. (1991) *National Identity*, London: Penguin Books.

Snyder, Louis (1990) *Encyclopedia of Nationalism*, New York: Paragon House.

Suzman, Mark (1996) *Ethnic Nationalism and the State*, Unpublished Dissertation, Oxford University.

Symmons-Symonlewicz, Konstantin (1968) *Modern Nationalism*, New York: Policy Institute of Arts and Sciences in America.

Tilly, Charles (1975) 'Reflections on the History of European State-Making' in Charles Tilly (ed.) *The Formation of National States in Western Europe*, Princeton: Princeton University Press.

Tilly, Charles (1978) *From Mobilization to Revolution*, New York: Random House.

Tilly, Charles (1993) 'National Self-Determination as a Problem for All of Us' in *Daedelus*, vol. 122, no. 3.

Vail, Leroy (1989) 'Ethnicity in Southern African History' in L. Vail (ed.) *The Creation of Tribalism in Southern Africa*, Berkeley: University of California Press.

Van den Berghe, Pierre (1981) *The Ethnic Phenomenon*, New York: Elsevier.

Waldron, Arthur (1985) 'Theories of Nationalism and Historical Explanation' in *World Politics*, vol. 37.

Weber, Max (1978) *Economy and Society, vols 1 and 2*, Guenter Roth and Claus Wittich (eds), Berkeley and Los Angeles: University of California Press.

IRELAND

Newspapers and Magazines

Christian Science Monitor
Cork Examiner

The Free State
Irish Felon
Irish Times
The Plain People
The Irish Republic (*Poblacht na-h-Eireann*)
Sinn Fein
United Irishman
Weekly Nation

Books, Pamphlets and Articles

Akenson, Donald Harman (1988) *Small Differences: Irish Catholics and Irish Protestants, 1815–1922*, Kingston: McGill-Queens University Press.
Alter, Peter (1974) 'Symbols of Irish Nationalism' in *Studia Hibernica*, vol. 14.
Beckett, J.C. (1986) *A Short History of Ireland*, London: Century Hutchinson.
Beckett, Ian F.W. (ed.) (1986) *The Army and the Curragh Incident*, Bodley Head/Army Records Society: London.
Bew, Paul (1987) *Conflict and Conciliation in Ireland, 1890–1910*, Oxford: Clarendon Press.
Bew, Paul, Gibbon, Peter and Patterson (1979) *The State in Northern Ireland 1921–72: Political Forces and Social Classes*, Manchester: Manchester University Press.
Boyce, D. George (1982) *Nationalism in Ireland*, London: Routledge.
Boyce, D. George (1988) ' "One Last Burial": Culture, Counter-Revolution and Revolution in Ireland 1886–1916', in D. George Boyce (ed.) *The Revolution in Ireland 1879–1923*, London: Routledge.
Bradshaw, Brendan (1989) 'Nationalism and Historical Scholarship in Modern Ireland' in *Irish Historical Studies*, vol. xxvi, no. 104.
Brailsford, H.N. (1903) *Some Irish Problems*, London: S.H. Bonsfield.
Carroll, Francis M (1978) *American Opinion and the Irish Question 1910–23: A Study in Opinion and Policy*, Gill and Macmillan: Dublin.
Clark, Samuel (1975) 'The Political Mobilization of Irish Farmers' in *Canadian Review of Sociology and Anthropology*, vol. 12.
Connolly, James (1949) *Labour and Easter Week: A Selection from the Writings of James Connolly*, Desmond Ryan (ed.), Dublin: Sign of the Three Candles.
Coogan, Tim Pat (1990) *Michael Collins*, London: Hutchinson.
Corish, Patrick J. (1961) 'Cardinal Cullen and the National Association of Ireland' in *Reportorium Novum*, vol. 3.
Cromerford, R.V. (1981) 'Patriotism as Pastime: The Appeal of Fenianism in the mid-1860s' in *Irish Historical Studies*, vol. xxii, no. 87.
Dail Eireann (1919a) 'Ireland's Case for Independence' in *Official Documents from Ireland*, New York: Friends of Irish Freedom.
Dail Eireann (1919b) 'Ireland's Address to the Free Nations of the World', Dublin: Fergus O' Connor.
Dail Eireann (1919c) 'The Declaration of Irish Independence', Dublin: Fergus O'Connor.
Davie, Donald (1960) in Conor Cruise O'Brien (ed.) *The Shaping of Modern Ireland*, London: Routledge and Kegan Paul.

Davis, Thomas (1914) [1842–45] in Arthur Griffith (ed.) *Thomas Davis the Thinker and Teacher: The Essence of His Writings in Prose and Poetry*, Dublin: M.H. Gill.

De Blacam, A (1921) *What Sinn Fein Stands For*, Dublin: Mellifort Press.

De Valera, Eamonn (1924) *The Hundred Best Sayings of Eamonn De Valera*, Dublin: Talbot Press.

De Valera, Eamonn (1926) 'Fianna Fail – A National Policy Outlined', Dublin: Wood Printing.

De Valera, Eamonn (1944) *Peace and War: Speeches by Mr. De Valera on International Affairs*, Dublin: M.H. Gill & Son.

De Vere White, Terence (1960) 'Arthur Griffith', in Conor Cruise O'Brien (ed.) *The Making of Modern Ireland*, London: Routledge and Kegan Paul.

Dickson, David, Keogh, Daire and Whelan, Kevin (eds) (1993) *The United Irishmen: Republicanism, Radicalism and Rebellion*, Dublin: Lilliput.

Dillon, Myles (1960) 'Douglas Hyde' in Conor Cruise O'Brien (ed.) *The Making of Modern Ireland*, London: Routledge and Kegan Paul.

Dudley Edwards, Owen (1987) *Eamonn De Valera*, Cardiff: GPC Books.

Dudley Edwards, Ruth (1971) *Patrick Pearse: The Triumph of Failure*, London: Faber & Faber.

Duffy, Charles Gavan (1848) *The Creed of 'The Nation': A Profession of Confederate Principles*, Dublin: Mason Booksellers.

Duffy, Charles Gavan (1894) 'The Revival of Irish Literature' in *The Revival of Irish Literature and Other Addresses*, London: T. Fisher Unwin.

Ellis, Steven G. (1986) 'Nationalist Historiography and the English and Gaelic Worlds in the Late Middle Ages' in *Irish Historical Studies*, vol. XXV, no. 97.

Ellis, Stephen G. (1991) 'Historiographical Debate: Representations of the Past in Ireland: Whose Past and Whose Present?' in *Irish Historical Studies*, vol. XXVII, no. 108.

Feingold, William L. (1975) 'The Tenants Movement to Capture the Irish Poor Law Boards, 1877–1886' in *Albion*, vol. 7.

Fitzpatrick, David (1987) 'The Geography of Irish Nationalism, 1910–21', in C.H.E. Philpin (ed.), *Nationalism and Popular Protest in Ireland*, Cambridge: Cambridge University Press.

Foster, R.F. (1987) 'Introduction' in C.H.E. Philpin (ed.), *Nationalism and Popular Protest in Ireland* Cambridge: Cambridge University Press.

Foster, R.F. (1988) *Modern Ireland, 1600–1972*, London: Penguin Books.

Gallagher, M (1980) 'The Pact General Election of 1922' in *Irish Historical Studies*, vol. xxi.

Garvin, Tom (1981) *The Evolution of Irish Nationalist Politics*, Dublin: Gill and Macmillan.

Garvin, Tom (1987) *Nationalist Revolutionaries in Ireland, 1858–1928*, Oxford: Clarendon Press.

Gibbon, Peter (1975) *The Origins of Ulster Unionism: The Formation of Popular Protestant Politics and Ideology in Nineteenth Century Ireland*, Manchester: Manchester University Press.

Griffith, Arthur (1906) *The Sinn Fein Policy*, Dublin: James Duffy & Co.

Harkness, David W. (1969) *The Restless Dominion: The Irish Free State and British Commonwealth of Nations, 1921–1931*, London: Macmillan.

Harkness, David W. (1981) 'Ireland since 1921' in J. Lee (ed.) *Irish Historiography 1970–79*, Cork: Cork University Press.

Henry, Robert Mitchell (1920) *The Evolution of Sinn Fein*, London: T. Fisher Unwin.

Hopkinson, Michael (1988) *Green against Green: The Irish Civil War*, Dublin: Gill and Macmillan.

Hoppen, K. Theodore (1984) *Election, Politics and Society in Ireland, 1832–1885*, Oxford: Clarendon.

Hoppen, K. Theodore (1989) *Ireland since 1800: Conflict and Conformity*, London: Longman.

Hutton, Sean and Stewart, Paul (1991) 'Perspectives on Irish History and Social Studies' in S. Hutton and P. Stewart (eds), *Ireland's Histories: Aspects of State, Society and Ideology*, London: Routledge.

Hyde, Douglas (1894) 'The Necessity for De-Anglicising Ireland' in *The Revival of Irish Literature and Other Addresses*, London: T. Fisher Unwin.

Johnson, Daniel S. and Kennedy, Liam (1991) 'Nationalist Historiography and the Decline of the Irish Economy: George O'Brien Revisited' in S. Hutton and P. Stewart (eds) *Ireland's Histories*, London: Routledge.

Kee, Robert (1972) *The Green Flag, Volume II: The Bold Fenian Men*, London: Penguin Books.

Kennedy, Liam (1978) 'The Early Response of the Irish Catholic Clergy to the Cooperative Movement' in *Irish Historical Studies*, vol. xxi, no. 81, pp. 55–74.

Kiernan, V.G. (1987) 'The Emergence of a Nation' in C.H.E. Philpin (ed.) *Nationalism and Popular Protest in Ireland*, Cambridge: Cambridge University Press.

Lee, J. (1966) 'Money and Beer in Ireland 1790–1875' in *Economic Historical Review*, xix.

Lee, J. (1973) *The Modernisation of Irish Society, 1848–1918*, Dublin: Gill and Macmillan.

Lee, J. (1981) 'Irish Economic History since 1500' in J. Lee (ed.) *Irish Historiography 1970–9*, Cork: Cork University Press.

Lee, J. (1989) *Ireland 1912–1985: Politics and Society*, Cambridge: Cambridge University Press.

Lee, J. (1991) 'The Irish Constitution of 1937' in S. Hutton and P. Stewart (eds), *Ireland's Histories: Aspects of State, Society and Ideology*, London: Routledge.

Lyons, F.S. (1971) *Ireland since the Famine, 1850 to the Present*, London: Weidenfeld and Nicolson.

Lyons, F.S. (1979) *Culture and Anarchy in Ireland, 1890–1939*, Oxford: Clarendon Press.

MacArdle, Dorothy (1960) 'James Connolly and Patrick Pearse' in Conor Cruise O'Brien, *The Making of Modern Ireland*, London: Routledge and Kegan Paul.

MacDonagh, Oliver (1983) *States of Mind: A Study of Anglo-Irish Conflict, 1780–1980*, London: Pimlico.

Macintyre, A. (1975) *The Liberator: Daniel O'Connell and the Irish Party 1830–47*, London.

McCartan, Patrick (1932) *With De Valera in America*, Dublin: Fitzpatrick.

McCracken, Donal (1982) *The Irish Pro-Boers, 1877–1902*, Johannesburg: Perskor.

McCracken, J.L. (1967) 'Northern Ireland, 1921–66' in T.W. Moody and F.X. Martin *The Course of Irish History*, Cork: Mercier Press.

McDowell, R.B. (1960) 'Edward Carson' in Conor Cruise O'Brien (ed.) *The Making of Modern Ireland*, London: Routledge and Kegan Paul.

McDowell, R.B. (1964) *The Irish Administration 1801–1914*, London: Routledge.

Maltby, Jeremy (1990) *Inventing an Irish Identity: The Creation of National Spirit through the Arts 1870–1923*, Honours Thesis, Harvard University.

Mandle, W.F, (1977) 'The IRB and the Beginning of the Gaelic Athletic Association', *Irish Historical Studies*, vol.xx.

Mandle, W.F. (1987) *The Gaelic Athletic Association and Irish Nationalist Politics 1884–1924*, London: Christopher Helm.

Mansergh, Nicholas (1940) *Ireland in the Age of Reform and Revolution*, London: George Allen and Unwin.

Mansergh, Nicholas (1960) 'John Redmond' in Conor Cruise O'Brien (ed.) *The Making of Modern Ireland*, London: Routledge and Kegan Paul.

Mansergh, Nicholas (1976) *The Prelude to Partition: Concepts and Aims in Ireland and India*, Cambridge: Cambridge University Press.

Martin, F.X (1967) *Leaders and Men of the Easter Rising: Dublin 1916*, London: Methuen.

Miller, David W. (1968) 'The Roman Catholic Church in Ireland, 1898–1918' in *Eire – Ireland*, vol. iii.

Miller, K.A. (1985) *Emigrants and Exiles: Ireland and the Irish Exodus to North America*, New York: Oxford University Press.

Mitchell, Arthur and O'Snodaigh, Padraig (1989) *Irish Political Documents 1869–1916*, Dublin: Irish Academic Press.

Moley, Raymond (1974) *Daniel O'Connell: Nationalism without Violence*, New York: Fordham University Press.

Moody T.W. (1967) 'Fenians, Home-Rule and the Land War, 1850–91' in T.W. Moody and F.X. Martin (eds) *The Course of Irish History*, Cork: Mercier Press.

Moran, D.P. (1905) *The Philosophy of Irish Ireland*, Dublin: James Duffy.

Moxon-Browne, Edward (1983) *Nation, Class and Creed in Northern Ireland*, Aldershot: Gower.

Mulvey, Helen F. (1971) 'Nineteenth Century Ireland, 1801–1914' in T.W. Moody (ed.) *Irish Historiography 1936–70*, Dublin: Dublin University Press.

Mulvey, Helen F. (1971) 'Twentieth Century Ireland, 1914–1970' in T.W. Moody (ed.) *Irish Historiography 1936–70*, Dublin: Dublin University Press.

Nowlan, Kevin Barry (ed.) (1969) *The Making of 1916: Studies in the History of the Rising*, Dublin: Stationery Office.

O'Brien, Conor Cruise (1957) *Parnell and His Party*, Oxford: Clarendon Press.

O'Brien, Conor Cruise (1988d) 'The Irish Mind: A Bad Case of Cultural Nationalism' in *Passion and Cunning and Other Essays*, London: Weidenfeld & Nicolson.

O'Brien, William (1892) 'The Influence of the Irish Language on Irish National Literature – A Lecture', Cork: Guy & Co.

O'Brien, William (1923) *The Irish Revolution and How it Came About*, London: George Allen & Unwin.

O'Connor, Batt (1929) *With Michael Collins in the Fight for Irish Independence*, London: Peter Davies.

O'Connor, James (1925) *History of Ireland 1798–1924*, London: Edward Arnold.

O'Connor Lysaght, D.R. (1991) 'A Saorstat is Born: How the Irish Free State Came into Being' in S. Hutton and P. Stewart (eds) *Ireland's Histories*, London: Routledge.

O'Day, Alan (1987) 'Introduction' in *Reactions to Irish Nationalism*, London: Hambledon Press.

O'Day, Alan and Stevenson, John (eds) (1992) *Irish Historical Documents since 1800*, Barnes and Noble Books: Savage, Maryland.

O'Tuathaig, M.A.G. (1981) 'Ireland, 1800–1921' in J. Lee (ed.) *Irish Historiography*, Cork: Cork University Press.

Pakenham, Thomas (1993) 'Brother by Oath' in *The Times Literary Supplement*, no. 4728, 12 November 1993.

Pearse, Patrick (1913) 'The Coming Revolution' in A.C. Hepburn (ed.) *The Conflict of Nationality in Modern Ireland*, London: Edward Arnold.

Pearse, Patrick (1914) 'The Sovereign People' in A.C. Hepburn (ed.) *The Conflict of Nationality in Modern Ireland*, London: Edward Arnold.

Pearse, Patrick (1915) 'Speech at the Burial of O'Donovan Rossa' in A. Mitchell and P. O'Snodaigh (eds) *Irish Political Documents 1869–1916*, Dublin: Irish Academic Press.

Pearse, Patrick (1980) *The Letters of P.H. Pearse*, (ed.) Seama O'Buachalla, Gerards Cross: Colin Smythe.

Philpin, C.H.E. (1987) *Nationalism and Popular Protest in Ireland*, Cambridge: Cambridge University Press.

Prill, Felicia (1975) *Ireland, Britain and Germany 1870–1914: Problems of Nationalism and Religion in Nineteenth Century Europe*, Gill and Macmillan: Dublin.

Redmond, John (1902) 'Why Ireland is Discontented', London: United Irish League.

Redmond, John (1910) *Speeches of John Redmond, M.P.*, R. Barry O' Brien (ed.), London: T. Fisher Unwin.

Rumpf, E. and Hepburn, A.C. (1977) *Nationalism and Socialism in Twentieth Century Ireland*.

Ryan, Desmond (1960) 'Stephens, Devoy and Tom Clarke' in Conor Cruise O'Brien *The Making of Modern Ireland*, London: Routledge and Kegan Paul.

Schrier, A (1958) *Ireland and the American Emigration, 1850–1900*, Minneapolis: University of Minnesota.

Stewart, A.T.Q. (1977) *The Narrow Ground: Aspects of Ulster 1609–1969*, London: Faber.

Stewart, A.T.Q (1993) *A Deeper Silence: The Hidden Origins of the United Irishmen*, London: Faber and Faber.

Townshend, Charles (1981) 'Modernisation and Nationalism: Perspectives in Recent Irish History' in *History*, vol. 66, no. 217.

Townshend, Charles (1983) *Political Violence in Ireland: Government and Resistance since 1848*, Oxford: Clarendon Press.

United Irish League (1903) 'Trial by Jury in Ireland in the Twentieth Century', Dublin.

Vaughn, W.E. and Fitzpatrick, A.J. (1978) (eds) *Irish Historical Statistics*, Dublin: Royal Irish Academy.

Walker, Brian M. (ed.) (1978) *Parliamentary Election Results in Ireland, 1801–1922*, Dublin: Royal Irish Academy.

Ward, Alan J. (1969) *Ireland and Anglo-American Relations 1899–1921*, London: Weidenfeld and Nicolson.

Watson, Robert Spence (1893) *Home Rule for Ireland – Fear or Hope?*, Gateshead: Howe Brothers.

Wright, Frank (1988) *Northern Ireland: A Comparative Analysis*, Dublin: Gill and Macmillan.

Yeats, W.B. (1987) *Autobiographies*, Papermac: London.

Younger, Carlton (1972) *A State of Disunion*, London: Fontana.

SOUTH AFRICA

Newspaper and Magazines

Die Burger
Die Huisgenoot
The Star
Die Transvaler
Die Vaderland

Books, Pamphlets and Articles

Adam, Heribert (1971) *Modernizing Racial Domination*, Berkeley and Los Angeles: University of California Press.

Adam, Heribert (1987) 'Black Unions and Reformist Politics' in David Welsh, Jeffrey Butler and Richard Elphick (eds), *Democratic Liberalism in South Africa*, Scranton: Harper and Row.

Adam, Heribert and Giliomee, Hermann (1979) *The Rise and Crisis of Afrikaner Power*, Cape Town: David Philip. (Published in the US as *Ethnic Power Mobilized: Can South Africa Survive?*, New Haven: Yale University Press).

Adam, Heribert and Moodley, Kogila (1993) *The Opening of the Apartheid Mind*, London: University of California Press.

Afrikaner Bond (1885) *Constitution of the Afrikaner Bond*, Bloemfontein.

Berger, Iris (1987) 'Solidarity Fragmented: Garment Workers of the Transvaal, 1930–1960'. In Shula Marks and Stanley Trapido (eds) *Politics of Race, Class and Nationalism in Twentieth Century South Africa*, New York: Longman.

Bloomberg, Charles (1990) *Christian Nationalism and the Rise of the Afrikaner Broederbond in South Africa, 1918–1948*, London: Macmillan.

Bottomley, John (1982) 'The South African Rebellion of 1914: The Influence of Industrialisation, Poverty and Poor-Whiteism', Africa Studies Seminar Paper, Africa Studies Institute, University of the Witwatersrand.

Bunting, Brian (1969) *The Rise of the South African Reich*, Harmondsworth: Penguin.

Cell, John (1982) *The Highest Stage of White Supremacy*, New York: Cambridge University Press.

Cronje, Geoff (1945) *'n Tuiste vir die Nageslag*, Johannesburg: Publicité.

Cruise O'Brien (1988e) 'What Can Become of South Africa?' in *Passion and Cunning and Other Essays*, London: Weidenfeld and Nicolson.

Davenport, T.R.H. (1966) *The Afrikaner Bond*, Cape Town: Oxford University Press.

Davenport, T.R.H. (1987) 'The Cape Liberal Tradition to 1910' in Jeffrey Butler, Robert Elphick and David Welsh (eds), *Democratic Liberalism in South Africa*. Scranton: Harper and Row.

Davenport, T.R.H. (1991) *South Africa – A Modern History*, London: Macmillan Press.

Davids, Achmat (1991) *The Afrikaans of the Cape Muslims from 1815–1915*, Durban: University of Natal.

Davies, Robert *et al.* (1976) 'Class Struggle and Periodization of the State in South Africa' in *Review of African Political Economy*, no. 7, Sept–Dec.

Department of Information (1952) *A Nation and Its Leader: Life and Policy of Dr D.F. Malan*, Pretoria.

Degenaar, Johannes (1978) *Afrikaner Nationalism*, Rondebosch: Centre for Intergroup Studies, University of Capetown.

Degenaar, Johannes (1987) 'Nationalism, Liberalism and Pluralism' in David Welsh, Jeffrey Butler and Richard Elphick (eds), *Democratic Liberalism in South Africa*, Scranton: Harper and Row.

De Klerk, W.A. (1975) *The Puritans in Africa: The Rise of Afrikanerdom*, London: Rex Collings.

De Villiers, René (1971) 'Afrikaner Nationalism' in Leonard Thompson and Monica Wilson (eds), *Oxford History of South Africa*, New York: Oxford University Press.

Denoon, Donald and Nyeko, Balam (1982) *Southern Africa since 1800*, London and New York: Longman.

Dickie-Clark, H.F. (1983) 'Ideology in Recent Writings about South Africa' in *Journal of Asian and African Studies*, XVIII, 1–2.

Diedrichs, Nicolaas (1936) *Nasionalisme as Lewensbeskouing En sy verhouding tot Internationalisme*, Bloemfontein: Nasionale Pers.

Du Plessis, E.P. (1964) *'n Volk Staan op: Die Ekonomiese Volkskongress en Daarna*, Cape Town: Human & Rousseau.

Du Toit, André (1975) 'Ideological Change, Afrikaner Nationalism and Pragmatic Racial Domination in South Africa' in Leonard Thompson and Jeffrey Butler (eds), *Change in Contemporary South Africa*, Berkeley and Los Angeles: University of California Press.

Du Toit, André (1981) 'Facing Up to the Future: Afrikaner Intellectuals and the Legitimation Crisis of the Afrikaner State' in *Social Dynamics*, 7.

Du Toit, André (1983) 'No Chosen People: The Myth of the Calvinist Origins of Afrikaner Nationalism and Racial Ideology', in *American Historical Review*, vol. 88.

Du Toit, André and Giliomee, Hermann (1983) *Afrikaner Political Thought: Analysis and Document, vol. 1, 1780–1850*, Berkeley and Los Angeles: University of California Press.

Floyd, T.B. (1975) *Afrikaner Nasionalisme*, Pretoria: The Author.

Floyd, T.B. (1977) *The Boer Nation's English Problem*, Pretoria: The Author.

Furlong, Patrick J. (1991) *Between Crown and Swastika: The Impact of the Radical Right on the Afrikaner Nationalist Movement in the Fascist Era*, Johannesburg: Witwatersrand University Press.

Gerhart, Gail (1978) *Black Power in South Africa: The Evolution of an Ideology.* Berkeley: University of California Press.

Giliomee, Hermann (1983) 'Constructing Afrikaner Nationalism' in *Journal of Asian and African Studies*, XVII, 1–2.

Giliomee, Herman (1987) 'The Beginnings of Afrikaner Nationalism 1870–1915' in *South African Historical Journal* (19).

Giliomee, Herman (1989) 'The Beginnings of Afrikaner Ethnic Consciousness' in Leroy Vail (ed.), *The Creation of Tribalism in Southern Africa*, Berkeley and Los Angeles: University of California Press.

Goldberg, Melvin (1983) 'The Nature of Afrikaner Nationalism' in *Journal of Modern African Studies*, 23, 1.

Hancock, W.K. (1962) *Smuts: The Sanguine Years, 1870–1919*, Cambridge: Cambridge University Press.

Hancock. W.K. (1968) *Smuts: The Fields of Force, 1919–1950*, Cambridge: Cambridge University Press.

Harrison, David (1981) *The White Tribe of Africa*, London: BBC.

Heard, Kenneth A (1974) *General Elections in South Africa, 1943–1970.* New York and London: Oxford University Press.

Hexham, Irwin (1981) *The Irony of Apartheid: The Struggle for National Independence of Afrikaner Calvinism against British Imperialism*, New York: Edward Mellan Press.

Hofmeyr, Isabel (1987) 'Building a Nation from Words: Afrikaans Language, Literature and Ethnic Identity, 1902–1924', in Shula Marks and Stanley Trapido (eds), *The Politics of Race, Class and Nationalism in Twentieth Century South Africa*, New York: Longman.

Hofmeyr, Jan Hendrik (1913) *The Life of Jan Hendrik Hofmeyr, Onze Jan*, in collaboration with F.W. Reitz, Cape Town: Van de Sandt De Villiers Printing.

Houghton, D. Hobart (1971) 'Economic Development 1865–1965', in Leonard Thompson and Monica Wilson (eds), *Oxford History of South Africa, vol. 2*, New York: Oxford University Press.

Kaplan, David (1976) 'The Politics of Industrial Protection', *Journal of Southern African Studies*, vol. 3, no. 1.

Kestell, J. D. (1939) *My Nasie in Nood*, Capetown: Nasionale Pers.

Kruger, D. W. (1935) *Die Viering van Dingaansdag 1838–1910*, Capetown: Nasionale Pers.

Leatt, James, Kneifel, Theo and Nurnberger, Klaus (1984) *Contending Ideologies in South Africa*, Cape Town and Johannesburg: David Philip.

Lewsen, Phyllis (1982) *John X. Merriman*, Johannesburg: A.D. Donker.

Lipton, Merle (1985) *Capitalism and Apartheid*, Totowa: Rowman and Allanheld.

Magubane, Bernard Makhosezwe (1979) *The Political Economy of Race and Class in South Africa*, New York: Monthly Review Press.

Malan, D. F. (1942) 'Die Britse Konneksie' in S.W. Pienaar (ed.) (1964) *Glo in U Volk*, Cape Town: Tafelberg.

Malan, D.F. (1943) 'Christendom and Communism', in S.W. Pienaar (ed.) (1964) *Glo in U Volk*, Cape Town: Tafelberg.

Malan, D.F. (1959) *Afrikaner Volkseenheid en my Ervarings op die Pad Daarheen*, Cape Town: Nasionale Boekhandel Beperk.

Malherbe, D.F. du T. (1942) *Afrikanervolkseenheid*, Capetown: Nasionale Pers.

Marks, Shula and Trapido, Stanley (1981) 'Lord Milner and the South African State', in *Southern African Studies, vol. 2*, Johannesburg: Ravan Press.

Marks, Shula and Trapido, Stanley (1987) 'The Politics of Race, Class and Nationalism', in Shula Marks and Stanley Trapido (eds), *The Politics of Race, Class and Nationalism in Twentieth Century South Africa*, New York: Longman.

Meyer, Piet J. (1941) *Die Afrikaner*, Bloemfontein: Nasionale Pers.

Meyer, Piet J. (1942) *Demokrasie of Volkstaat?*, Stellenbosch: ANS.

Milner, Alfred Lord (1931) in Cecil Headlam (ed.) *The Milner Papers, vol. 1, South Africa 1897–1899*, London: Cassell & Co.

Milner, Alfred Lord (1933) in Cecil Headlam (ed.) *The Milner Papers, vol. 2, South Africa 1899–1905*, London: Cassell & Co.

Moodie, T. Dunbar (1975) *The Rise and Crisis of Afrikanerdom: Power, Apartheid and the Afrikaner Civil Religion*, Berkeley: University of California.

Muller, C.F.J. (ed.) (1984) *500 Years: A History of South Africa*, Pretoria and Capetown: Academica.

Neame, L.E. (1930?) *General Hertzog*, London: Hurst and Blackett.

O'Dowd, M.C. (1966) 'The Stages of Growth and the Future of South Africa', reprinted in Lawrence Schlemmer and Eddie Webster (eds), *Change, Reform and Economic Growth in South Africa*, 1978, Johannesburg: Ravan Press.

O'Meara, Dan (1977) 'The Afrikaner Broederbond 1927–1934: Class Vanguard of Afrikaner Nationalism' in *Journal of South African Studies*, (3).

O'Meara, Dan (1978) 'Books Reviewed' in *Journal of South African Studies*, vol. 4, no. 2.

O'Meara, Dan (1983) *Volkskapitalisme: Class, Capital and Ideology in the Development of Afrikaner Nationalism 1934–1948*, New York: Cambridge University Press.

Pakenham, Thomas (1979) *The Boer War*, London: Weidenfeld and Nicolson.

Pelzer, A. N. (1979) *Die Afrikaner-Broederbond: Eerste 50 Jaar*, Cape Town: Tafelberg.

Pirow, Oswald (1957) *James Barry Munnik Hertzog*, Cape Town: Howard Timmins.

Reitz, Deneys (1975) [1929] *Commando: A Boer Journal of the Boer War*, London: Faber & Faber.

Robins, Eric (1953) *This Man Malan*, Cape Town: S.A. Scientific Publishing.

Saunders, Christopher (1988) *The Making of the South African Past*, Cape Town: David Philip.

Seidman, A. and N. (1978) *South Africa and U.S. Multinational Corporations*, Westport: Lawrence Hill.

Serfontein, J.H.P. (1978) *Brotherhood of Power*, Bloomington: Indiana University Press.

South Africa House (1949) *Dr. Malan Defines South Africa's Position in the Commonwealth*, Public Relations Office.

South Africa 1979: Official Yearbook of the Republic of South Africa (1979), Johannesburg: Chris Van Rensburg Publications.

Smuts, J.C. (1952) *Jan Christiaan Smuts*, London: Cassell & Company.

Sparks, Alistair (1990) *The Mind of South Africa*, London: William Heinemann.

Stultz, Newell (1974) *Afrikaner Politics in South Africa 1934–1948*, Berkeley and Los Angeles: University of California Press.

Thom, H.B. (1980) *D.F. Malan*, Cape Town: Tafelberg.

Thompson, Leonard (1960) *The Unification of South Africa 1902–1910*, Oxford: Clarendon.

Thompson, Leonard (1962) 'Afrikaner Nationalist Historiography and the Policy of Apartheid' in *Journal of South African History*, vol.3, no. 1.

Thompson, Leonard (1971) 'The Compromise of Union', in Leonard Thompson and Monica Wilson (eds) *Oxford History of South Africa*, New York: Oxford University Press.

Thompson, Leonard (1985) *The Political Mythology of Apartheid*, New Haven: Yale University Press.

Treunicht, A.P. (1975) *Credo van 'n Afrikaner*, Capetown: Tafelberg.

Vail, Leroy (1989) 'Ethnicity in Southern African History' in Leroy Vail (ed.), *The Creation of Tribalism in Southern Africa*, Berkeley and Los Angeles: University of California Press.

Van Jaarsveld, F.A. (1962) *The Awakening of Afrikaner Nationalism, 1868–1881*, Cape Town: Human and Rousseau.

Van Onselen, Charles (1982) *Studies in the Social and Economic History of the Witwatersrand, 1886–1914*, London: Longman.

Van Zyl Slabbert, F. (1975) 'Afrikaner Nationalism, White Politics and Political Change in South Africa' in Leonard Thompson and Jeffrey Butler (eds.), *Change in Contemporary South Africa*, Berkeley and Los Angeles: University of California Press.

Welsh, David (1971) 'The Growth of Towns' in Leonard Thompson and Monica Wilson (eds), *Oxford History of South Africa*, New York: Oxford University Press.

Welsh, David (1989) 'Afrikaner Women and the Creation of Ethnicity in a Small South African Town' in Leroy Vail (ed.) *The Creation of Tribalism in South Africa*, Berkeley and Los Angeles: University of California Press.

Wilkins, Ivor and Strydom, Hans (1978) *The Super-Afrikaners: Inside the Afrikaner Broederbond*, Johannesburg: Jonathan Ball Publishers.

Yudelman, David (1983) *The Emergence of Modern South Africa*, Cape Town: Creda Press.

Yudelman, David (1987) 'State and Capital in Contemporary South Africa' in Jeffrey Butler, Robert Elphick and David Welsh (eds), *Democratic Liberalism in South Africa: its History and Prospects*, Scranton: Harper and Row.

ZIONISM

Newspaper and Magazines

London Sunday Times
Manchester Guardian
Palestine Post
Palestine Weekly
Zion

Books, Pamphlets and Articles

Arab Federation (1935) 'Appeal to Members of the British Parliament by the Palestine Arab Party', Jerusalem: Arab Federation Press.

Arab Higher Committee (1937) 'A Memorandum Submitted by the Arab Higher Committee to the Royal Commission', Jerusalem: Modern Press.

Arab Higher Committee (1937) 'A Memorandum Submitted by the Arab Higher Committee to the Permanent Mandates Committee and the Secretary of State for the Colonies', Jerusalem: Commercial Press.

Arlosoroff, Chaim (1932) 'The Strategies of Zionism and Minority Rule' in Walid Khalidi (ed.) (1971) *From Haven to Conquest*, Beirut: Institute for Palestine Studies.

Baumkoller, Abraham (1930) *Le Mandat sur la Palestine*, Paris: Rousseau et Cie.

Beit-Hallahmi, Benjamin (1992) *Original Sins: Reflections on the History of Zionism and Israel*, London: Pluto Press.

Ben Gurion, David (1938) *Letters to Paula*, London: Valentine Mitchell.

Ben Gurion, David (1946) 'Analysis of the Foreign Secretary's Statement on Palestine', London: Jewish Agency.

Ben Gurion, David (1964) 'We Look towards America' in Walid Khalidi (ed.) (1971) *From Haven to Conquest*, Beirut: Institute for Palestine Studies.

Ben Gurion, David (1970) *Recollections*, London: Macdonald Unit Seventy-Five.

Ben Gurion, David (1972) *Israel: A Personal History*, London: New English Library.

Caplan, Neil (1986) *Futile Diplomacy: Volume Two, Arab–Zionist Negotiations and the End of the Mandate*, London: Frank Cass.

Cohen, Israel (1938) *The Progress of Zionism*, London: Zionist Organisation.

Cohen, Israel (1953) *Theodor Herzl: His Life and Times*, London: Jewish Religious Education Publications.

Cohen, Michael J. (1986) 'The Zionist Perspective' in William Louis and Robert Stookey (eds) *The End of the Palestinian Mandate*, Tauris: London.

Cohen, Michael J. (1988) *Palestine to Israel: From Mandate to Independence*, London: Frank Cass & Co, London.

Cohen, Michael J. (1990) *Truman and Israel*, Berkeley: University of California Press.

Cohen, Mitchell (1987) *Zion and State: Nation, Class and the Shaping of Modern Israel*, Oxford: Basil Blackwell.

Eisenstadt, S. N. (1967) *Israeli Society*, London: Weidenfeld and Nicolson.

Elon, Amos (1981) *The Israelis*, London: Penguin Books.

Encyclopedia of Zionism and Israel (1971), Rafael Patai (ed.), New York: Herzl Press/McGraw Hill.

Feuer, Leon I. (1944) *Why a Jewish State?*, London: APC Books.

Fisch, Harold (1978) *The Zionist Revolution*, London: Weidenfeld and Nicolson.

Flapan, Simha (1979) *Zionism and the Palestinians*. London: Croom Helm.

Flapan, Simha (1987) *The Birth of Israel: Myths and Realities*, London: Croom Helm.

Frankel, Jonathan (1981) *Prophecy and Politics: Socialism, Nationalism and the Russian Jews, 1862–1917*, Cambridge: Cambridge University Press.

Giladi, Dan (1975) 'The Economic Crisis during the 4th *Aliyah*, 1926–27', in Daniel Carpi and Gedalia Yogel (eds) *Zionism: Studies in the History of the Zionist Movement and the Jewish Community in Palestine*, Tel Aviv: Massada Publishing.

Gorni, Yosef (1975) 'Changes in the Social and Political Structure of the 2nd *Aliya* between 1904 and 1940', in Daniel Carpi and Gedalia Yogel (eds) *Zionism: Studies in the History of the Zionist Movement and the Jewish Community in Palestine*, Tel Aviv: Massada Publishing.

Gorny, Yosef (1987) *Zionism and the Arabs, 1882–1948*, Oxford: Clarendon Press.

Grose, Peter (1986) 'The President versus the Diplomats' in William Louis and Robert Stookey (eds) *The End of the Palestinian Mandate*, Tauris: London.

Ha'am, Ahad (1902) 'The Spiritual Revival' in Ahad Ha'am (1912) *Selected Essays*, translated Leon Simon, Philadelphia: Jewish Publication Society.

Halevi, Nadav and Klinov-Malu, Ruth (1968) *The Economic Development of Israel*, New York: Frederick A. Praeger.

Halpern, Ben (1969) *The Idea of the Jewish State*, Cambridge: Harvard University Press.

Hertzberg, Arthur (1959) *The Zionist Idea*, New York: Macmillan.

Herzl, Theodor (1946)[1896] *The Jewish State*, London: Rita Seal.

Hess, Moses (1959) [1881] *Rome and Jerusalem* in A. Hertzberg (ed.) *The Zionist Idea*, New York: Macmillan.

Hirst, David (1984) *The Gun and the Olive Branch*, London: Faber and Faber.

Horowitz, Dan and Lissak, Moshe (1978) *The Origins of the Israeli Polity*, London: University of Chicago Press.

Jewish Agency (1937) *Report of the Zionist Organisation of the Jewish Agency for Palestine*, Jerusalem: Zionist Organisation.

Jones, Martin (1986) *Failure in Palestine*, London: Mansell Publishers.

Katznelson, Berl (1937) 'Reaction against Progress in Palestine', London: Palestine Labour Studies Group.

Kedourie, Elie (1976) *In the Anglo-Arab Labyrinth: The McMahon–Husayn Correspondence and its Interpretations, 1914–1939*, Cambridge: Cambridge University Press.

Khalidi, Walid (1971) *From Haven to Conquest*, Beirut: Institute for Palestine Studies.

Khalidi, Walid (1986) 'The Arab Perspective' in William Louis and Robert Stookey (eds) *The End of the Palestinian Mandate*, London: Tauris.

Koestler, Arthur (1949) *Promise and Fulfilment: Palestine 1917–49*, New York: Macmillan.

Landau, Julian J. (1971) *Israel and the Arabs*, Jerusalem: Israel Communications.

Laqueur, Walter (1976) *A History of Zionism*, New York: Schocken Books.

Louis, W. Roger (1986) 'British Imperialism and the end of the Palestinian Mandate' in Roger Louis and Robert W. Stookey (eds) *The End of the Palestinian Mandate*, London: Tauris.

Lucas, Noah (1974) *The Modern History of Israel*, London: Weidenfeld and Nicolson.

Mansfield, Peter (1985) *The Arabs*, London: Penguin Books.

Muenzer, Gerhard (1947) *Labor Enterprise in Palestine: A Handbook of Histadrut Economic Institutions*, New York: Sharon Books.

O'Brien, Conor Cruise (1988a) *The Siege: The Story of Israel and Zionism*, London: Paladin Books.

O'Brien, Conor Cruise (1988c) 'Three Zionists: Weizmann, Ben Gurion, Katznelson', in *Passion and Cunning and Other Essays*, London: Weidenfeld and Nicolson.

Palestine Royal Commission Report (1937), [The Peel Commission] London: Government Records.

Patkin, A.L. (1943) *Zionism: Present Tasks and Post-War Aims*, London: Zionist Federation.

Pinsker, Leo (1959) [1881] 'Autoemancipation' in Arthur Hertzberg (ed.) *The Zionist Idea*, New York: Macmillan.

Rodinson, Maxime (1973) *Israel: A Colonial Settler State?*, New York: Monad Press.

Roosevelt, Kermit (1948) 'The U.S. and the Arab World, 1939–1945' in Walid Khalidi (ed.) (1971) *From Haven to Conquest*, Beirut: Institute for Palestine Studies.

Sacher, Harry (1943) *The Mandate and the Building of a New Palestine*, London: Zionist Federation.

Safran, Nadav (1978) *Israel: The Embattled Ally*, London: Belknap Press.

Said, Edward (1992) *The Question of Palestine*, Vintage Books: London.

Sankowitz, Shoshanna Harris (1947) *A Short History of Zionism*, Bloch Publishing: New York.

Shafir, Gershon (1989) *Land, Labour and the Origins of the Israeli–Palestinian Conflict, 1882–1914*, Cambridge: Cambridge University Press.

Shalev, Michael (1992) *Labour and the Political Economy in Israel*, Oxford: Oxford University Press.

Shapira, Anita (1992) *Land and Power*, Oxford: Oxford University Press.

Shapiro, Yonathan (1976) *The Formative Years of the Israeli Labour Party: The Organisation of Power, 1919–1930*, London: Sage Publications.

Shlaim, Avi (1990) *The Politics of Partition: King Abdullah, the Zionists and Palestine, 1921–1951*. Oxford: Oxford University Press.

Simon, Leon (1912) 'Introduction' in *Selected Essays by Ahad Ha'am*, Philadelphia: Jewish Publications.

Simon, Leon (1944) 'Forerunners of Zionism', London: Zionist Federation of Great Britain and Ireland.

Smith, Charles D. (1992) *Palestine and the Arab-Israeli Conflict*. New York: St. Martin's Press.

Smolensky, Oleg M (1986) 'The Soviet Role in the Emergence of Israel' in William Louis and Robert Stookey (eds) *The End of the Palestinian Mandate*, London: Tauris.

Stein, Leonard (1961) *The Balfour Declaration*, London: Vallentine, Mitchell & Co.

Stookey, Robert W. (1986) 'Historiographical Essay' in William Louis and Robert Stookey (eds) *The End of the Palestinian Mandate*, London: Tauris.

Szereszewski, Robert (1968) *Essays on the Structure of the Jewish Economy in Palestine and Israel*, Jerusalem: Israel Universities Press.

Taylor, Roger (1959) *Prelude to Israel: An Analysis of Zionist Diplomacy, 1897–1947*, New York: Philosophical Library.

Teveth, Shabtai (1985) *Ben Gurion and the Palestinian Arabs: From Peace to War*, Oxford: Oxford University Press.

Teveth, Shabtai (1987) *Ben Gurion: The Burning Ground, 1886–1948*, Boston: Houghton Mifflin Co.

United Nations Special Committee on Palestine (1947) 'The Political History of Palestine under British Administration – A Memorandum by His Britannic Majesty's Government', Jerusalem.

Vital, David (1987) *Zionism: The Crucial Phase*, Oxford: Clarendon Press.

Wasserstein, Bernard (1978) *The British in Palestine: The Mandatory Government and the Arab-Jewish Conflict, 1917–39*, London: Royal Historical Society.

Wasserstein, Bernard (1991) *Herbert Samuel: A Political Life*, Oxford: Clarendon Press.

Weizmann, Chaim (1931) 'The Zionist Movement 1916–1931 – A Statement of Policy submitted to the XVIIth Zionist Congress' London: Zionist Federation of Britain and Ireland.

Weizmann, Chaim (1946) 'Presidential Address to XXIInd Congress', London: Jewish Agency.

Weizmann, Chaim (1949) *Trial and Error*, London: Hamish Hamilton.

Weizmann, Chaim (1968–75) *The Letters and Papers of Chaim Weizmann, vols I–VII*, Leonard Stein (ed.), London: Oxford University Press.

Wolffsohn, Michael (1987) *Israel: Polity, Society and Economy, 1882–1986*, Atlantic Highlands, NJ: Humanities Press.

World Zionist Organisation (1935) *Report of the Executive of the Zionist Organisation submitted to the XIXth Congress*, London: Zionist Organisaton.

Zionist Federation (1945) *A Short History of Zionism, Lectures I–VI*, London: Zionist Federation.

Zionist Organization of America (1919) *The American War Congress and Zionism*, New York: Zionist Organization.

Zureik, Elia T. (1979) *The Palestinians in Israel: A Study in Internal Colonialism*, London: RKP.

Index